THE DECISION

THE DECISION OF FAITH

Can Christian Beliefs Be Freely Chosen?

Kevin Kinghorn

t&t clark

T&T Clark International
A Continuum imprint

The Tower Building	15 East 26th Street
11 York Road	New York, NY 10010
London SE1 7NX, UK	USA

www.tandtclark.com

British Library Cataloguing-in-Publication Data
A catalogue record for this book is available from the British Library.

ISBN: HB: 0-567-03067-9
PB: 0-567-03068-7

Library of Congress Cataloguing-in-Publication Data

Kinghorn, Kevin Paul, 1967–
The decision of faith : can Christian beliefs be freely chosen? / Kevin Kinghorn. p. cm.
Based on the author's thesis (D. Phil.)—University of Oxford.
Includes bibliographical references (p.) and index.
ISBN 0-567-03067-9 – ISBN 0-567-03068-7 (pbk.)
1. Faith development. 2. Free will and determinism. 3. Belief and doubt. 4. Psychology, Religious. I. Title.

BT771.3.K57 2005
234'.23–dc22   2005041880

Typeset by Data Standards Ltd, Frome, Somerset, UK
Printed and bound in Great Britain by MPG Books Ltd, Cornwall.

For Barbara

CONTENTS

ACKNOWLEDGMENTS

The central question addressed in this book became a concern of mine upon reading Richard Swinburne's *Faith and Reason*. Some time after first reading that work, I was fortunate enough to have Professor Swinburne supervise my DPhil project, which was an attempt to answer this central question and which became an early form of this book. Those familiar with Swinburne's writings on faith and belief will undoubtedly see that his ideas have influenced my own work, and I am grateful for his many suggestions and clarifications from which I have benefited in writing this project. Of course, in providing my own account of the relationship between faith and belief, I have not always advanced his own suggested ways of resolving difficult issues; and any remaining errors in this book are certainly to be attributed to me alone.

I would be remiss if I did not also single out another former teacher. Jerry Walls introduced me to the study of philosophy of religion and has provided ongoing support in ways far too numerous to list here. His influence on the direction of my life has been profound.

I was able to complete my DPhil work with the financial help of A Foundation for Theological Education, through which I continue to benefit by being part of the community of John Wesley Fellows. I would also like to thank The Queen's College, which awarded me a Holwell Studentship during my time as a research student at Oxford University.

I have used portions of previous articles in this present work: 'Why Doesn't God Make his Existence More Obvious?' *Asbury Theological Journal* 57:2 (2003); 'What is it to Put One's Faith in God?' *Quodlibet Journal* 6:3 (2004). I thank the publishers for permission to reprint the material here.

I am both grateful for and blessed by the benefits that come from being a member of the Kinghorn and Wallace families. Especial thanks to my parents, Ken and Hilda, for their long-standing investments in my education.

Finally, I am glad to have the opportunity here to express my appreciation for my wife Barbara's overwhelming love and support during every phase of the writing process for this book. You are a pearl of great price. Our young daughter Anna Keren's influence on future projects is warmly anticipated.

INTRODUCTION

This project centres on a problem that arises from one of the fundamental claims of the Christian religion: namely, that our eternal fate hinges on whether we voluntarily put our faith in God. The seriousness of the problem is such that the very coherence of the notion of 'voluntary faith' comes under threat.

The Christian tradition as a whole has affirmed that it is by 'putting one's faith in God' that heaven is attained. The Christian tradition has also generally wanted to affirm that the act of putting one's faith in God is an act people freely perform (though there has been disagreement over what constitutes a free act). As to the nature of faith, Christian theologians have historically described faith in God as containing a fundamental element of 'belief'. After all, if one has faith in another person, one must at least believe such things as that the person exists and has a certain sort of character.[1]

In supposing faith to be a voluntary matter for which people can rightly be held morally responsible, Christian theologians have largely assumed that the 'belief' element within faith is voluntary. However, philosophers in recent times have provided strong arguments that we are *not* capable of freely deciding which beliefs we will hold. Rather, we simply *find ourselves believing* things as the evidence before us seems to dictate. So then, if belief is indeed an involuntary matter, and if certain beliefs are requisite for Christian faith, how can faith be the kind of voluntary matter through which we have the opportunity to attain heaven?

In Part 1 I press this objection against the Christian theist, examining along the way the nature of belief and the nature of faith. In Part 2 I explore a line of argument the Christian theist might use to respond to this objection. To frame our discussion properly, we will need to make certain assumptions at the outset as to which kinds of responses would *not* constitute adequate rebuttals to the pending objection.

First, I shall assume that the Christian theist is committed to assigning Jesus Christ a unique role in the process of human reconciliation to God. More specifically, I shall assume that the Christian theist understands the atoning work of Jesus Christ to constitute the one and only means by which sinful humans can be reconciled to God. The overwhelming majority of the Christian tradition has affirmed this understanding of Jesus Christ's unique role in human reconciliation to God. And so I shall assume that the Christian theist cannot satisfactorily get round the objection facing her by suggesting that some people might attain salvation through means other than Christ's passion.

As part of this first assumption, I assume that Christ's passion has no salvific efficacy unless a person appropriates it. That is, I assume that one must explicitly offer Christ's passion to God as atonement for one's own sins in order to attain heaven. This is not to say that those who are not Christian theists cannot in this life experience any aspects of God's grace. It is simply to say that full and final reconciliation with God is not possible without a recognition of, and proper response to, the atoning work of Christ. This position has certainly been the majority position within the Christian tradition and does, I think, follow from the Christian affirmation that it is only through appreciating the sacrifice of Christ that we can fully understand the status of our relationship to God and the extent to which God, in forgiving us, absorbs the injury to our fellowship with him brought about by our sins.[2]

Second, I shall assume that any judgment the Christian God makes as to a person's eternal fate would be consistent with the attribute of perfect goodness.[3] Thus, the Christian theist must affirm that, should God consign a person to final separation from himself – as opposed to accepting the person into the heavenly community – God's action would not undermine his perfect goodness. The challenge, then, is for the Christian theist to offer a defence of God's goodness in the face of the objection outlined above.

In considering defences of God's goodness, we should regard as inadequate, I think, any defence that seeks to make too great a distinction between divine 'goodness' and human 'goodness'. Some Christian theists have sought to reconcile God's goodness with the various evils in his created world by claiming that God's attribute of 'goodness' is simply very different from our human understanding of 'goodness'.[4] Thus, even if a certain attitude or pattern of behaviour would not be consistent with us saying of a man that 'he is good', we cannot, so this line of argument goes, make similar conclusions about God's activities. For we humans do not know what divine 'goodness' actually amounts to.

To see the inadequacy of this line of argument, we can begin by noting that it seems to empty the affirmation 'God is good' of any meaningful content. For, if we do not start with some basic understanding of what divine 'goodness' would amount to – e.g. that what is good promotes the flourishing of personal agents – then the claim that 'God is good' merely amounts to the claim that 'God is God'.

The bulk of the Christian tradition has, I think, been much more confident in identifying parallels between God's goodness and the best examples of human goodness. We would not describe a human father as loving and good if, in having children, he decided that, for some of his children, he would make no sustained effort to ensure that they found love, joy or peace in life. Similarly, it seems quite implausible that we could in any meaningful sense describe God as good if he decided to make no sustained effort to reconcile all people to himself – whom Christians understand to be the one source of such fulfilment. Any adequate defence of God's goodness, then, will not rely on the claim that God's goodness is radically different from what we typically mean in saying of a virtuous man that 'he is good'. In short, the Christian theist cannot get round the objection facing her simply by contending that God's plan for some people is that they never be reconciled to himself.

Third, I shall assume that the kind of relationship with God that accomplishes the ends of the Christian religion cannot be unilaterally established by God. Some within the Christian tradition have affirmed that God can unilaterally establish a personal relationship with an individual; and they have understood faith as that which affirms what has already been unilaterally established. Against this understanding of faith, I shall assume that a personal relationship between any two agents *cannot* be unilaterally established by one of the agents. That is, I shall assume the theological point that, subsequent to God's invitation to a personal relationship, a person enters into that relationship through an act of faith. Thus, it is the act of faith that establishes[5] a relationship with God – as opposed to serving as a sign that the relationship has already been established.

In stipulating this point, I mean also to commit myself to a certain understanding of the extent to which God is involved in a person's act of faith. Almost all the Christian tradition has affirmed that people cannot come to faith unless they are 'drawn' by the Holy Spirit. Most would agree, that is, with the Council of Trent's summary that humans cannot escape their sinful state without being 'aroused and assisted by divine grace'.[6] However, the Christian tradition has been divided over the question of whether this 'drawing' is irresistible – this division perhaps being seen most clearly during the period of the Protestant Reformation. Many of the Protestant Reformers followed the later Augustine in their understanding of faith, as Calvin put it, as something 'merely passive'.[7] Against Chrysostom and the other 'Greek fathers', Calvin described the prompting of God's grace as 'one which affects us efficaciously' – as opposed to 'a movement which thereafter leaves us the choice to obey or resist it'.[8] In contrast, the Council of Trent – in words later adopted by Vatican I – affirmed that a person can respond to God's invitation 'by agreeing to, and cooperating with His grace, which he could resist'.[9]

I shall assume that people *can* indeed resist God's grace. I take this to be the majority position within the Christian tradition as a whole, although I shall not argue this point here. At any rate, it is this position that is consistent with our preceding assumption that God, in his goodness, would work toward reconciling all people to himself. After all, the Christian tradition has affirmed as a real possibility that some people might fail to exercise faith in God and consequently be for ever separated from God. And if the Christian theist is to account for this possibility – and at the same time preserve God's commitment to seek the salvation of all people – she will need to do so in terms of the choices a person makes in resistance to God's attempts to draw that person to himself.

In connection with this third assumption, I shall assume, fourthly, that a person cannot rightly be considered morally culpable for a decision or action unless she performs that action free from causal determinism. Most philosophers have wanted to affirm the link between culpability and 'free' decisions or actions.[10] Of course, philosophers have long debated what *kind* of freedom is needed to ground culpability. This debate often centres on whether a causally determined action might yet be the kind of freely performed action for which it is sometimes appropriate to praise or blame someone. So-called compatibilists affirm the compatibility of freedom with causal determinism, while libertarians insist that causal determinism violates some fundamental condition of freedom – such as an alternate possibilities condition or an ultimate responsibility condition.

Consonant with the intuition among philosophers that culpability presupposes freedom, the bulk of the Christian tradition from early on[11] has affirmed that the act of faith is voluntary and that those who culpably lack this faith do so because they freely reject God. As is the case in the philosophical literature, the *kind* of freedom one exhibits when one freely puts or fails to put one's faith in God has been disputed within the Church. I shall assume that a person would not be free – and therefore not culpable – for an action if that action was causally determined by God. Against this assumption, some within the Christian tradition have affirmed an understanding of divine predestination whereby God causally determines all human actions, while at the same time leaving human freedom and responsibility intact. However, this view gives rise to the problematic question: If God could cause all people to exercise a saving faith in him without overriding their freedom, then why does he not do so? And so in affirming theological determinism we would again be led into a conflict with our working assumption that a perfectly good God would work toward reconciling all people to himself.

A fifth assumption I shall make involves the more specific conditions that must obtain if a person is rightly to be held culpable by God for a given decision one makes or action one performs. Culpability for a decision or action presupposes that one is morally responsible for that decision or action. And moral responsibility not only presupposes free decisions (as was discussed in our preceding assumption), it presupposes free decisions of a specific type: namely, morally significant decisions. We shall need to spend the next few paragraphs examining how morally significant decisions arise and how one might be culpable for them. We shall then be in a position to identify the types of decisions for which God might rightly hold someone culpable.

Our decisions may be good or bad for different reasons. When someone refers to one of my decisions as 'good' or 'bad', he may have moral or prudential considerations in mind. Specifying what makes a decision *morally* significant is not always easy.[12] Following Kant,[13] R.M. Hare has emphasized that the goodness or badness of moral decisions stems from *universal* considerations.[14] If it would be a morally good thing for Mr Jones to give money to Ms Smith, then this is because it would be a good thing for anyone in Mr Jones's position to give money to anyone in Ms Smith's position. In response to this criterion, one might submit that it is always a good thing to serve white wine with fish – and yet such a decision is hardly a moral one. Thus, in order to distinguish matters of morality from matters of taste or preference, we will need to describe those universal considerations that make a decision or action morally good or bad as being of a certain kind. Commonly, moral matters are described as being supreme, or overriding. Thus, to accept an obligation as moral is to accept that it should be met – whatever else may be said against doing so. In response to this criterion for distinguishing moral matters from non-moral matters, Philippa Foot has raised the possibility that an individual might come to view the act of clapping his hands three times in an hour as a good thing – perhaps a good thing of pre-eminent importance.[15] If we wish to deny that such a judgment constitutes a true *moral* judgment, there are various ways we might go about narrowing the scope of what qualifies as moral. Some writers have wanted to identify moral significance with that which promotes or undermines human happiness. To vary this characterization of the moral slightly, we might identify moral value with the flourishing of humans, or the flourishing of personal agents, or perhaps the flourishing of all living things. Alternatively, we might note that there exists widespread agreement among humans over which types of universal considerations contribute to a matter having overriding importance. As Richard Swinburne has pointed out:

> Of course people have different moral beliefs – some men believe euthanasia (in the sense of helping someone who wishes to die to do so) to be morally right, others do not, and so on. But most of those who dispute about particular moral issues agree that the considerations adduced by their opponents have some force; that is, would show the action (e.g.) right but for the considerations which they adduce on the other side.[16]

Thus, even the opponent of euthanasia will acknowledge that, all things being equal, it is a good thing to give to others the kind of help for which they ask us. And the advocate of euthanasia will admit that, in general, there is great potential value in human life. As Swinburne notes, in a case like this, 'Both the disputants appeal to considerations which their opponent will admit to have some weight, although they assess and apply them differently'.[17]

I shall not attempt here to explore the various ways in which one might seek to sharpen further the distinction between moral decisions and non-moral decisions. It will suffice for our purposes to note that there is wide agreement among people that some kinds of action are of special, overriding importance in virtue of the universal properties they believe confer positive or negative worth on those actions. In my subsequent use of the term 'moral decisions', I mean to refer to decisions about actions of this kind.

I assume here that people's moral judgments about the worth of actions involve moral *beliefs* – contrary to the non-cognitivist claim that to express a moral conviction is simply to express an attitude of some sort, such as approval/disapproval (*emotivism*) or a recommendation/admonition (*prescriptivism*). It seems obvious enough that most people assume this much in everyday reflections and conversations. We sometimes find ourselves believing that a certain course of action is wrong, even though we may wish it were not so, and we often consider others to be mistaken in their beliefs about whether certain practices are morally acceptable. Moreover, to think that a certain action – e.g. committing violence against a particular ethnic group – is wrong is to think it would be wrong even if one had been brought up by one's parents to think otherwise. Thus, the assumption that we have beliefs about what is right and wrong seems an entirely plausible one.[18]

In specifying which moral decisions are ones for which a person is morally culpable, we can note that some of our beliefs about what is morally good or bad involve questions of where our obligations lie. Some morally good acts are obligatory; others are not. It is both a good thing and obligatory that I provide adequately, as I am able, for any children I might have. Yet, it is not obligatory that I give 70 per cent of my salary to charitable causes – even if it would be a good thing that I do so. As for morally bad acts, sometimes they violate obligations and sometimes they do not. It may be a bad thing for scholars to watch television sitcoms instead of maximizing their intellectual gifts, but they will probably not violate an obligation if they watch in moderation. At times, however, morally bad acts clearly *do* violate an obligation, as when I decide to watch television instead of keeping an appointment with a friend. A morally bad act that also violates an obligation I take to be a morally *wrong* act. Thus, decisions for which one is morally culpable will involve situations in which one's moral beliefs are about where one's obligations lie.

It has long been recognized that moral beliefs differ from most other beliefs in that people are motivated to act in accordance with what they recognize as morally good. Indeed, it seems odd to suggest that someone could be convinced on moral grounds that it would be a good thing – perhaps even an obligatory thing – to visit his sick grandmother and yet not be motivated to any degree to do so. Philosophers are divided as to the source of such motivation. 'Internalists' maintain that moral judgments themselves provide motivation to act; and they appeal to the idea that one cannot sincerely ascribe goodness to some action without accepting that there is at least a prima facie good reason to perform that action. 'Externalists', on the other hand, claim that moral judgments do not by themselves account for motivation; and they posit such external things as a logically independent desire to be a moral person in explaining why people might act in accordance with their moral beliefs.

It seems on empirical grounds that either internalism is correct or that the vast majority of people have certain desires to act in accordance with their moral beliefs. However the debate between internalists and externalists should be settled, it is enough for our purposes to recognize that people are motivated to act in accordance with their moral beliefs. That is, people will in fact perform the action they believe to be morally good – assuming that they have no other, contrary motivations. Of course, a person often *will* have other motivations. If a person believes that he has an obligation to visit his grandmother, he may still have desires to refrain from doing so. These desires might range from a cruel wish to hurt her feelings to a slothful wish simply to remain comfortably seated on the living-room couch. In cases where one believes that one is obligated to act a certain way, but also possesses a desire the realization of which (one believes) is at odds with one's perceived obligation, one is faced with a moral decision. When one then acts (or attempts to act) contrary to one's perceived obligation, one does something – I shall take as a fifth working assumption – for which one is morally culpable. Accordingly, if God is perfectly good, he will hold people culpable only for these types of decisions.

My sixth and final assumption is that, among those people who do not hold the beliefs requisite for Christian faith, some would choose to exercise Christian faith if only they *did* hold these requisite beliefs. William Lane Craig, in an attempt to reconcile God's goodness with the fact that unevangelized people do not have the opportunity to exercise saving faith in Christ, has argued that perhaps God knows (via middle knowledge) that no unevangelized person would in fact respond positively to the Christian gospel message if he or she were to hear that message.[19] Adopting this line of argument, one might suggest that God has ordered the world such that there simply are no people who fail to respond positively to God in faith solely because they lack the beliefs requisite for faith. Assuming such is the case, so the suggestion would then go, God's goodness is in no way undermined if unbelievers are not given (what ends up amounting to) an opportunity to explicitly reject the gospel message.

In response to this line of argument, we can acknowledge that it is logically possible that, among the group of people (numbering even today in the billions) who go through life on earth without ever holding the beliefs requisite for Christian faith, not one person would go on to exercise saving faith if he were to hold these requisite beliefs. Yet, such a possibility seems very implausible. Christian missionaries have generally had at least some success in whatever community with which they have engaged. And it is difficult to imagine that, among all the previous generations of a newly reached community, no person would have responded positively to the gospel message if he or she had been reached by earlier missionaries. In addition, the suggestion in question leads to the counter-intuitive demographic conclusion that, for a number of centuries, white individuals of European descent just happened to comprise the majority of those people who would exercise Christian faith if they came to hold the beliefs requisite for such faith. It seems quite implausible, then, to claim that God ensures that there are no persons who both (1) persist in unbelief throughout their earthly lives, and (2) would exercise Christian faith if only they had come to hold the beliefs requisite for Christian faith. I shall assume that the Christian theist cannot get round the objection facing her by making this claim.

In spelling out the objection that comprises Part 1 of this project I shall proceed as follows. In Chapter 1 I shall examine various aspects of the nature of belief. In Chapter 2 I shall argue that beliefs are not the kinds of mental states a person can hold simply by choosing to hold them. Moreover, I shall show that a person who desires to hold a particular belief may exhaust every means at his disposal in an attempt to acquire that belief and yet fail to acquire it. In Chapter 3 I shall provide an account of what it is to put one's faith in God, and in Chapter 4 I shall identify those beliefs one must hold if one is to be in a position to exercise faith. I shall conclude Part 1 by pressing the objection: if belief is involuntary, and if certain beliefs are requisite for Christian faith, then how can the exercise of faith be a voluntary decision through which all people have the opportunity to attain heaven?

In Part 2 I shall explore whether the Christian theist can rebut this objection. In Chapter 5 I shall examine why it is that some people fail to hold Christian beliefs, and I shall note the explanation from some Christian writers that a person may fail to hold such beliefs because he has become 'spiritually blinded'. In Chapter 6 I shall explore the psychological literature on self-deception to make sense of the idea of spiritual blindness, and I shall carefully distinguish culpable nonbelief from *in*culpaple nonbelief. After discussing in Chapter 7 why God would allow inculpable nonbelief to exist at all, I shall explore in Chapter 8 the possibility that the inculpable nonbeliever might yet exercise faith. I shall argue that, on my account of faith put forward in Chapter 3, this is indeed possible. For those individuals without specifically Christian beliefs nonetheless have the opportunity to exercise *implicit* faith. I conclude that the Christian theist can indeed defend God's goodness in the face of the objection outlined in Part 1 – but only if she adopts my account of the nature of faith, which provides a sharper distinction between faith and belief than is generally found in accounts of faith within the Christian tradition.

Notes

[1] It might be argued that one can have faith in a literary or some other fictional character whom one does not believe exists. Still, given that our concern with the exercise of faith will be with how faith can establish an interpersonal relationship between two people who *do* exist, the idea of faith in fictional characters need not concern us.

[2] But see Reichenbach (1999), who argues that, even on a sacrificial theory of the atonement, one need not have specific knowledge of Christ's atoning work in order to make the kinds of subjective decisions through which this atoning work is appropriated.

[3] As to why we should think that the Christian understanding of God entails that God is motivated by love both when he includes people in, and excludes people from, heaven, see Kvanvig (1993: 107–19).

[4] Cf. Hume's character, Demea, in Hume (1779).

[5] 'Establishes' not in the sense of setting the parameters of the relationship, but rather in the sense of marking the final activity needed for the relationship to begin.

[6] *Enchiridion Symbolorum* 1957: 798.

[7] Calvin 1559: III, xiii, §5.

[8] Calvin 1559: III, iii, §10. Cf. II, ii, 4.

[9] *Enchiridion Symbolorum* 1957: 1791. Cf. *Enchiridion Symbolorum* 1957: 814.

[10] But see Adams (1985) for a contrary analysis in support of the notion of 'involuntary sins'.

[11] Cf. Irenaeus c. 180: IV, xxxvii, 5 and Clement of Alexandria c. 202: II, 2.

[12] See Wallace and Walker (1970) for a good overview of how philosophers have sought to make this distinction.

[13] See Kant 1785: II, §421–4.

[14] See Hare 1955. But see MacIntyre (1957), who argues to the contrary. For Hare's fuller account of the moral, which includes an emphasis on the prescriptive nature of moral judgments, see Hare (1952) and (1963).

[15] See Foot 1978: 118f.

[16] Swinburne 1997: 221.

[17] Swinburne 1997: 221.

[18] But see, e.g. Blackburn (1984: Ch. 6) who seeks to account for the 'objectivity' within moral judgments in non-cognitive terms.

[19] See Craig 1989.

PART 1

THE NATURE OF BELIEF

1.1 *Truth and propositional belief*

There is a conceptual connection between what one believes and one's understanding of what is true about the world. In stating my belief that Bombe Alaska will be served for dessert, I am claiming that I believe it true that Bombe Alaska will in fact be served. Similarly, in professing my agreement with the statement, 'Bombe Alaska was served last evening', I can rightly be taken to have assented to the truth of this statement. As Bernard Williams puts it, there is a sense in which we might describe beliefs as 'aiming at truth',[1] for they are the kinds of things meant to be accurate reflections of the way the world is. Beliefs are representational in character; they are one's 'map' of how things are.

I can *imagine* that a special dessert both is and is not being prepared for me in the next room. Having mixed feelings about eating rich food, I can have both a *desire* that the dessert is, and a desire that it is not, being prepared for me in the next room.[2] However, I cannot – with full awareness of what I believe and a rational understanding of what my beliefs entail – have a *belief* that a dessert is being prepared and at the same time have a belief that it is not being prepared. For beliefs are restricted by our understanding of the way the world is in ways in which imaginations and desires are not. The contrasting ways in which beliefs and desires are connected with one's understanding of the world is neatly described by Mark Platts: 'falsity is a decisive failing in a belief, and false beliefs should be discarded; false beliefs should be changed to fit with the world, not vice versa. Desires aim at realization, and their realization is the world fitting with them.'[3]

Thus, I may both believe that there is, and desire there to be, a glass of water behind me. Upon turning around to discover that there is no glass of water, I naturally find myself giving up my belief. However, I do not necessarily give up my desire, and I may in fact attempt to procure a glass of water, thus attempting to change the world to make it fit with my desire. So, we might say that desiring has a different 'direction of fit' with the world than does believing.[4]

Whether or not our beliefs turn out to be true beliefs will depend on facts about the world. It is this shared assumption about what

makes beliefs true that enables us to engage in the everyday practice
of disagreement. When you challenge my belief – e.g. 'the Loch Ness
monster is not real' or 'it is your turn to wash up the dishes' –
offering your own belief instead, you are claiming that your belief
'corresponds' with the facts about the world in a way in which my
belief does not. Your belief, if indeed true, is true in virtue of this
correspondence; whereas my belief, if false, is false because it lacks
this correspondence.

Typically, talk of believing can be analysed in terms of what we
might call 'belief-that' or 'propositional belief'. Consider the
statements, 'I believe there is a computer in front of me'; 'I believe
I was not in Chicago last year'; 'I believe the weatherman'. Put in
propositional form, these statements can be taken to mean 'I believe
that there is a computer in front of me', '*that* I was not in Chicago
last year', and '*that* the weatherman is giving me accurate
information'. A proposition, as William Sessions roughly defines
it, is

> whatever can have a truth-value of true or false; a 'statement' is the
> linguistic expression of a proposition, inscribed (or uttered, or whatever)
> in some particular 'sentence.' Persons may take various 'propositional'
> attitudes toward propositions; they may entertain, doubt, affirm, or
> assume them. Belief is one such propositional attitude.[5]

One might question whether, in believing a computer now to be in
front of me, I am really taking an attitude toward a proposition.
That is, strictly speaking it is not that I form an attitude toward the
proposition 'there is a computer in front of me'; rather, I form an
attitude toward some piece of the world itself. In response to this
point we can agree that we do not usually have beliefs *about*
propositions; rather, we have beliefs about computers, tables,
chairs, and so forth. Still, the *content* of one's beliefs can (typically
at least) be expressed in propositional form. And so it is appropriate
to speak in terms of one believing propositions.

Of course, one may often have difficulty expressing in propositional form precisely what one believes. A skilful detective – with his
highly developed 'gut impression' – may not himself be able to
specify every single proposition he believes in reaching the conclusion that a certain suspect is lying. Similarly, a basketball player
with keen 'court vision' may not be able to specify all his beliefs
about the positions of other players when asked to explain his
choice to throw a cross-court bounce-pass that led to a winning
basket. However, this does not mean that what the detective and the
basketball player believe is not express*ible* in terms of individual
propositions. Indeed, if we had a complete understanding of the
mental inner workings of the two individuals, it would seem possible

in theory for us to express all that they believe in terms of individual propositions.

There is, however, another type of possible objection to the idea that we can express beliefs through propositional statements. This objection stems from the fact that propositional statements are made in the context of a given language. As noted earlier, our beliefs are typically *about* tables, chairs and other things in the world – and not about propositions or propositional statements themselves. It seems plausible to suggest that in some instances there might remain a gap between what is actually believed and the best attempts to give that belief linguistic expression in the form of a propositional statement (or statements). In other words, there may be a shortage of adequate public language to capture precisely in words what one believes about the world.[6] This issue seems better left for larger discussions within the philosophy of language; but the lack of resolution of this issue should not trouble us too much. For it still seems open to us to analyse beliefs in terms of propositional statements, even if we acknowledge that these propositional statements may not always be perfect expressions of our beliefs. In the end, any sort of possible 'gap' between our beliefs and the linguistic expression we are capable of giving them should not affect our discussions in any critical way.

1.2 *Identifying beliefs from a 'third-person' perspective*

It is possible to analyse the notion of 'belief' either from what we might call a 'third-person' perspective or from a 'first-person' perspective. Discussions of belief from a third-person perspective usually focus on the relationship between a person's beliefs and his or her public behaviour. In contrast, discussions of belief from a first-person perspective centre on the believer's own mental life. Let us first consider beliefs from a third-person perspective.

In using a person's public behaviour as the starting-point for examining that person's beliefs, Alexander Bain wrote nearly a century and a half ago that 'belief has no meaning except in reference to our actions'.[7] While twentieth-century writers in the behaviourist tradition tended towards a more moderate position that takes more seriously the existence of conscious mental states, they continued to focus on the link between one's behaviour and what one believes. R.B. Braithwaite, for instance, remarked: 'It seems to me that my belief in [the proposition that the physical object which I am seeing is a pencil] consists, apart from its entertainment, in appropriate actions, e.g. in trying to write with the pencil; and that my reasons for believing that I believe it are inductive'.[8] One of the insights stemming from third-person analyses of belief is that we can make inferences as to a person's beliefs by examining that person's public behaviour. For example, if we know that Jane intentionally took the X90 bus from Oxford in an attempt to get to London, we can deduce that she held certain beliefs about the travel route of the X90 leaving Oxford. And the behaviourist need not stop with public behaviour, for his theory of belief can be extended to include inferences to persons' beliefs made from their *hypothetical* behaviour. In commenting on his own behavioural theory of belief, Braithwaite noted: 'my *differentia* of belief is not a set of actual actions, but a set of dispositions to action, dispositions which will not be actualized except in suitable circumstances'.[9] If the behaviourist accurately surmises how a person is disposed to act in a given situation, it may be possible for him to make accurate inferences as to that person's beliefs. Suppose the behaviourist can accurately predict that Jane would take the X90 bus to London in a certain 'suitable circumstance' – e.g. her wanting to travel to London. The behaviourist's inferences about what Jane believes the X90's route to be would be the same inferences he would have made had this 'suitable circumstance' actually been realized and Jane had in fact taken the bus to London.

Continuing our third-person analysis, we must add that, in order to gauge accurately another person's beliefs, we must know more than merely that person's actions (or dispositions to act). I may see Anne flirt with Tom and infer that her action stems from her belief that such behaviour will attract Tom. However, I may well be mistaken. Perhaps Anne is not interested in Tom, but is instead interested in Joe. Her action in flirting with Tom, it may turn out, stemmed from her belief that such behaviour would make Joe jealous and thereby attract Joe. What is needed accurately to infer Anne's beliefs is the knowledge of her actions *plus* knowledge of her *purposes* in acting.[10] Consider what Bernard Williams has called 'the trio of project,[11] belief, and action'.[12] He points out that, with respect to

(1) S's projects,
(2) S's beliefs and
(3) S's actions,

if we know (3) and (1), then we can infer (2). For example, if we know that (3) John gave his mother flowers, and if we know that (1) John's purpose in acting was to make his mother happy, then we can infer that (2) John believed that giving his mother flowers would make her happy.[13]

But is it *always* the case that beliefs can be accurately inferred if we know the believer's actions and purposes in acting? Richard Swinburne – in rightly pointing out that 'a given stretch of a man's public behaviour is compatible with his having various beliefs and purposes'[14] – has argued that we cannot always correctly infer a person's belief even if we know her action *and* her purpose in acting. Swinburne begins by distinguishing 'means–end' beliefs (one's 'beliefs about the probability of different actions attaining his goal') from more theoretical beliefs (from which specific means–end beliefs follow).[15] He then describes cases in which 'the same public action may for men of the same purpose, be a case of acting on different theoretical beliefs'.[16] Let us consider the kind of example Swinburne has in mind:

> If, seeking baked beans, I open a certain can, that perhaps shows that I believe that opening the can will get me baked beans. But people normally hold means–end beliefs because they hold more theoretical beliefs from which those means–end beliefs follow; and a particular course of conduct does not show which more theoretical beliefs a man has. Thus I may hold the means–end belief, that opening the can will secure baked beans for me, because I hold the more theoretical belief that there are baked beans in the can. But there are other more theoretical beliefs from which the means–end belief also follows. It follows from the belief that the tin contains peas, and that if I open it, my wife will find and open for me a tin of baked beans. It also follows from the belief that there is a genie whom I can force to give me baked beans by opening this magic can.[17]

Does this thought experiment demonstrate that different beliefs can properly be inferred from the same combination of purposes and actions? Consider again the scenario in which I open a certain can, believing that in so doing I will secure baked beans for myself, where this belief is consistent with any of the following more theoretical beliefs:

(1)   that the can contains baked beans;
(2)   that the can contains peas and that, if I open it, my wife will find and open for me a tin of baked beans;
(3)   that this can is magical and that, by opening it, I can force a genie to give me baked beans.

It is certainly true that these beliefs differ and that they are consistent with the same action of opening a can. But is it correct to say that these beliefs are all consistent with the same action *and the same single purpose* of securing baked beans for myself? The answer seems to be 'no'. For, among these three scenarios, not only do my beliefs vary, but *my purposes vary as well*. In the case consistent with my theoretical belief (1) I have the purpose of obtaining beans. In (2) I have the purpose (we might call it an *intermediate* purpose) of doing that which will lead to my wife opening a can of beans for me

– which I believe will help toward my larger, longer-term purpose of securing beans for myself. In (3) I have the intermediate purpose of obtaining the help of a genie – which I believe will help toward my larger, longer-term purpose of securing beans for myself. Purposes are linked with goals; to seek to achieve a purpose is to seek to achieve a goal. In scenario (1) I have one goal. In scenarios (2) and (3), it would seem, I have two goals and therefore two purposes.

Of course, it is possible to define purposes and goals so that all purposes and goals are ultimate ones. On this more restricted account of purposes, the combination of a person's action and her purpose in acting will indeed in many situations be consistent with varying beliefs she might hold. A person may, for the ultimate purpose of staying alive, avoid a certain bridge because she believes that the bridge might not support her weight, or because she believes she might fall off, or because she believes bandits hide on the bridge, and so forth. But if we allow for the conceptual possibility of intermediate purposes, we will not describe this person as merely having a *single* purpose – viz. remaining alive. Rather, while acknowledging that her (ultimate) purpose of staying alive is consistent with her having a number of intermediate purposes – avoiding dangerous heights, avoiding bandits, and so forth – we will insist that, when we consider *all* the purposes (both ultimate and intermediate) she has, then we *can* accurately identify at least one specific belief she holds. Given that people often do pursue certain purposes (e.g. winning a marathon race) by focusing on the pursuit of other purposes (e.g. finishing a daily training run), it seems appropriate to allow that bona fide purposes may be either ultimate or intermediate. We conclude, then, that any complete analysis of the ways in which purposes and beliefs combine to explain one's actions will take account of the role played by intermediate purposes.

A different type of possible challenge to the thesis that we can accurately infer a person's beliefs if we know his actions and purposes comes in the form of Jonathan Cohen's distinction between belief and acceptance. For Cohen, to accept that *p* is 'to have or adopt a policy of deeming, positing, or postulating that *p* – that is, of going along with that proposition ... as a premiss in some or all contexts for one's own and others' proofs, argumentations, inferences, deliberations, etc'.[18] Belief, on the other hand, is described as 'a disposition to feel it true that *p*, whether or not one goes along with the proposition as a premiss'.[19] According to Cohen, the model whereby we explain the actions of others in terms of their beliefs and desires is too simple. In some cases, he maintains, people's actions and desires may point to what they *accept*, not to what they believe. Take, for example, Newton's theory of motion.

Cohen notes that, because of the minor anomalies in the theory: 'We should be wrong to believe the theory, in the sense of feeling it to be true. But we can certainly accept it, in the sense of going along with it as a premiss, for all the purposes to which it is applicable'.[20] Following Cohen, we can imagine a case where a science student, if she has no better theory available, might well accept a theory – i.e. use the theory as a premise in experiments and calculations about the world – even though she does not believe the theory to be an accurate reflection of the way the world is. So if we know that Sarah is making calculations about the world using Newton's theory, and if we know that Sarah's purpose is to make discoveries about the world, do we have only firm information about what she *accepts* and not what she *believes*?

This would be the wrong conclusion. That we cannot infer that Sarah believes 'that Newton's theory of motion is true' does not mean that we cannot make *other* inferences as to what she believes. We can infer, for instance, that she believes 'that Newton's theory of motion is approximately true and thus likely to lead to certain discoveries about the world'. It is not hard to imagine other scenarios – e.g. Sarah taking a physics test with the purpose of giving correct answers – where we could discover from a third-person perspective whether Sarah believes Newton's theory of motion to be true.

Not only is Sarah's experimentation using Newton's theory explicable in terms of purposes and beliefs, but Sarah's *acceptance itself* of Newton's theory is also explicable in terms of purposes and beliefs. Cohen describes acceptance as a 'choice of which propositions to take as [one's] premisses';[21] by his own account, acceptance is an action. As an action, acceptance seems to be explicable in terms of purposes and beliefs. Taking the case of Sarah, her acceptance of Newton's theory can be quite naturally explained in terms of, e.g. her purpose to discover facts about the world and her belief that using Newton's theory as a premise in experimentation could help lead to such discoveries.

In sum, our examination of beliefs from a third-person perspective helps us see the role beliefs play in action explanation. Stated roughly, beliefs explain why a person attempts to achieve her purposes through a particular means, or action, instead of through some other means.

Notwithstanding this insight into the link between belief and intentional action, though, there does seem to be more to the concept of a belief than the fact that it might be inferred – from a third-person perspective – from one's actions and purposes. If I am questioned whether I believe that I bought milk yesterday, I do not have to (a) wait until I have the purpose of eating cereal, then

(b) observe whether I head to the refrigerator or head to the market, then (c) infer from my actions and my purposes whether I believe I bought milk yesterday. Instead, I can give an answer immediately, for I am directly aware of my belief upon introspection.[22]

1.3 Identifying beliefs from a 'first-person' perspective

Considering the kind of privileged access (i.e., through reflection) we have to what we believe, it might seem obvious that beliefs are mental states that can be analysed from a first-person perspective. Some philosophers, though, have denied that a mental realm exists. So-called eliminative materialists acknowledge that we use terms like 'beliefs' and 'desires' as part of our everyday, 'folk psychology' terminology. However, they deny that, strictly speaking, there are such things as beliefs and other mental attitudes; instead, they insist, there are only brain states.

There is reason to question just how seriously we should take the eliminativist challenge. Lynne Rudder Baker points out that when new scientific theories such as Copernican astronomy have replaced old ones, the new theories have generally been able to account for the mistakes of the old ones and to show where they went wrong. Baker then asks:

> But from the point of view of the eliminativist's denial of the common-sense conception [of mental states such as beliefs], how is the error of the common-sense conception even to be intelligible? ... What needs to be shown, and what has not been shown by anyone denying the common-sense conception, is how, in the absence of attitudes identified by content, physicalist psychology can characterize cognitive error as error at all.[23]

That the eliminativist must, like everyone else, rely on the notion of beliefs in formulating his thesis surely helps uphold the plausibility of the common-sense assumption that there in fact are such things as mental states.

Given the problems with trying to deny a mental realm, some philosophers have granted the existence of a mental realm but have argued that mental states such as beliefs are reducible to physical states.[24] An assessment of the plausibility of various reductive theses is best left for larger discussions within the philosophy of mind.[25] It is enough for our purposes that we be able to proceed on the plausible assumption that there do exist mental states such as beliefs.

David Hume is generally credited for laying the groundwork for attempts to analyse belief from what we are calling a 'first-person' perspective. Hume's own proposal reflects the difficulties in trying to identify from a first-person perspective exactly what distinguishes a belief from any other idea in the mind.

belief is nothing but an idea, that is different from a fiction, not in the nature, or the order of its parts, but in the *manner* of its being conceiv'd. But when I wou'd explain this *manner*, I scarce find any word that fully answers the case, but am oblig'd to have recourse to every one's feeling, in order to give him a perfect notion of this operation of the mind. An idea assented to *feels* different from a fictitious idea, that the fancy alone presents to us: And this different feeling I endeavor to explain by calling it a superior *force*, or *vivacity*, or *solidity*, or *firmness* or *steadiness*.[26]

To illustrate the phenomenological difference between believing something to be true and merely imagining that it is or might be true, Hume described two people who read the same work – one who reads the work as history and the other who reads the work as fiction. Of the two readers, Hume maintained, the former enters into the concerns of the characters and gives credit to the testimony of the author in a way in which the latter does not. Hume stressed that this difference is not one of *content*; instead the difference lies in the *'feeling* or *sentiment'* toward that which one considers.[27] Hume acknowledged that his descriptions of 'force' and 'vivacity' do not adequately capture the phenomenological difference between an 'idea assented to' and a 'fictitious idea', conceding that "tis impossible to explain perfectly this feeling' associated with believing.[28] Still, Hume stated that 'every man is every moment conscious of the sentiment represented' by belief. Thus, despite the difficulty in articulating the phenomenological aspect of belief, Hume concluded that 'no one is ever at a loss to know the meaning of that term'.[29]

It seems plausible to assume that most people do have similar psychological experiences that distinguish their beliefs from other mental attitudes of which they are aware. However, identifying a phenomenological element common to all instances of belief seems impossible in view of the complex and various feelings and emotive states that can accompany instances of belief. H.H. Price remarked that beliefs can be manifested, among other ways, 'in emotional states such as hope and fear; in feelings of doubt, surprise, and confidence'.[30] Perhaps Price's own appeal to the notion of surprise comes closest to providing a reliable link between a phenomenological state and a belief. Price called attention to those feelings that occur when a proposition one is considering is doubted, challenged, or shown to be false.[31] His idea is that we can test whether, and with what strength, we believe a proposition by imagining how surprised we would be upon finding out that this proposition is not true.

While Price's discussion of surprise provides insight into the phenomenology of believing, his discussion does stand in need of a bit of refinement. First, Price states that surprise 'is the feeling which we have when some proposition which we believe turns out to be false'.[32] Strictly speaking, though, feelings of surprise do not occur simply when one's belief 'turns out to be false'. Rather, one feels surprise when one comes to *believe* that the proposition one had been believing is false. Second, we need to be clear in distinguishing surprise from other emotive states such as shock. While watching a National Geographic television special, a person might find out – contrary to what he thought he clearly remembered correctly from primary school – that porpoises are generally smaller than dolphins. Yet, the person might not experience a great deal of emotion. On the other hand, the same person might believe, but only very tentatively, that he will survive his company's employee cutbacks. Upon discovery that he had believed falsely, he might still experience intense feelings of emotion.

Clearly, the different levels of emotion in these examples primarily have to do with how important the subject matter is to the individual. If we are to insist that feelings of surprise vary according to the degree of strength of one's belief, then we will need to be explicit in defining surprise as that emotion that stems from the consideration of the *falsity itself* of a proposition – as opposed to the (non-epistemic) implications of that proposition being false. Thus, in the two examples cited, we can say that the first person actually experiences greater surprise, although the second person clearly experiences a higher level of emotion, which we might characterize as shock, trauma or some other emotional state. With this understanding of surprise, Price's general point about surprise seems most plausibly put as follows: a belief *b* manifests itself in feelings of surprise (or in imaginations of how one would feel surprised) when one comes to believe (or imagines that one might come to believe) that that belief *b* is not true.

Price prudently did not insist that beliefs will *always* be manifested in feelings of surprise when one finds that things are not as one had believed. Still, the notion of surprise involves the discovery (or, again strictly speaking, the belief that one has made the discovery) that something about the world is not as one had expected. And it is this feeling of expectancy, it seems to me, that best captures the phenomenology of believing. To form a belief is to form an opinion about the way the world is. In considering a proposition and 'taking a stand' with respect to whether it is true or false, one comes to have a certain expectation – possibly we should call it an anticipation – of how things are. Perhaps it is best at this point to follow Hume's lead and appeal to common experiences by suggesting that this expectation has a particular, common feel to it that we seem able to recognize through introspection as being unique to, and indicative of, the mental state of believing.

Of course, in order for a child initially to distinguish some specific feeling he comes to identify with the term 'belief' from other feelings, he will need to observe the term being used with reference to public behaviour. For example, his parents may tell him, when he looks in a certain drawer for his favourite toy that he 'believes' the toy to be in the drawer. He may then come to associate a certain feeling with the notion of what it is to believe something. Clearly, though, the fact that references to public behaviour are necessary in order for us initially to come to recognize our own beliefs does not mean that we cannot over time become adept at identifying our own beliefs simply through reflection.

1.4 *Belief and awareness*

Having looked at how one can be aware of a belief one holds, we can now ask whether a belief 'that p' *must* involve some kind of first-person awareness that one believes 'that p'. This question should not be confused with the more general matter of whether someone *believes* that she has certain beliefs. This distinction becomes clear when we consider the hypothetical case of Jill, who becomes alarmed at her own increasingly frequent, cruel remarks to Jack as their relationship deepens and they contemplate marriage. After a number of sessions with a prominent psychotherapist, Jill is told that she is 'projecting' the unreliability of her own father onto Jack. The purpose of her cruel remarks toward Jack, she is told, is to avoid getting hurt again; for (she is also told) she believes that Jack will cause her pain by someday leaving her if she allows herself to get too close to him.[33] Though Jill still possesses no first-person awareness of any belief on her part regarding Jack's unreliability, she comes to see (from a third-person perspective) that such an unconscious belief is the most plausible explanation for her actions. Let us assume that Jill does in fact have this unconscious belief; that is, she believes the proposition, 'Jack will leave me someday'. We can now say that Jill does have a certain belief and in fact believes that she has this certain belief – even though she still finds herself unable to become aware of any such belief through first-person introspection.

Returning now to the question of whether the nature of beliefs necessitates that one has first-person awareness of what one believes, it seems clear that I need not be currently thinking about a fact about the world for me still to hold a belief about that fact. After all, it would be odd to say that I cease to believe that $2 + 2 = 4$ even when I am not thinking about it. But what of beliefs of which I have *never* been aware? Michael Dummett comments with initial plausibility that 'I can hardly be said to believe some proposition which has never occurred to me'.[34] However, assuming it is the kind of conscious awareness through first-person introspection we are considering here, closer analysis seems to show that one might indeed hold a belief without ever being aware of it.

In a number of places throughout the world laws have been passed prohibiting certain subliminal advertising practices. One advertising practice that is widely outlawed involves a process by which a picture is presented to consumers for a time period shorter than that time necessary for humans to become aware that they have seen a picture. For instance, a picture might be spliced into the frames of a film-reel so that the picture appears on a screen being watched by a consumer – but only for a small fraction of a second. Although the consumer is not aware that she is seeing the picture, she still 'takes in' the information and her behaviour can be influenced by what she has seen.

Suppose that a certain consumer, Kate, is presented with such a picture one day while viewing the previews of a movie in the cinema. The picture is the marketing creation of a certain dairy company, Brand Z, and is a shady attempt to undermine consumer confidence in Brand Z's main competitor, Brand A. The picture is of a sick and clearly anaemic boy holding in each hand a carton of Brand A milk. Some time after viewing the picture, Kate goes to the grocery store with a shopping list that includes milk. One of Kate's primary goals in buying milk is to ensure that her children remain healthy. Though a regular customer of Brand A milk, she has an uneasy feeling this day when she looks at the Brand A milk cartons and decides to purchase Brand Z milk instead. We assume in this example that Kate's decision is a result of the subliminal advertisement she viewed. At the same time it is plausible to suppose that, if later asked why she believed Brand Z better ensured milk that was good for her children, Kate would be unable to give any reason. Yet, her uneasiness at purchasing Brand A milk stemmed in fact from her (unconscious) belief that Brand A milk might somehow be linked with certain illnesses. Examples such as this one – as well as our previous example involving Jill – illustrate the possibility of holding a belief despite having no awareness that one holds that belief.

At the same time, it does not seem correct to say that one might hold a belief even though one *could* not become aware of it. As a mental state, a belief seems to be the kind of thing to which by definition it must be possible for the believer to have privileged, first-person access – at least in ideal conditions. Suppose that – through hypnosis, psychotherapy, or some other means of discovery – one gained complete first-person access to, and appreciation of, all one's mental states. If, under these ideal conditions, one still was not aware of a purported belief, then we should not, I think, describe the person as having this particular belief. For to do so would require that we define the term 'belief' far outside its normal use.

It is true that beliefs are notoriously difficult to categorize according to psychological levels. K.V. Wilkes remarks that, in addition to

> unconscious, subdoxastic, and conscious beliefs ... there appear to be numerous kinds of states which can readily be described as belief states to which one might want to append adjectives such as 'preconscious', 'subconscious', or 'nonconscious'. ... For example: climbing up stairs I trip at the top and fall. Dusting myself down I explain, 'I thought there was another step.'[35]

Whatever the psychological level of belief, it seems most natural to stipulate in a definition of 'belief' that the believer must, in ideal conditions, be able to become aware of his beliefs through reflection. However, as we have seen in this section, a person may, in practice, hold a belief even if he is unable at the time readily to identify that belief through reflection.

1.5 *Belief and evidence*

Let us now turn to the question of why someone might form a belief about the world. Suppose a friend tells me that he recently passed by the bicycle shed and did not see my bicycle. Do I form the belief that my bicycle has been stolen? I may need to consider a number of things. First, I need to consider that a number of bicycles have been stolen recently from the bicycle shed, and this lends credence to my friend's testimony. On the other hand, I think I remember locking my bicycle to a railing; and if I did lock it up, then a theft would seem quite improbable. Of course, I will need to consider that my wife might have borrowed my bicycle without telling me. She has never done so before, but she does have a key to my bicycle padlock. Also, I will need to consider the manner in which my friend told me that he noticed my bicycle missing. Did his voice have a hint of surreptitiousness that would suggest he is pulling a prank on me? Did his voice have a casualness to it that suggests he merely glanced at where he thought my bicycle would be – as opposed to looking closely around the entire bicycle shed out of fear that it might have been stolen? There are a number of things I will need to consider as I begin to form a belief about whether my bicycle has been stolen. Whatever the belief is that I form, I will have formed the belief on the basis of *evidence*.[36] That is, the testimony of my friend, my evaluation of his tone of voice, the firmness of my memory that I locked my bicycle, and so forth, will all serve as my evidence in reaching my conclusion as to whether my bicycle has been stolen.

Of course, the evidence to which I give weight may or may not be *good* evidence by objective standards. Suppose that, having a faulty understanding of the 'law of averages', I incorrectly infer that it is very unlikely that I will ever have another bicycle stolen since I had a bicycle stolen once before. We might even suppose that I believe that this evidence from the 'law of averages' outweighs all my other evidence, which, taken by itself, points toward a different conclusion. What is important here, though, is that this faulty evidence seems *to me* like good, relevant evidence; it is *my* evidence and, as such, serves as the basis for my belief. So we must allow that individuals may differ over whether a purported piece of evidence (e.g. the 'law of averages' regarding repeated bicycle theft) bears on the truth or falsity of a given proposition (e.g. that my bicycle was stolen). Moreover, even where there is agreement over *which* pieces of evidence are relevant to the truth or falsity of a proposition, individuals may differ over *what bearing* each piece of evidence has on the truth or falsity of that proposition.

When one assesses evidence for and against a given proposition, will one's resulting belief about that proposition always be simply the conclusion to which one takes the evidence on balance to point? Although I ultimately do wish to affirm as much, certain examples may seem initially to suggest that this is not so. Take the cases of people who suffer panic attacks when they are in confined spaces. Some sufferers will find it too upsetting to perform tasks such as driving through a mechanized car wash. Such a person, in explaining why she is unable to bring herself to go through a car wash, might remark, 'I just know that I'm going to get trapped'. When probed further, she might acknowledge that, to her knowledge, the car wash machine has never malfunctioned before. And she might concede that, if the machine were to malfunction, the workers at the car wash would be able to turn off the machine and come to her aid. Nonetheless, she may still persist in avowing that she will become trapped if she enters the car wash.[37]

There are various ways we might go about trying to explain plausibly the behaviour and beliefs of the person from our example. We might deny, contrary to her testimony, that she does in fact fervently believe that she will become trapped. Instead, we might account for her behaviour by suggesting that, although she believes it very unlikely that she will in fact become trapped, the scenario of becoming trapped so terrifies her that she resists performing those actions that she sees as involving even the remotest of possibilities that she might become trapped. Assuming, though, that she *does* in fact firmly believe that she will become trapped, how are we to account for her belief? One approach here would be to suggest that people are capable of (irrationally) holding a belief 'that p' even when the balance of their evidence[38] – which comes in the form of other beliefs they hold – points to the falsity of p. However, it seems questionable whether this scenario is coherent. Given that beliefs are what one takes to be true about the world, it is difficult to imagine how a person, however irrational, could believe both that p is true and that there is most reason, all things considered, to think that p is false.

How then are we to account for the panic attack sufferer who both believes she will become trapped and also acknowledges evidence that seems decidedly to undermine this belief? The most plausible suggestion here seems to be that the person has private evidence of which she is not fully conscious. Perhaps a repressed memory of a childhood trauma involving the feeling of being trapped has left her with the unconscious belief that becoming trapped is an all-too-likely prospect. David Pears considers the possibility that some irrational beliefs are nature's way of ensuring that certain goals are met. For example, a husband may have as a goal the elimination of any rivals for his wife's romantic attentions. As a means of achieving this goal, nature's 'programme' may include the formation of irrationally jealous beliefs that appear to outsiders to have little or no evidential support.[39] Perhaps the panic attack sufferer's belief that she will become trapped is similarly in some sense part of 'nature's way' of ensuring that certain survival goals are met. That is, perhaps an earlier trauma of feeling trapped has led to an exaggerated – and, by objective, inductive standards, clearly irrational – belief as to the likelihood of her becoming trapped again.

A repressed memory of a childhood trauma is only one possible way of explaining how the panic attack sufferer might have private evidence in the form of unconscious beliefs. Whatever the source of her private evidence, though, it seems most plausible to describe her as having *some* kind of private evidence for her belief that she will become trapped in the car wash. Not being able to articulate this private evidence, she may describe her belief as a 'gut-feeling' or a 'strong hunch'. In the end, though, there seems no good reason to deny that her belief is simply the conclusion to which her other beliefs (which serve as her evidence) point – even if her conclusion is not reached through conscious inference. That a belief is irrational does not mean that it is not still based on one's evidence.

Having looked at how beliefs can follow from one's assessment of evidence, we can now consider the question: *which* of our beliefs are formed in the context of evaluating evidence? In cases where a belief 'that p' stems from one's evaluation of evidence for and against the truth of p, one's evidence for p, as already noted, will be some other propositional belief(s) one holds. Thus, I believe I will not have to walk downtown tomorrow in the shoes I am now wearing because I believe I will again have possession of my favourite shoes sometime this afternoon. I believe I will have my favourite shoes by then because I believe the cobbler has them re-soled and ready for me to pick up today. I believe the cobbler has them ready because I believe that he called with the message that they are ready. I hold this latter belief because I read a note indicating that the cobbler called to say he had finished with my shoes. I believe that the note was intended for me because it was in my pigeonhole and appeared to be in the handwriting of my wife. And, of course, I believe that the handwriting was that of my wife because of still other beliefs I hold. Now, assuming that I hold $belief_a$ on the basis of $belief_b$, and $belief_b$ on the basis of $belief_c$, and so forth, it seems natural to ask where this evidential chain of beliefs ends. Foundationalism and coherentism represent two well-known and different ways of answering this question. Foundationalists insist that the chain of beliefs does end, as one eventually forms a belief that is not (entirely)[40] based on other beliefs one holds. Thus, the foundationalist posits 'foundational', or 'basic', beliefs such as self-evident beliefs $(2 + 2 = 4)$ and beliefs that are evident to the senses (I see something that appears as red to me). Coherentists, on the other hand, conceive of chains of beliefs as 'circular' and thus deny that chains of belief must end. On the coherentist account, one's evidence for any belief is the complex, interconnected web of beliefs one already holds.

Part of the difficulty in settling the question of whether there are such things as basic beliefs stems from our inability to identify how basic beliefs, if they exist, necessarily differ phenomenologically from non-basic beliefs. As noted earlier, the fact that a belief is based on other beliefs one holds does not necessarily mean that conscious inference was involved. Thus, a person who forms a non-basic belief 'that p' may describe the formation of that belief by saying that it simply seemed to him at some point that p is true. A person who forms a basic belief may, of course, give the same phenomenological description. Whether or not there are such things as basic beliefs,[41] however, the central point of this section remains: Where a belief *is* formed on the basis of evidence (i.e., other beliefs one holds), one's belief will be the conclusion to which one sees (consciously or unconsciously) one's evidence as pointing.

1.6 *Belief and probability*

It seems clear that I do not have to be absolutely certain that a proposition *p* is true in order to believe 'that *p*'. I believe that my ninth birthday marked the date I was given my first baseball mitt; but, like most things I believe, I am not certain of this fact. For that matter, I am not absolutely certain that my last birthday marked the time that I received the framed picture that now hangs in my hallway – though I am more certain in this belief than in my belief regarding my ninth birthday present.

Normally, as in the cases just described, when I reflect on whether I believe a certain proposition, I contrast the proposition with its negation. Thus, in believing that 'I received a picture on my last birthday', I might be described as believing that this proposition is more probably true than its negation: 'It is *not* the case that I received a picture on my last birthday'.[42] However, as Richard Swinburne has pointed out,[43] a proposition might be contrasted with more than one alternative. For instance, someone might be asked whether she believes that Brazil will win the next World Cup. If she answers 'yes', she might mean that she believes the proposition 'Brazil will win the World Cup' to be more probable than the *combined* chances of the other competing national squads. However, unless Brazil has a dominant squad, she will perhaps mean by answering 'yes' merely that she believes it more probable that Brazil will win the World Cup than that any other *single* squad will win. Thus, we conclude with Swinburne that the meaning of 'believes that *p*' can depend on the alternative(s) with which *p* is being contrasted.

Nevertheless, it seems counter-intuitive to define beliefs in such a way that one could believe a proposition if one believes the probability of its being true to be less than 0.5. As there seems no non-arbitrary probability value between 0.5 and 1 that we could point to as the minimum requirement for a 'genuine' belief, it seems most natural to characterize belief such that one does in fact believe 'that *p*' if one believes that the probability that *p* is true is greater than 0.5.[44] So what of the person who believes that Brazil's chances in the next World Cup are greater than any other single nation's chances – yet does not believe that Brazil's chances are better than the combined chances of the other nations? Perhaps she assigns the proposition, 'Brazil will win the World Cup', a probability somewhere around 0.3, assigning, of course, a lower probability to the prospect of any other team winning. In such a case, we will want to say that, strictly speaking, she does not actually believe the proposition, 'Brazil will win the World Cup'. At the same time, we can recognize that her probability assignment of 0.3 can play a role in action explanation. Suppose that she has the purpose of choosing the World Cup winner for an office pool and that she enters Brazil as her pick. Clearly, the action-guiding belief here will be something like: 'Brazil's chances of winning the World Cup are greater than any other nation's chances'. She will assign *this* proposition a probability of 1 – something that follows logically from her probability assessments that Brazil's chances of winning are around 0.3 and that every other nation's chances are even lower.

So, one's probability assessments can play a central role in guiding one's actions even when these assessments do not meet the requirements for a bona fide belief – i.e., even when the assessments are not greater than 0.5. Indeed, one can perform a certain action in the pursuit of a certain purpose even when one does not, strictly speaking, believe that the action will in fact achieve that purpose. All that is needed for action explanation is for one to believe that there is no *other* available course of action that has a *better* chance of achieving that purpose.

It might be objected at this point that probability assessments have little to do with standard instances of belief, given that people do not typically make probability assessments as they interact with the world each day. William Alston puts the point as follows.

> Every day I form innumerable, usually short-lived ... beliefs. I glance out of my window and note that the new building opposite is not finished yet ... Did I form the belief that the proposition that the building is not yet finished is rendered more probable than some alternative – such as its negation ... ? If so, I regularly carry out such doxastic operations in a way ideally calculated to escape my notice.[45]

Alston is certainly correct in noting that we do not typically make *conscious* judgments of comparative probability as we manoeuvre through the world. What seems less clear, however, is whether we do not commonly make *unconscious* probability assessments in daily life. It seems plausible to suggest that many of our everyday, 'short-lived' beliefs are rife with rather complex (albeit less than fully conscious) probability assessments. Suppose that Sue is driving her car down a highway with three lanes. Sue is in the middle lane, with a truck beside her in the outside lane, and another car beside her in the inside lane. Sue sees the truck's indicator light flash as the truck begins to turn into her lane. She considers speeding up to pull ahead of the truck, but she estimates that her car does not have the horsepower to pull ahead of the truck before it fully enters the middle lane. She considers putting on the brakes and even takes her foot off the accelerator for a moment, but again she estimates that there is not sufficient time to avoid the truck. She honks her horn while moving to the inside line of the middle lane, away from the truck. As it grows less and less likely from her perspective that the truck will respond to her horn, Sue reaches the point where she estimates that her best chance to avoid an accident is to swerve into the inside lane. She realizes that there is another car next to her, but she deems it more likely that the driver of that car will swerve onto the shoulder of the road (thus avoiding Sue's swerving car) than that the driver of the truck will finally realize that Sue is in the middle lane. This seems to be a case where a number of probability assessments are made[46] – all within the space of two to three seconds. While Sue, even upon reflection, may have difficulty identifying all the probability assessments she made during this event, some type of probability assessment seems to be the only plausible candidate for explaining her series of actions.

Even when we make thoughtful attempts to achieve a certain purpose, we often are not aware of all the probability assessments we routinely make. During a power cut one evening, I may decide to light a candle and subsequently rummage through drawers trying to find a box of matches I remember buying some time ago. I naturally begin with the drawer in which I think the matches are most likely to be found. If the matches are not there, I then continue my search through other drawers. The order of the drawers I search will correspond (roughly, at least) with the descending order of probability I assign to propositions of the kind: 'This drawer contains the matches'. Thus, I will search the tool drawer before I search the household cutlery drawer, but not before I search the candle drawer. That my selection of drawers to search is not arbitrary seems to show clearly that I am making (at some psychological level) comparative probability assessments. However, I may be no more conscious of assigning rough probabilities to propositions than Sue the driver was from our previous example. I might explain my actions in rummaging through drawers by saying that I was simply trying to light a candle as quickly as possible – just as Sue will explain her driving by saying she was simply trying to avoid an accident. What is important for our larger project is that we do often make assessments as to how probably true propositions are of the kind: 'Action A will achieve purpose P'. And, as we have seen, assessing the probability of such propositions can guide one's actions even when one's assessments do not rise to the level of a bona fide belief.

Conclusion

Noting the connection of beliefs with truth, propositions and evidence, we have examined the notion of belief from both a first- and third-person perspective. We have found that beliefs are mental states to which one may have privileged access. At the same time, we have seen that one may not always be aware of the beliefs one holds. Analysing beliefs from a third-person perspective, we can point to beliefs as explaining why someone attempts to achieve a certain purpose in the way she seeks to achieve it. And we have seen that probability assessments can play the role beliefs play in action explanation – even if these probability assessments are best characterized as something short of bona fide beliefs.

Notes

[1] See Williams 1970: 136f.

[2] I understand a desire to be an inclination to act – an inclination that will result in one attempting to realize one's desire (provided one believes this realization is possible) unless one has a contrary desire or some reason to act otherwise.

[3] Platts 1979: 256–7.

[4] For a fuller discussion see Smith (1994: 111–15).

[5] Sessions 1994: 52. Sessions notes that 'there are difficulties in characterizing more precisely such notions as "proposition," "truth," "statement," "sentence," "language," or "attitude" ' (52, n. 46).

[6] But see Sessions (1994) who remarks:

> I tend to think that it is not possible for S to believe that p without S being able, in some way and to some degree, to give linguistic expression to p. After all, how could someone hold some proposition to be true but have no way of expressing which proposition she is holding? Would she properly be said to be holding anything at all to be true? (52).

This qualification for having a belief, though, leads to the counter-intuitive conclusion that animals and infants do not have beliefs.

[7] Bain 1859: 568.

[8] Braithwaite 1933: 36.

[9] Braithwaite 1933: 34.

[10] I understand one's pursuit of a 'purpose' to be one's deliberate attempt to achieve a goal one desires to realize and/or believes there is good reason to achieve.

[11] As the terms are used in our discussion, one's *projects* are synonymous with one's *purposes*.

[12] Williams 1970: 144. This kind of theory of action Williams advances has its roots in David Hume's analysis that it is one's desires plus one's beliefs that explain one's actions.

[13] Typically, we infer someone's beliefs and purposes together. That is, we observe someone's public behaviour and infer what combinations of 'beliefs + purposes' most plausibly explain this behaviour.

[14] Swinburne 1981: 13.

[15] Swinburne 1981: 9.

[16] Swinburne 1981: 12.

[17] Swinburne 1981: 12.

[18] Cohen 1989: 368.

[19] Cohen 1989: 368.

[20] Cohen 1989: 386.

[21] Cohen 1989: 370.

[22] Frequently, the first-person perspective will be the more reliable means of determining someone's belief. For example, when a person's public actions are compatible with a number of 'belief + purpose' combinations, the person might be able

to tell us with reliability exactly what she believes. On the other hand, in cases where one is deceived about – or, at least, not fully aware of – what one believes, greater reliability might well lie in third-person assessments than in asking a person what she believes.

[23] Baker 1987: 124–5.

[24] Foster (1991) outlines the two general forms a reductive thesis might take. *Analytical* reductionism involves the claim that statements about mentality can be reformulated, by conceptual analysis, in non-mentalistic terms. *Metaphysical* reductionism, by contrast, does not preserve the ontology of mental items, as it involves the claim that mental facts are wholly constituted by non-mental facts (26).

[25] For a defence of the philosophically fundamental nature of beliefs and other mental states against various reductive theses, see Baker (1987) and Foster (1991).

[26] Hume 1739–40: 628–9.

[27] Hume 1739–40: 623.

[28] Hume 1739–40: 629.

[29] Hume 1748: V, II, §40.

[30] Price 1969: 294.

[31] Price 1969: 275f.

[32] Price 1969: 276. Price also notes that we 'feel some surprise, though not so much, when we come across evidence against some proposition which we believe, even though this adverse evidence is by no means conclusive' (276). However, we need not pursue the more complicated examples where one feels surprise upon coming to believe that a particular belief one holds *might* not be true.

[33] Collins (1969) discusses cases where an analyst might persuade his patient that the patient's own unconscious beliefs provide the best explanation for the patient's behaviour.

[34] Dummett 1973: 286.

[35] Wilkes 1981: 93–4. For some of the difficulties in trying to identify exactly what makes a belief 'conscious', see Hookway (1981).

[36] My evidence comes in the form of other beliefs of mine of which I may have various degrees of confidence.

[37] I take this example from the actual testimony I once witnessed of a panic attack sufferer.

[38] Again, by 'their' evidence I mean their own understanding of what evidence exists and their own criteria in determining how a piece of evidence bears on the truth of a given proposition.

[39] See Pears 1984: 44.

[40] While descriptions of foundationalism within the philosophical literature do not always include the term 'entirely' as it is used here, foundationalism is only plausible if we include this qualification.

[41] Though I shall not argue the point, my own view is that foundationalism is correct in positing basic beliefs.

[42] The kind of probability at issue here is evidential probability, as opposed to statistical probability, which is an empirical matter.

[43] Swinburne 1981: 4f.

[44] Swinburne's view seems to be that believing 'that p' *consists in* believing that p is more probable than some alternative(s). That is, to believe that p is to have a view about the probability of p. The discussion here involves the weaker claim that, *when* one *does* hold a view about the probability of p, one's probability assessment of p will not amount to a belief if it is not above 0.5.

[45] Alston 1994: 26. Cf. Hookway (1981) 'we seem to sort propositions into those we believe, those we disbelieve, and those that we are agnostic about' (78).

[46] In some of these probability assessments, the probability of p is compared with the probability of not-p; in others, the probability of p is being compared with the probability of q, r ... and so forth.

THE INVOLUNTARINESS OF BELIEF

2.1 *Direct versus indirect volitionalism*

There are any number of reasons why one might wish to hold a certain belief. A woman who must testify in court and dreads choosing between honesty and loyalty may wish that she could believe that her friend is innocent. A religious person may be convinced that the way in which God judges the lives of people depends at least in part on whether they believe certain propositions contained in a creed. However, even though we may very much want to believe certain propositions, is it the case that we can believe what we want to believe?

It is clear that when we form beliefs where we do not reflect on whether we have evidence for them – e.g. perceptual, memory and self-evident beliefs – we are not exercising choice. There simply is no room for choice when, without reflection, I form the perceptual belief that there is a computer in front of me. Of course, subsequent reflection on the evidential support for and against such beliefs might lead us to give them up, as when I look in my diary and realize that my memory about the time of a pending dinner engagement is inaccurate. Still, it does not seem in such cases that I *decide* to give up the belief; rather, I *find myself* giving up the belief. It further seems that reflection does not afford me any opportunity to *acquire* such beliefs by way of choice. I cannot choose to believe that I am now seeing a palm tree, that I grew up in the sixteenth century, or that $2 + 2 = 5$; no matter how much I reflect on these matters. But what of other beliefs, such as those involving morality, politics, or religion? We do seem to deliberate over questions in these areas, often 'going back and forth' about what we believe before finally 'changing our minds'. Is it the case that, with respect to at least some kinds of beliefs, we can sometimes choose what to believe?

Our language occasionally suggests that we do consider belief to be a matter of choice. Consider the phrases: 'I refuse to believe that'; 'Why won't you believe me?'; 'I've decided that such a course of action would be imprudent', and so forth. Moreover, given that we share Kant's intuition that 'ought' implies 'can', we seem to assume an optional element in believing when we say that the Nazi officers ought not to have believed Hitler's rhetoric as they did. We sometimes even criticize others for whether or not they form *any* belief, claiming that they are irresponsibly naïve in believing too easily, or that they are unduly cynical in not being willing to believe. In the following two sections we shall explore the question of whether or not beliefs really are the kinds of things we can sometimes choose to hold. But before we look at that question, we need a clear understanding of the two types of ways in which one might seek to hold a belief – and this leads us into the distinction between direct and indirect belief acquisition.

In order to acquire a belief *directly*, one's act of believing would need to be a *basic* act – one performed through no intermediate means.[1] As Trudy Govier puts it, a person could directly acquire a belief – i.e., believe something 'by fiat' – if he could 'decide that he would like to believe something and then, simply in virtue of having taken that decision, believe it, just like that'.[2] By contrast, someone acquires a belief *in*directly if he takes steps that bring it about that he believes a certain proposition.[3] Whereas direct belief acquisition is said to occur by a 'single fiat of will', *in*direct belief acquisition might be described as a voluntary cultivation of a belief.[4] As an analogy to the distinction between direct and indirect belief acquisition, consider Bernard Williams's remarks on blushing:

> What would it be to blush at will? You could put yourself in a situation which you would guess would make you blush. That is getting yourself to blush – by a route – but it could not possibly count as blushing at will. Consider next the man who brings it about that he blushes by thinking of an embarrassing scene. That is getting a bit nearer to blushing at will. The best candidate of all would be somebody who could just blush in much the way that one can hold one's breath.[5]

Like blushing at will, one can only believe at will if one does nothing to acquire the belief except make the decision to believe it.[6]

With respect to the relationship between our daily decisions and our beliefs, it is uncontroversially true that our voluntary decisions often affect which beliefs we come to hold. For example, my decision about what rural route to take during a drive in the country may help determine what I come to believe about shapes in the clouds that day. Clearly, one's choices affect one's beliefs even when one is not seeking to hold any particular belief. The more controversial question in which we are interested, however, is whether one can choose to acquire some particular belief one specifically desires to hold but does not yet hold. In section 2.3 we shall consider the kind of influence on belief that one might be able to exert by choosing to take intermediate steps in an attempt to acquire a belief one desires to hold. But let us turn first to the question of whether one can choose to hold a desired belief simply by choosing to hold it.

2.2 *Logical constraints of direct belief acquisition*

It seems obvious on phenomenological grounds that it is psychologically impossible for at least many people to hold all the beliefs – including religious beliefs – they want to hold simply through the basic act of choosing to hold them.[7] Many people report wishing they could hold various religious beliefs – or wishing they could hold them with a greater degree of confidence. Yet, unlike the performing of basic acts like raising one's arm or focusing one's attention on a problem at hand, one's success in acquiring such beliefs does not depend simply on the extent of *trying* to do so.

Similar phenomenologically based arguments might also be made as to the impossibility of holding only those desires and emotions we choose to hold. Yet, unlike desires and emotions, there are logical constraints particular to belief by fiat that help shed light on why the very idea of belief by fiat is in principle problematic. To see these logical constraints, let us consider Bernard Williams's argument as to the logical impossibility of choosing one's beliefs.

Williams contends that our inability to believe by fiat is not merely a contingent fact about us – like the fact (if it is a fact) that we are unable to blush at will. Instead, he argues, the logical implications of beliefs, themselves, preclude the possibility of believing by fiat. In a well-known passage Williams writes:

> If I could acquire a belief at will, I could acquire it whether it was true or not; moreover I would know that I could acquire it whether it was true or not. If in full consciousness I could will to acquire a 'belief' irrespective of its truth, it is unclear that before the event I could seriously think of it as a belief, i.e. as something purporting to represent reality. At the very least, there must be a restriction on what is the case after the event; since I could not then, in full consciousness, regard this as a belief of mine, i.e. something I take to be true, and also know that I acquired it at will. With regard to no belief could I know – or, if all this is to be done in full consciousness, even suspect – that I had acquired it at will.[8]

We have already noted that beliefs are propositional attitudes characterized by a certain kind of expected correspondence between the proposition one considers and some fact about the world. Again, as Williams puts it, there is a sense in which our beliefs 'aim at truth'. Williams's line of argument in the passage here points to a general reason for regarding as incoherent the notion of direct, voluntary belief acquisition: if one knows that one's belief 'that *p*' stems from one's own will, one will know that this belief was acquired irrespective of whether it 'purports to represent' a fact about the world. And if I know that the reason I came to believe 'that p' had nothing to do with whether or not p represents a fact about the world, then it does not make sense to say that I actually believe p to be true.

In analysing Williams's line of argument we must first recognize a certain ambiguity contained in it. At the beginning of the passage quoted above, Williams speaks of the difficulty in coming to believe 'that p' when one believes that one *could* acquire that belief by willing to believe it. At the end of the passage, however, Williams asserts that it is impossible to believe 'that p' when one believes that one *has acquired* the belief 'that p' by willing to believe it. So, in a case where we imagine one acquiring a belief 'that p' by fiat, Williams can be taken as claiming that that belief would be undermined by one or both of the following:

    (a) the belief that one could acquire the belief 'that p' through an act of the will.

    (b) the belief that one has acquired the belief 'that p' through an act of the will.

Strictly speaking, neither belief$_{(a)}$ nor belief$_{(b)}$ by itself would undermine a person's belief 'that p'. However, Williams's point seems to be that belief$_{(a)}$ and belief$_{(b)}$ each lead to further beliefs about the unreliability of the means by which the belief 'that p' is (or was) acquired. Now, it is true that, given the sense in which beliefs 'aim at truth', any belief a person holds will be undermined by the further belief that it has been acquired (and sustained)[9] through unreliable means. But does belief$_{(a)}$ and/or belief$_{(b)}$ necessarily lead to the conclusion that a belief formed via the will has been acquired through unreliable means?

Let us first consider belief$_{(a)}$. It is true that a person must think she has at least *some* chance of succeeding when she attempts to believe a proposition by fiat; after all, the notion of trying to perform an action seems incompatible with the belief that that action is impossible.[10] So, in order to believe 'that p' by fiat one must believe (at the time one attempts through an act of the will to believe 'that p') that there is at least a chance that one will be successful. However, from the belief that one *could* acquire – or *possibly has the ability* to acquire – the belief 'that p', it does not necessarily follow that, once one acquires the belief 'that p' by fiat, one will believe that this belief was acquired through unreliable means. To see why this is so, consider a case where I believe that I am capable of believing 'that p' by fiat, and I attempt to acquire the belief 'that p' in this fashion. Despite my thinking myself *capable*, broadly speaking, of believing 'that p' by fiat, perhaps I strongly doubt that I will in fact be successful in this particular case. As it turns out, however, I *am* successful in believing 'that p' by fiat. Still, I continue to doubt that I was successful, attributing my new belief to the process of deliberation that accompanied what I regard as my failed attempt to acquire a belief by fiat. Given such a scenario, I would have no cause to think that my belief 'that p' was acquired through unreliable means.

So much for belief$_{(a)}$; let us turn to belief$_{(b)}$. It does seem difficult to imagine how one could hold belief$_{(b)}$ and yet not also believe that one's belief 'that p' was acquired through unreliable means. However, even on the understanding that the further belief regarding unreliability necessarily follows from belief$_{(b)}$, we still cannot formulate a successful argument against the logical possibility of acquiring the belief 'that p' by fiat. For it is not logically necessary to hold a belief$_{(b)}$ in order to acquire a belief 'that p' by fiat. As we saw in the previous example, it is logically possible for one to acquire a belief by fiat without being aware that one is doing so. Additionally, it is conceivable that one might, subsequent to acquiring a belief by fiat, forget that one has done so. In these cases, one who acquires a belief by fiat will not hold belief$_{(b)}$. And without belief$_{(b)}$ one's original belief 'that p' will not be undermined.

Although Williams' line of argument fails to demonstrate a strict logical impossibility in the idea of belief acquisition by fiat, it does offer sufficient reason why, in most situations, people find it impossible to believe things at will. As stated in section 1.1, beliefs are representational in nature; they are one's 'map' of how the world is. By analogy, choosing a belief would be like a cartographer choosing where various European countries' boundaries should be drawn on a map. If he is conscious of the fact that the boundary lines he is drawing stem from his own personal decisions and do not necessarily reflect the actual borders of France, Italy, and so forth, then the boundary lines he is drawing do not in fact constitute a map.

To be sure, it is possible to concoct various scenarios to escape the logical constraints associated with belief by fiat. Yet, these logical constraints stemming from the nature of a belief do help us understand why beliefs are not propositional attitudes people can (typically, at least) acquire through the basic act of trying to acquire them. At the very least, it seems safe to conclude that many people might not find themselves in the position to acquire a desired belief simply by virtue of a decision to hold it.

This modest conclusion is all we need reach at this point in our discussion. As outlined in the Introduction, our larger project is concerned with the Christian theist's affirmation that faith in God is voluntary. We noted in the Introduction that certain beliefs are requisite for the exercise of faith, and we shall explore this point in some depth in Chapter 4. Even now, though, we can see emerging a general difficulty with the Christian theist's affirmation about the voluntary nature of faith: if beliefs are not the kinds of mental states individuals can always hold simply by deciding to hold them, and if beliefs are indeed necessary for the exercise of Christian faith, then how can the voluntary exercise of faith be a bona fide option for all individuals?

Still, we must not be too quick to conclude from one's inability to acquire a given belief by fiat that the belief lies outside one's ultimate control. Though one might not be able to acquire a belief simply by deciding to hold it, there might still be other ways in which one can voluntarily exercise control over which beliefs one comes to hold. It is these other means of acquiring desired beliefs we shall now consider.

2.3 *The extent to which we can exercise control over our beliefs*

If I find myself unable to acquire a desired belief by simply willing to acquire it, I might still try to acquire it through some indirect means. If I want to believe that a friend is innocent of his co-worker's criminal accusations, I might choose not to examine closely the evidence against my friend and instead choose to look into the co-worker's background in an attempt to find something that would undermine the co-worker's testimony. Similarly, someone who wants to believe the articles of faith contained in a Christian creed might choose to stock her bookshelves with the works of C.S. Lewis and Richard Swinburne, staying well away from anything written by Bertrand Russell or J.L. Mackie. In such cases, one takes steps with the hope that one's actions will (indirectly) result in one coming to hold the desired belief. One's attempts at indirect belief acquisition may sometimes be successful; that much seems uncontroversial. A more difficult question involves the extent to which one can exercise control over what one will come to believe. Specifically, are there certain choices the nature of which *guarantees* that one will (indirectly) come to hold the belief one desires to hold?

This notion of guaranteed success is crucial for our larger discussion, which involves the Christian affirmation that God will someday judge *all* people according to whether or not they freely put their faith in him. Thus, if even one person cannot, despite her best efforts, voluntarily acquire the beliefs requisite for the exercise of faith – with the voluntary exercise of faith therefore not a bona fide option to her – then the Christian theist's original affirmation is undermined. Though direct belief acquisition certainly allows for the kind of guaranteed success needed to make one's beliefs

voluntary and within one's ultimate control, we have already seen
that individuals are not (always, at the very least) in a position to
acquire beliefs in this manner. Yet, do individuals possess the ability
to make certain kinds of other choices through which they can
ultimately control what they come to believe?

Toward answering that question, let us consider the proposal of
Robert Holyer, who has argued that, in addition to the act of
believing by fiat, there remain other choices one can make that
amount to direct influence on one's beliefs.

> Those who have denied the will any direct influence have been concerned
> almost completely with belief by fiat, without considering other possible
> kinds of direct influence. ... [T]o rule out belief by fiat is not necessarily
> to rule out other directly volitional elements in belief nor is it to offer
> very sound argument for the view that belief is a passive response to
> evidence.[11]

It is important at this point to recognize that Holyer's understanding of 'direct influence' differs from 'direct volitionalism' as we have
been using the term. We have used 'direct volitionalism' to denote
the acquisition of a belief through the basic act of trying to hold it.
Holyer's understanding of 'direct influence', though it obviously
includes more than the basic act of belief by fiat, is not altogether
clear. He does not attempt to give a precise definition, conceding
that 'once we exclude belief by fiat, it is not immediately clear what
is at issue in asserting or denying a direct role for the will in belief'.[12]
Still, as we 'dig deeper for the real issues', Holyer states, we find that
one of the primary ones is 'whether assent follows automatically
from an understanding of the evidence'.[13] Thus far, I have suggested
that, once we exclude belief by fiat, any attempt to acquire a belief
will amount to an (indirect) attempt whereby one performs a certain
act and then hopes that at some point one will (involuntarily) come
to hold the belief one desires to hold. While this standard
description of indirect belief acquisition assumes that our assent
will follow involuntarily from our assessment of the evidence we
encounter, Holyer wants to stress that 'in the matter of belief we are
not simply the unwitting victims of the evidence we encounter'.[14]
His claim seems to be that the kind of control we can exercise over
our beliefs is somehow greater, or more 'direct', than in the standard
description of indirect belief acquisition.

Our primary concern in this section is with whether a person can
exercise control over what he believes to the extent that his attempts
to hold a desired belief are guaranteed to succeed. Thus, whatever
else Holyer's arguments might originally have been intended to
show, for our purposes we shall consider Holyer's arguments for the
possibility of 'direct influence' as arguments for the possibility of

guaranteed success in one's attempt to hold a desired belief by means of performing some action (aside from the action of believing by fiat). Correspondingly, we shall take the term '*in*direct influence' to denote the attempt to acquire a desired belief, where one's attempts are *not* guaranteed to succeed. With this understanding of how 'direct' and 'indirect' influence are to be read henceforth in this section, let us consider Holyer's line of argument for the possibility of direct influence over what one believes.

To illustrate the kinds of choices that can amount to direct influence over what one believes, Holyer provides the following example:

> Consider the case of the seasoned atheist who encounters a particularly persuasive religious believer. In the course of extended discussion, the believer unfolds a compelling case for his beliefs by presenting a number of philosophical and historical arguments and by showing the atheist how religious beliefs are implied by some of his basic values and beliefs. The atheist finds the arguments coherent, historically plausible and in agreement with the facts so far as he knows them. Thus, he proceeds to confront the believer with his long-standing objections to religion, only to find that the believer can answer them all satisfactorily. In the end, the atheist has to admit that, so far as he can tell, the case for religious belief is impeccable. Yet, he does not at once assent; instead he goes away to mull the issues over in his own mind, to search for other objections, to consult his atheist friends to see if they can shed new light on the matter, and to check the believer's facts and interpretations against reputedly expert opinion. But, as it turns out, he can find nothing that seriously detracts from the believer's case, and at length, his conviction grows and he finally gives up his atheism to become a believer.[15]

In support of the conclusion that the atheist's belief can rightly be called voluntary, Holyer identifies five ways in which the atheist demonstrates direct control over his beliefs:

(1)   The atheist exercised choice in 'continuing his discussion with' and 'pay[ing] attention to' the believer.

(2)   The atheist exercised choice 'in that he selected certain epistemic norms or criteria by which to evaluate what the believer had to say – in this case by its coherence and agreement with historical fact'.

(3)   The atheist displayed a capacity to 'withhold assent in the face of strong evidence'.

(4)   The atheist exercised choice 'in that the termination of his deliberation was to a degree arbitrary'.

(5)   The atheist had the capacity to 'exercise some control' over

his emotions, which could well have had an influence on his 'initial reluctance to believe as well as his eventual assent'.[16]

The decisions Holyer's atheist makes that (allegedly) directly influence his beliefs seem to fall within two broad categories. First, (1) and (4) are decisions regarding *what* evidence he considered. Second, (2), (3) and (5) are decisions as to *how* this evidence was evaluated. In determining the extent to which these decisions demonstrate control over his beliefs, let us begin by looking at decisions (1) and (4).

At first glance, (1) appears to be a clear case of *in*directly cultivating a belief. For a decision to listen to another person's arguments is simply a decision to examine certain evidence. While one may *hope* that one will (involuntarily) form a certain belief in the light of examining certain evidence, there surely is no *guarantee* that the belief one ends up forming will be the belief one had originally hoped to form. Holyer suggests that this line of argument misses a crucial point. In a letter to Louis Pojman, Holyer writes:

> You in effect ask, 'if I choose to do A and A effects B, how is this choosing to do B'? This is a succinct way of putting the issue, but it leaves unspecified one crucial factor: do I know that A effects B? If I don't know that doing A will effect B, then we've got a clear case of indirect influence. But what if I do know? What if I direct my attention to certain kinds of evidence knowing (at some level from full consciousness on down) that this will prevent me from having reasons to hold a particular belief? If I do, it seems we have a clear case of a direct influence of the will on belief.[17]

So, Holyer allows, if I do not know that my choice to look at certain evidence for *p* will necessarily lead to my belief 'that *p*', then my choice amounts to standard indirect influence. However, if, in deciding to look at certain evidence for *p*, I *do* know that my looking at the evidence will bring about my belief 'that *p*', then in making this decision I exercise definite control over whether I come to believe 'that *p*'.

But how are we to envision a case that falls within Holyer's description of knowing that certain evidence for *p* will effect my belief 'that *p*'? If I know that looking at certain government documents will convince me that Abraham Lincoln was the sixteenth president of the United States, cannot I be said *already* to believe this fact, even though my evidence is not as extensive (and my belief perhaps not as firm) as if I had looked through the government documents? Assume that *E* represents a given collection of evidence that supports a proposition *p*. If I have enough evidence to know (or believe) that E, if I look at it, will effect my belief 'that p', then this evidence, *itself*, is enough to effect my belief 'that p'.

Perhaps one might rejoin that there could be cases in which a person knows that looking at a given piece of evidence will effect a belief – despite not knowing precisely which belief will be formed. But what would a case like that look like? Suppose I want to form a true belief into which city is the capital of Switzerland. Knowing that I will form a true belief on this subject by looking at a globe, I do just that and instantly form the belief that Bern is the capital of Switzerland. My decision to look at certain evidence has led immediately to the belief that Bern is the capital of Switzerland. But is it accurate to say that I knew that looking at the globe would effect the belief that Bern is the capital of Switzerland? The answer is 'no'. I may have known that looking at the globe would lead to a certain belief about the capital of Switzerland; but I could not have known that this act would lead to the belief that *Bern* is the capital of Switzerland. If I had known this, I would have already believed that Bern is the capital of Switzerland.

Admittedly, it is possible to think of rather imaginative scenarios in which one does exercise control over the holding of a belief by choosing to do some action A while knowing that A will effect the holding of that belief. A person might conceivably take a certain drug or visit a hypnotist, knowing that her action will begin a chain of events resulting in her holding the desired belief. Alternatively, we might assume a Freudian theory of separately rational 'systems' within an individual, where one's unconscious system 'knows' that action A will effect a certain belief within one's conscious system.[18] Given that the unconscious system can influence behaviour, and given that the conscious system is unaware of the unconscious system's 'plan' of action, then we might suppose that it is possible sometimes to control through one's decisions (at an unconscious level) whether one comes to hold a certain (conscious) belief. Still, it is only by constructing rather imaginative scenarios such as these that we escape the logical constraints associated with Holyer's description here of direct influence. At the very least, it seems safe to conclude that many people might not ever find themselves in the position of knowing that some particular action A will effect the holding of a particular belief they desire to hold.

Holyer's description of the fourth way in which the atheist exercised control over his beliefs is less problematic, but only because it involves a limited and relatively uncontroversial kind of control. Holyer comments that the atheist exercised choice 'in that the termination of his deliberation was to a degree arbitrary'. This decision to terminate enquiry is a decision to leave one's belief as it is. However, what concerns us in this section is the more difficult issue of whether one can exercise control over the *acquisition* of some belief one wants to hold (but does not yet hold). We might try to amend Holyer's description so that the atheist – at time t_1 and before he holds a certain belief – decides to terminate his enquiry at t_2 so that he will come then to hold that belief. But this amendment leads us back to the previously discussed problems with the notion that we can control what beliefs we acquire by choosing to look at selective evidence.

Let us now turn to the second category of ways in which Holyer's atheist is alleged to have exercised direct control over his beliefs through acts of the will: namely, by choosing how he evaluated the evidence under his consideration. Commenting on decision (2), Holyer states that

> The atheist ... exercised choice in that he selected certain epistemic norms or criteria by which to evaluate what the believer had to say – in this case by its coherence and agreement with historical fact. Although there might be widespread agreement that he chose the correct norms, he could have chosen others, and, if he had, he would have come to a different assessment of the evidence. For example, he may have reasoned: The believer is defending his own beliefs; therefore, all of what he has to say is based on self-interest. Since self-interested arguments are always false, I can disregard it.[19]

Holyer's suggestion is that the atheist's criteria for evaluating evidence might have included something like the following: 'When a person has a vested interest in defending a proposition he believes, his arguments in favour of that proposition will constitute very poor evidence in support of the truth of that proposition'. It is certainly conceivable that this criterion for evaluating evidence *might* have been the atheist's criterion. But is it correct to say that the atheist could have *chosen* that this criterion be the one with which he evaluated the evidential support for the truth of the proposition(s) in question?

Paul Helm has argued that although people are not free to choose their beliefs, they are free to choose their *belief-policies*. Helm defines a belief-policy as 'a strategy or project or programme for accepting, rejecting, or suspending judgement as to the truth of propositions in accordance with a set of evidential norms'.[20] Now, it is certainly true that a person may be free to adopt a certain policy of evidence evaluation. And it is also possible that one might adopt a given policy for reasons that have nothing to do with the goal of holding true beliefs. For example, a person might wish that she were not so cynical in evaluating the evidence of other people's testimony; or, she might wish that she were not so naïve in doing so. Such a person might then resolve to cease/begin investigating the motives behind other people's testimony in an attempt to become a less/ more cynical person. Here, the person's goal is not to hold true beliefs; rather, her goal is to hold those beliefs characteristic of a less/more cynical person. So, we can acknowledge that one might seek to evaluate evidence using a criterion that one does not also believe serves as the most reliable means of getting at the truth.

At the same time, given the conceptual connection between one's beliefs and one's understanding of what is true of the world, it would not be accurate to say that one is free to choose whether a given criterion is the most reliable means of getting at the truth. For this would amount simply to choosing whether one will hold a belief – specifically, the belief 'that this given criterion is the most reliable means of assessing truth'. And we saw in section 2.2 the problems with the idea that one can hold a belief simply by choosing to hold it. Yet, if Holyer's atheist cannot choose whether a given criterion is the most reliable means of getting at the truth, then any choice he might make to adopt a particular belief-policy would not amount to a choice about how he will assess the truth of the believer's argument. In short, it would not amount to the exercise of control over whether he believes the believer's conclusion to be true.

Of course, Holyer's atheist may choose to take steps in an attempt to come to believe that his favoured evidence evaluation criterion is in fact the most reliable means of assessing truth. But this brings us back to the question of the extent to which one can exert control over the acquisition of a belief – in this case, the belief 'that this given criterion is the most reliable means of assessing truth' – by performing some action A as a means of acquiring it. And, again, we have already discussed in this section the limitations associated with such a scenario.

These same limitations arise yet again when we consider the alleged control Holyer's atheist exercised over his beliefs by making decision (5). In making this decision, Holyer remarks, the atheist exercised control over his emotions, which could well have influenced what he came to believe. Aside from any problems regarding the extent to which it is psychologically possible to exercise control over one's emotions, we again find the logical difficulties associated with the notion that a person can, by means of performing some action A, control whether he comes to hold some specific belief he desires to hold.

The final way in which Holyer's atheist allegedly exercised control over his beliefs involves his 'withholding assent in the face of strong evidence'. The atheist's decision to withhold assent, a decision we classified earlier as decision (3), is purportedly made despite hearing a compelling presentation from the believer, whose case the atheist concedes is 'impeccable'. There are a number of ways we might plausibly explain why the atheist might not have assented to the conclusion following from the believer's impeccable argument – ways that have nothing to do with any decision the atheist might have made.[21] Perhaps the atheist believed that, since he and his fellow atheists probably held their views for good reason, there might be evidence that would undermine the believer's testimony – even if he, the atheist, could not think at the moment what that evidence is. Perhaps he was unsure what weight to give to the believer's argument and found himself neither believing nor disbelieving the conclusion put forward by the believer. In describing the atheist as 'withholding assent', Holyer seems to suggest that the atheist's action was a straightforward case of arriving at a belief – namely, 'that the believer's conclusion may not be true' – simply by choosing to hold it. But this amounts, of course, to belief by fiat, which, again, is problematic for reasons discussed in section 2.2.

In the end, once we exclude belief by fiat, it becomes difficult to see how people's efforts to acquire a desired belief can be guaranteed to succeed. Admittedly, we can construct fairly imaginative scenarios – e.g. ones that involve taking a drug or visiting a hypnotist – in which one might know that, by performing a certain action A, one will certainly come to hold a desired belief b. However, more common attempts at this kind of belief acquisition are surely those in which one acts with the hope – as opposed to the knowledge – that one's actions will result in one coming to hold a desired belief. Sometimes one's efforts may be successful; at other times they may not be. At the very least, it is conceivable that some individuals might exhaust every available option in an attempt to acquire a desired belief b and still fail to acquire it.

Before moving on, we can note a possible theological rejoinder to the conclusions of this chapter. It might be argued that there are various ways in which God could conceivably work around any logical constraints stemming from the nature of beliefs so as to ensure that people do acquire the beliefs requisite for Christian faith[22] whenever they earnestly seek to hold them. God might, for instance, aid in direct belief acquisition[23] by enabling a person at t_2 to forget that she had acquired a belief by fiat at t_1. Alternatively, God might aid in indirect belief acquisition simply by ensuring that any person who sought to acquire true religious beliefs via indirect means would go on to see her evidence as pointing to the truth of those beliefs requisite for Christian faith.

The problem with this suggestion is that it seems obvious that God does *not* in fact ensure that all people who seek to hold true beliefs about him go on at some point in their earthly lives to hold those beliefs requisite for Christian faith. We noted in our introduction the implausiblity of supposing that of the group of people who fail to hold the beliefs requisite for Christian faith, *every* person would fail to exercise Christian faith if only he or she were to acquire these beliefs. That is, it would be implausible to suppose that *all* people who do not hold the beliefs requisite for Christian faith are disposed to reject the picture of God they would acquire if they came to hold those beliefs. Following on from this conclusion, it would seem implausible to suppose that among the group of people who do not hold the beliefs requisite for Christian faith, no one seeks with the right attitude to acquire true religious beliefs.

To put the matter slightly differently, there is not a direct correlation between one's honest attempts to acquire true religious beliefs and one's holding of Christian beliefs in one's earthly life.[24] Thus, the Christian theist cannot plausibly assert that God ensures that all people who earnestly try (via belief by fiat or via indirect means) to acquire true religious beliefs go on to acquire at some point in their earthly lives the beliefs requisite for Christian faith. Seeking to hold true religious beliefs – even among those disposed to exercise Christian faith if they were to acquire the beliefs requisite for such faith – is no guarantee that one will acquire Christian beliefs at any point in one's earthly life.

Conclusion

We have distinguished two ways in which a person might attempt to acquire a belief she desires to hold: by directly acquiring the belief through the basic act of trying to hold it; and by choosing to perform actions that indirectly lead to the acquisition of the belief. Apart from our common experience of finding belief by fiat psychologically impossible, there are logical constraints associated with belief by fiat that show why such an undertaking is in principle problematic in most situations. The notion of *in*direct belief acquisition is less problematic – but only inasmuch as we assume a person's efforts to carry no guarantee of success. Admittedly, it is possible to build guaranteed success into an imaginative description of a case of indirect belief acquisition. But to avoid logical constraints, we must appeal to what surely are uncommon scenarios – such as the taking of a drug one knows will lead to one holding a certain belief – in describing how a person might know that by performing a certain action A he will come to hold a given belief b he does not already hold. Our conclusion, then, is that a person who desires to hold a particular belief may yet find that there is no decision available to him by which he can ultimately control whether or not he holds the belief.

I stated in the Introduction that the Christian theist faces the following possible objection to his affirmations about the voluntary nature of faith: if belief is an involuntary matter, and if certain beliefs are requisite for Christian faith, how can people rightly be 'judged' by God according to whether or not they have voluntarily put their faith in him? Having come to the conclusion that belief (for some people, at the very least) is indeed an involuntary matter, we are now halfway through spelling out this objection. It remains for us to explore whether (and which) beliefs really are requisite for the exercise of Christian faith. So let us turn now to examine the nature of Christian faith.

Notes

[1] Shooting a gun, for example, is *not* a basic act because I do something else – namely, squeeze my finger – in order to do it. However, the act of squeezing my finger *is* a basic act because (presumably) there is nothing I do (apart from trying to move it) as a means to squeezing my finger. Cf. Danto (1965) on basic actions. With respect to the distinction in Baier (1971) between a causally basic act and a teleologically basic act, we are speaking here of teleologically basic acts.

[2] Govier 1976: 642. Presumably, Govier's point is not that one could 'just like that' either (a) choose that he would *like*, or *want*, to have a certain belief, or (b) choose to acquire a belief *without* having any *desire* or *reason* to do so. Rather, direct belief acquisition involves a scenario where, given that one desires to have a belief, one arrives at the belief via the single act of choosing to hold it.

[3] Cf. Clarke 1986: 39f. and Pojman 1986: 144. Govier (1976) provides a good description of this process: 'One decides that it would be a good thing if he believed something; one thinks of actions he could take which would be likely to result in his coming to hold this belief; one takes these actions; and, if all works well, one then believes as desired' (652).

[4] Cf. Price 1969: 222.

[5] Williams 1970: 148.

[6] As I use the terms here, 'believing at will', 'directly acquiring a belief', 'believing by fiat' and 'believing as a basic act' can be used interchangeably without loss of meaning.

[7] For a discussion of philosophers who have argued for the psychological impossibility of voluntary belief acquisition, see Pojman (1986: viii, 159f.).

[8] Williams 1970: 148.

[9] Barbara Winters (1979) has pointed out that a person might discover that she had acquired a belief at will (assuming this is possible), yet continue to hold the belief because she now has good evidence for holding the belief. Her principle with respect to believing at will is an improvement on Williams's initial account: 'it is impossible to believe that one believes *p* and that one's belief of *p* originated and is sustained in a way that has no connection with *p*'s truth' (243). For simplicity of discussion, we shall assume in the examples that follow that one does not obtain new evidence after the initial acquisition of the belief 'that *p*'.

[10] But see Winters (1979) for her argument to the contrary (255).

[11] Holyer 1983: 274.

[12] Holyer 1983: 275. For a good discussion of the ways in which one might seek to distinguish direct from indirect belief acquisition, see Alston (1988: § IV-VI).

[13] Holyer 1983: 275.

[14] Holyer 1983: 275.

[15] Holyer 1983: 276.

[16] Holyer 1983: 276–9.

[17] As quoted in Pojman (1984: 697).

[18] Perhaps Holyer has in mind examples of this kind when he states that knowing might occur 'at some level from full consciousness on down'.

[19] Holyer 1983: 277.

[20] Helm 1994: 58.

[21] Cf. Alston (1988: 124–7) for a discussion of cases where belief by fiat is sometimes alleged – but where other explanations that do not involve belief by fiat are more plausible.

[22] We shall discuss in Chapter 4 precisely what the beliefs requisite for Christian faith are.

[23] Here I am using 'direct' to denote the basic act of belief acquisition by fiat – as opposed to the sense in which Holyer's atheist was alleged to have exercised direct influence over what he came to believe.

[24] We shall discuss this point in some detail in Chapter 7.

THE NATURE OF FAITH

3.1 *A definition of faith*

The term 'faith' is commonly used in varying, everyday contexts to denote quite different things. When a father suspects that his teenage son is not telling the truth, he might nonetheless 'act as though he believes' his son, describing his own behaviour as 'showing faith' in his son. When someone is told that her lottery ticket has little chance of paying off, she might respond by saying, 'Well, you've got to have faith.' Magazine articles sometimes encourage us to have faith in principles, institutions or economic policies. Within religious contexts, Christians will understand the notion of faith quite differently than will Sŏn Buddhists, who typically deny that faith has any object at all. Even within the Christian tradition, one finds a host of different emphases as to what lies at the heart of Christian faith. Some Christian writers have sought to define faith in terms of belief[1] – or, at least, belief formed in love[2] – while other writers have emphasized the notion of trust.[3] Still other writers have been concerned to stress the roles of obedience,[4] confession[5] or hope.[6]

The varying points of emphasis in accounts of faith within the Christian tradition become understandable as one recognizes that the Bible uses the term 'faith' – which is the typical translation of the Hebrew `amān in the Old Testament and the Greek πίστις in the New Testament – to express a host of varied ideas. The term 'faith' is used at times to denote a commitment to Christian discipleship (2 Tim. 1.5). In various places it is linked with propositional belief (Heb. 11.6), with obedience (Heb. 11.17), and with that which makes obedience possible (Rom. 1.5). It is sometimes used to indicate teaching that is faithful to the apostolic message (Jude 3), and sometimes used to indicate faithfulness to one's covenant with another person (Mal. 2.14). Faith is identified as a spiritual gift, along with other gifts such as teaching, prophecy and healing (1 Cor. 12.9); and yet, faith is also identified as that which makes healing and other miracles possible (Mt. 17.18-20). Faith is sometimes described as something that admits to degrees, or measure (Rom. 12.3). And while one can confess one's faith (Jn 12.42), one can also 'put one's faith in' someone else (Jn 2.11).

Following these biblical references, there seem to be a number of different meanings one might, within the Christian religion, legitimately assign to the term 'faith'. The understanding of faith on which I want to focus involves the kind of faith distinctive of the redeemed. The Christian tradition has wanted to identify the people who are reconciled to God – and thus saved from eternal separation from God after their lives on earth – with those who have put their faith in Jesus Christ. But what is it to put one's faith in someone else? The Bible does not provide a straightforward definition along these lines. Avery Dulles comments that 'The apostolic fathers show no interest in formulating precise definitions of faith or speculative theories about the subject. Their concern is rather to motivate their readers to persevere and grow in the life of faith.'[7] Surely the same can be said with respect to the primary concerns of the biblical writers, who were understandably more concerned with exhorting their readers to reach out to God than with providing a philosophically subtle account of that in which this reaching consists.[8] Still, one thing that does appear clear from the biblical writers and from later Christian theologians is that the redeemed are in fact the redeemed in virtue of a certain kind of *relationship* they enjoy with God. And in my examination of Christian faith, I start from this premise.

In the Introduction we stipulated that God's relationship with an individual – as in any interpersonal relationship – cannot be unilaterally established by God. Instead, some kind of human response of faith is necessary if a personal relationship with God is to be established. It is my aim in this chapter to spell out my own specific account of the kind of decision that lies at the heart of virtuous Christian faith. Instead of relying on terms such as trust or hope in describing the nature of Christian faith, I shall attempt to provide more philosophical precision than is perhaps possible with these commonly used, but general, terms. Still, I mean my own account of faith essentially to be a spelling-out of what the Christian tradition has always wanted to affirm regarding the nature of faith – specifically, that it is in the response of faith that individuals enter into the right kind of personal relationship with God.

Our question, then, is this: under what account of faith would one enter, in virtue of having such faith, into the kind of personal relationship with God that accomplishes the ends of the Christian religion? With this question in mind, I wish to defend the following account of what it is to have faith in someone:

> Person S has faith in person G inasmuch as S, in response to G's invitational statement(s) to S, accepts G's authority in the areas to which this statement(s) indicates that G's authority extends.

I propose that, when one has faith in God under this description, one enters into the kind of relationship with God commended by the Christian religion. In unpacking this account of faith, let us begin by examining the importance of G's invitational statements to S.

3.2 The nature and role of 'invitational statements'

Any personal relationship involves a mutual recognition of, and response to, the agency of the other person. Consequently, if S places her faith in G, this act will not establish a personal relationship between the two if G has not already extended an invitation to S to enter into a personal relationship. Such an invitation to S will come in the form of some type of communication from G to S. Robert Adams comments:

> I think the sin of unbelief always involves rejection of something God has said to the sinner ... Butterflies presumably do not believe in God, but they are not therefore guilty of the sin of unbelief. If we, unlike butterflies, are guilty of the sin of unbelief, it is not because we are supposed to be able to *figure out* divine truth for ourselves, but because God has spoken to us.[9]

We can acknowledge that there might well be cases in which one person is obligated to respond to another person even if that other person has not attempted to communicate with him. For example, a father might be obligated to respond to his infant daughter wandering off by searching for her. However, with respect to humans responding to God, Adams seems correct in suggesting that such a response should not be expected if one has had no communication from God to respond *to*.

The Christian tradition has affirmed with wide accord (and near unanimity for its first 1,500 years) that God does communicate with humans and that such communication is fundamental to the Christian religion. Following the many biblical narratives describing God's communication with humans, the Christian tradition has allowed that God can communicate with people by actually 'speaking' to them.[10] This is not to say that the Christian tradition must be committed to the idea that God has vocal cords through which he makes utterances, or hands through which he writes down his thoughts. That one can perform speech acts without such corporeal features becomes understandable upon consideration of the distinction J.L. Austin has made between *phatic* acts and the kinds of *force* phatic acts can have. A phatic act is an uttering of an intelligible sentence, such as 'The door is still open'. The *locutionary* force of a phatic act involves the sense and reference of the utterance; and the *il*locutionary force is what one means to do (e.g. issue a command or make a promise) in making the utterance. Thus, the locutionary force of 'The door is still open' is the predication of something of a piece of wood; and the illocutionary force of this utterance may be that of a reprimand or an exclamation of exasperation or a comment on the draftiness of a room.

Now suppose my intention is to request that someone shut the door. I might make this request by performing the phatic act of uttering the sentence, 'Would you please shut the door?' However, I might also make this request by looking someone in the eye, raising my eyebrows, and pointing to the door. These physical movements carry the illocutionary force of a request just as the utterance 'Would you shut the door?' carries the force of a request. The general point is that one can do things like issue commands and make promises by means other than the acts of uttering and inscribing words. Indeed, humans have devised a number of ways to discourse with one another, including the use of winks, nods, shoulder shrugs, sign language, smoke signals, light flashes, and so forth. Granted, these further means of communication involve corporeal features; and God does not have such features. But is it nonetheless possible that God might communicate through means that do *not* involve any corporeal features?

One of the ways in which God might, despite not having corporeal features, communicate with people is by directly bringing it about that they hold a true conviction that God is asking or asserting something.[11] Alternatively, and perhaps more straightforwardly, it seems open to God to bring it about that someone perceives she is hearing something like a unique-sounding 'still, small voice'. Apart from communicating with people through direct means such as these, the Christian tradition has affirmed that God does speak to people through more indirect means, such as a preacher or sacred scripture. In examining how one can perform speech acts through the words or writings of someone else, consider the oft-cited example of a secretary who writes a letter on behalf of an executive.[12] While the secretary types or writes down the words of the letter, the executive signs the letter, which becomes the means by which the executive says something to the letter's recipient. The executive may dictate the letter, or he may explain to his secretary the crux of what he wants to say and leave it to her to compose the specifics of the letter. Possibly, the secretary will compose a letter with no prior instructions from the executive to do so; for instance, a secretary might compose a thank-you note which she thinks the executive would want to send. In all these cases, the letter becomes the executive's speech act if he *authorizes* the letter – that is, if he does something that counts as his performing a speech act. In this example, what counts as his performing a speech act is his signing the letter. We should note that the extent of the executive's involvement in the specific composition of the letter – i.e. whether he dictated it or was unaware that his secretary was writing it – is an issue quite different from the issue of authorization. Indeed, an executive may dictate a letter and decide in the end not to sign or send it. What makes the letter a medium of *his* speech is his authorization of the letter, which, again, he accomplishes by signing the letter (or by authorizing his secretary to sign his name for him).

With respect to God speaking through, e.g. a preacher or sacred scripture, again the key issue is authorization. We saw that the executive authorizes the letter written by his secretary by signing it; but how might God authorize the utterances of a preacher or the writings of scripture? Two straightforward methods God might use are *deputization* and *appropriation*. Deputization occurs as one party (e.g. the president of a country) authorizes another party (e.g. an ambassador) to speak on his behalf. According to Christian tradition, Jesus, at one point in his earthly ministry, sent out 70 followers into neighbouring towns, commissioning them with the words, 'He who listens to you listens to me; he who rejects you rejects me.'[13] There seems to be no reason why God could not today deputize gifted teachers and preachers to speak to others on his behalf.

Unlike deputization, appropriation does not involve commissioning someone else ahead of time to speak on one's behalf. Instead, appropriation is a matter of making someone else's speech acts one's own. That is, it is a matter of declaring, 'That discourse of someone else speaks for me'. We might appropriate another person's discourse by signing a petition, nodding, saying 'Hear, hear!' and so forth. Nicholas Wolterstorff argues that divine appropriation of human discourse[14] is the most plausible way to understand the claim that God authorizes sacred scripture as his own speech, noting that 'If it is the Christian Bible we are speaking of, the event which *counts as* God's appropriating this totality as the medium of God's own discourse is presumably the rather drawn-out event consisting of the Church's settling on the totality as its canon'.[15] Whether authorization is accomplished through deputization, or through appropriation, or through some other means, authorization represents a way for God to speak to one human by means of the phatic utterances and written words of another human.

The Christian tradition has often affirmed that God can communicate different messages to different people who are all listening to the same sermon or reading the same passage of scripture. The idea is that God can use the general points made in a sermon or in scripture and speak to an individual about the specific circumstances with which he or she is currently faced. How is this possible? Perhaps an example will show how God might accomplish this feat. Suppose that I have a relationship with three persons who represent three generations of a certain family. Suppose further that my relationships with all three persons are based partially on conversations we have had about finding the right vocation. Let us assume that the following is also the case: the eldest of these three persons, 'Senior', once gave me advice on finding the right vocation. He emphasized how important it is to have a career plan and to stick to it, and his advice proved valuable. The next member of the family, 'Junior', who is a contemporary of mine, has had trouble finding the right career. My advice to him has been that he has been too quick to change jobs when feelings of monotony have begun to emerge; and I have urged him, when he contemplates career changes, to set aside temporary emotions that seem to run his life and to use sober thinking in making important decisions. The last member of the family, 'Tre', is only a teenager, but I have told him that it is not too early for him to begin thinking about career choices.

Now suppose that I am in a room with all three persons and that we are listening to a vocational counsellor talk about career choices. At one point the counsellor says, 'Sometimes we need to sit down and really think about the future'. Upon hearing this assertion I say out loud, 'Hear, hear!', thereby appropriating the counsellor's assertion as my own speech act. My appropriated speech act is aimed at all three persons with me. To Tre, I mean to suggest that it would be a good thing for him to set aside time to make tentative plans for the future. To Junior, I mean to re-emphasize my earlier advice that cool *thinking* should supplant emotional *feelings* in planning for the future. To Senior, I mean to say 'thank you' for helping me understand the value of planning for the future. This case is one in which I use the same propositional content of my appropriated discourse to say different things to different people.[16] I am able to accomplish this feat because I have a different history of experiences with each person. Each person's interpretation of my remark, as well as my expectations of how each will interpret my remark, is shaped by the nature of the relationship we have. Indeed, all interpretations of other people's speech acts are shaped by what we know of them. If God, then, has a unique relationship with each person who hears a particular sermon or reads a particular passage of scripture, then we have a way to make sense of the claim that

God can say many different things to many different people through
the same divinely authorized human discourse.

In the example regarding vocational planning, my use of a single
comment to say three different things to three different people was
not at all difficult. The ease of this task stemmed from the fact that
the vocational counsellor's comment seemed perfectly suited to my
purpose of using it to convey my intended messages to the three
people. According to the Christian religion, God 'inspired' the
writing of sacred scripture in much the same way that he inspires
certain teachers and preachers.[17] If God does inspire such human
discourse, one of his primary reasons for doing so may well be to
guarantee that he has human discourse at his disposal that is
exceptionally well suited to his purpose of using it to say the many
different things he wants to say to many different people.

Having briefly sketched some of the ways in which God might
speak to people – either directly or through divinely authorized
human discourse – let us turn to the role speech acts play in the
account of faith I have given. As stated earlier, S's faith in G will
establish a personal relationship between the two only if G has
already extended to S an invitation to enter into a personal
relationship. Such an invitation is issued to another person, I
contend, any time one makes a statement of a certain sort – let us
call it an *invitational statement* – to that other person. Invitational
statements can be, among other things, commands, promises, or
assertions that one person makes to another person/s. Invitational
statements differ from non-invitational statements in two ways.
First, in making an invitational statement, the speaker claims that
she has the authority-making features that establish her right to
make the statement. Such a claim might be explicitly or implicitly
stated. For example, a military officer may issue a command to his
subordinate by explicitly saying, 'As your superior, I command you
to perform this task'. On the other hand, a woman may say to her
friend, 'It's wrong of you to cheat on your income tax and it's clear
that you should stop!' In this latter example, the woman makes an
implicit claim to be enough of a moral authority to know what is
morally required of her friend. It is this moral authority, so the
implicit claim goes, that gives the woman the right to tell her friend
she should stop cheating. Promising and asserting, when they are
invitational statements, also carry explicit or implicit authoritative
claims. If I promise someone that I will meet him for lunch, I am
claiming that I am in a position to ensure that that promise is
realized.[18] If I assert to someone that Jerry had salad for lunch
yesterday, I am claiming to be in a position to know and accurately
to report what Jerry had for lunch yesterday. It is being in this

position that gives me the right to testify to the truth of my statement.

Before introducing the second common feature of invitational statements, it is worth noting Nicholas Wolterstorff's comments on the 'normative' qualities of speech acts such as promising and commanding.

> Speaking consists not in communicating or expressing knowledge (or true belief) but in taking up a certain sort of *normative stance*, as I shall call it … The intended function of promising and commanding is not to inform us of what we don't know but to take on duties *toward* us and to require things *of* us.[19]

As an example of someone who acquires a normative standing with others, Wolterstorff describes a car-driver who signals left by flipping the car's left-hand blinkers. By flipping the blinkers (which constitutes a speech act, presumably the conveying of an intention)[20] the driver takes on prima facie duties; and those motorists around the driver also find themselves with prima facie duties – namely, to treat the driver 'as one who has signaled a left turn'.[21]

For our purposes, what is important about the car-driver who signals left is that she desires that the motorists around her *respond* to her speech act – i.e., her flipping the car's left-hand blinkers – in a certain way. We noted earlier that, in making an invitational statement, the speaker claims that she has the authority-making features that establish her right to make this statement. We can now state the second common feature of invitational statements: when making an invitational statement to a given person(s), the speaker desires that that person respond to her authoritative claims in a certain kind of way.

To illustrate this element of invitational statements, consider the example of a newspaper columnist who gives marital advice. It may be the case that the columnist hopes that her readers will read the column, realize that the assertions made in the column make perfect sense, and then proceed to change their habits. It will not matter to the columnist whether the readers even notice who wrote the column. Her only interest is that the statements in her column resonate with her readers. If all this is true of the columnist, then her statements do not constitute an invitation to enter into a personal relationship any more than finding a copy of an ancient poem by an anonymous poet constitutes an invitation by that poet to enter into a personal relationship. For the columnist is inviting her readers to respond to her *statements themselves*; she is not inviting them to respond to *her* as a personal agent. Consequently, the columnist's statements do not amount to invitational statements.[22]

On the other hand, it may be the case that the columnist insists that her newspaper byline carry the inscription: 'PhD in psychology with over 20 years experience as a marriage therapist'. Here, the columnist desires that her readers follow her advice, at least in part because of her qualifications as an expert on marriage relationships. Her statements in her column constitute invitational statements because (a) they carry with them the claim to have authority-making features that establish her right to make these statements, and (b) she desires that her readers respond to this *authoritative claim*, as opposed to responding merely to her statements themselves. The columnist has invited her readers to respond to *her* as a personal agent. Her statements are invitational statements; they constitute an invitation to her readers to relate at some level to her.[23]

But what of the Christian theist's positive response to what she perceives as God's directives? The Christian religion summarizes its core teachings as the 'gospel', or (from the Greek εὐαγγέλιον) the 'good message'. And one might argue that it is (sometimes, at least) more natural to think of people responding to God's *message* to them than to think of them responding to the *authoritative claims* that accompany God's message. What should we make of the proposal that one's positive response might be to the good news contained in God's message – rather than to the fact that it is God who has communicated this message?

To offer a rejoinder here, the crucial factor on my account will be whether the person responds to God's message *within the context* of relating to God. Put another way, we might ask: does the person recognize the message as coming from a personal agent who invites her into a relationship? If so, then the content of the message itself might largely be what *motivates* her to respond; but this fact is not unusual within the give and take of personal relationships. A man's spouse may tell him the good news that she is willing to go on holiday with him to his favourite destination. The thought of going to this destination may indeed be good news to him; but surely his positive response to his wife's message will be shaped partly because it is the conveying of his *wife's* willingness to go with him. If we suppose that his reaction would be exactly the same no matter *who* expressed a willingness to accompany him on holiday, then perhaps we will want to say that his response truly is merely to the message itself, that someone is willing to share a holiday with him. But surely (or, at least, hopefully) this will not be the case. Surely the man's response to the message will be shaped in large part because it comes from his wife. Similarly, the Christian theist's response to the promises contained in the gospel message – e.g. the possibility of eternal life, forgiveness, peace – is shaped in large part because these promises are seen as coming from God. After all, the theist presumably would not respond positively to these promises if they were made to him by just *anyone*. That the theist's response to the gospel message is shaped in part by the understanding that it comes from God shows that the theist is recognizing and responding to the agency of God.

3.3 *Faith as the acceptance of another's authority*

When G makes an invitational statement to S, any response by S to the authoritative claims that accompany this statement will establish a personal relationship with G. We shall now consider the *kind* of positive response S might make to God's invitational statement(s) that would establish the *kind* of personal relationship with God commended by the Christian religion.

Let us invent a fictional country of Aarvak and suppose that Sue is preparing for a meeting to discuss whether a communiqué should be issued condemning the recent overthrow of the Aarvakian president by the Aarvakian military. Suppose further that, before the meeting, Gary tells Sue that the former president's administration was corrupt in ways that do not seem to be appreciated by most members of the media who have reported the overthrow. As discussed earlier, for Gary's assertion to Sue to serve as an invitational statement,[24] Gary must desire that Sue respond to his assertion because *Gary himself* made it. In other words, Gary must desire that considerations of his own authority-making features play a part in Sue's decision to respond to his statements. When Sue responds to the authoritative claims that accompany Gary's assertion, she establishes a type of personal relationship with him. She may choose to undermine his authority, in which case she will help to establish a kind of 'negative' personal relationship with Gary. However, with respect to the kind of response that signifies *faith in* Gary, Sue will need in some way to *accept* Gary's authority.

At this point it is important to distinguish my use of the term 'accept' from other possible ways in which the term might be used. Paul Tillich, for example, relied on a certain understanding of acceptance in his well-known exhortation as to how one should respond to God: 'Do not seek for anything; do not perform anything; do not intend anything. *Simply accept the fact that you are accepted!*'[25] Whatever the full implications of Tillich's understanding of 'acceptance' here, it is clear that acceptance is to be contrasted with the performance of any act and even with the formation of an intention. In contrast with this use of 'acceptance', we saw in section 1.2 how Jonathan Cohen distinguished 'acceptance' from 'belief', stipulating that 'accepting' a proposition is a matter of adopting it for use in further deliberations. This use of 'acceptance' is also employed by William Alston in a line of argument we shall later consider in section 4.3.

My own use of the term 'accept' carries its own implications and should not be confused with these, or other possible, uses of the term. In using the term 'accept' in my own account of faith I wish to specify that *what S is accepting is G's invitation to relate to G on certain terms*. We have seen in this section that such an invitation comes in the form of an invitational statement, which G issues to S and which is accompanied by explicit or implicit authoritative claims. As I shall discuss in more detail shortly, the type of authoritative claims that accompany G's invitational statements will determine the type of relationship into which G invites S. On my use of the term 'accept', to say that S accepts G's authority is to say that S agrees to relate to G on the terms indicated by the authoritative claims that accompany G's invitational statement(s) to S.

In accepting Gary's authority, Sue might perform any number of actions. She might vote a particular way at her meeting based on what Gary told her; or encourage others to vote the same way; or relay to others the statement Gary made; or decide to rethink her policy of generally not questioning the accuracy of media reports about foreign countries. All these actions might well be examples of accepting Gary's authority. The ways in which Sue might legitimately make such a positive response to Gary's authority will be limited by two factors. First, the content of Gary's statements will narrow the range of ways in which she can respond to his authority in a way that constitutes genuine acceptance of it. If Gary tells Sue that she is morally obligated to vote a particular way at the meeting, then she will not accept his authority by urging others to vote this particular way while not doing so herself. Second, the ways in which Sue can genuinely accept Gary's authority will vary according to the type of authority she recognizes Gary as having. If Sue recognizes Gary as an authority on *the workings of the former Aarvakian government*, then she might demonstrate her acceptance of Gary's authority by acting in ways that assume that most of the media really do not know the full extent of the Aarvakian government's activities. If she recognizes Gary as an authority on *the true moral insidiousness of government corruption in general*, then she might seek to demonstrate her acceptance of Gary's authority by acting in ways that assume that the media, when it reported the government's actions, did not fully understand just how immoral those acts truly were.

In stating that S's acceptance of G's authority must be in 'the areas to which G's statements indicate that G's authority extends', I mean to suggest that there must be a kind of 'meeting of the minds' between G and S as to the type and extent of authority that lie behind G's statements. Put another way, the authoritative claims that accompany G's statements to S must to a certain degree correspond to the claims of authority S understands G as making. The relationship Gary seeks to have in making invitational statements to Sue may be of any number of kinds. He may seek a relationship with her where he is a mentor or a protégé; where he is a peer or a parent; where his advice is expected to be taken with a grain of salt, or seriously considered, or unquestioningly followed. Suppose that Gary, in making statements to Sue about the media's underappreciation of the Aarvakian government's immorality, means to convey to her that he is – in addition to being a knowledgeable person in the areas of Aarvak and the media – a moral expert in a way that Sue is not. Here, Gary's statements might be described as an invitation to have a relationship with Sue where he assumes the role of a spiritual mentor by virtue of his moral expertise. However, if Sue understands Gary only to be making the implicit authoritative claim to be one who knows about the media and governments, she will misunderstand the type of relationship into which he has invited her. If Sue responds positively to Gary's statements on the grounds that he has authority simply as one who possesses knowledge of the media and governments, does she thereby establish a personal relationship with Gary? This would depend primarily on whether Gary is willing to accede to a personal relationship with Sue in which she recognizes his authority as a knowledgeable person but not as a mentor. Perhaps Gary will go on to state explicitly to Sue that he wishes their relationship to be one of spiritual mentor and protégé – possibly a relationship in which Gary advises Sue on a wide range of moral issues. If Sue nonetheless refuses to recognize his authority as a moral mentor, but still seeks to relate to him as one who has the authority-making features (merely) of a media expert, then Gary will need to decide whether he is willing to accede to a personal relationship with her on *these* terms.[26] Of course, we can also imagine a case where Sue recognizes Gary as making *more* claims to authority than he intended to make. For example, she might recognize and seek to make a positive response to Gary's authority as a moral arbiter – where he had only meant to convey that he knew a bit about the media. In such a case, Gary will have to decide whether he is willing to 'offer' that part of himself to Sue by relating to her on a 'deeper' level than he had initially intended.

Turning now to the thought of God making invitational statements, it seems telling that, within every book of the New Testament, the writer refers to Jesus Christ as 'Lord'. Whatever else this term may mean in the context of the New Testament, I understand the term to carry the following implication. To relate to

God as Lord is, roughly, to allow him to make (if he so chooses) all the final decisions that a created human is obligated to allow her creator to make regarding how she lives her life. If God does want us to relate to him as Lord, then presumably any invitational statement he issues to us will carry the invitation to relate to him in that way.

Of course, on the Christian understanding of the universal nature of human sin, it would seem that no one accepts God's authority as Lord with perfect consistency. In Chapter 8, we shall consider the criteria God might use in determining whether or not to agree to an ongoing (and eternal) relationship with someone who falls short of making such an ideally consistent response. For now, we can make the following general point. From the Christian perspective, although God invites people to relate to him as Lord, no one in this life meets the strictest terms of this relationship. As to the question of whether a positive, personal relationship with God is nonetheless established when a person falls short of making this kind of perfectly consistent positive response to God, the answer – as with any case in which G's authoritative claims are not fully understood and/or accepted by S – will simply depend on whether God is willing to accept a relationship with the person on these terms.

3.4 The role of 'accepting God's authority' in action explanation; and the Augustinian objection to idolatry

In describing what it is for S to accept G's authority, I have given examples of actions S might take that would constitute, in the appropriate situation, the acceptance of G's authority and that would thereby establish a personal relationship with G. But it would be too quick a move to conclude that S, upon hearing G's invitational statements, simply makes a decision whether or not to accept G's authority. Things are not so simple. For it would be quite implausible to suppose that the acceptance of G's authority is the *ultimate purpose* S seeks to achieve whenever she performs those actions that in fact constitute an acceptance of G's authority.

Returning to a previous example: suppose that Sue's ultimate purpose in voting against a communiqué condemning the overthrow of the Aarvakian government is the furthering of justice in the world. Let us suppose further that her action of voting is explained in terms of (a) this ultimate purpose and (b) her belief that by accepting the authority of Gary – who has advised her how to vote and whom she recognizes as an authority on government corruption – she will achieve her ultimate purpose. In this case, Sue's acceptance of Gary's authority would constitute an *intermediate* purpose as she seeks to achieve her ultimate purpose of furthering justice in the world.

Similarly, it seems plausible to suppose that a person might, in the context of certain invitational statements she believes God to have issued, accept his authority as a means to some other ultimate goal. For example, a person may offer up petitionary prayers in response to Jesus's recorded statement, 'Come to me, all you who are weary and burdened, and I will give you rest',[27] because she wants to be free from certain burdens that have become unbearable. Likewise, a person may follow with a repentant attitude Jesus's instructions to take Holy Communion because she can no longer live with feelings of guilt and wants to experience forgiveness. In these examples, one demonstrates an acceptance of God's authority and thus an agreement to relate to God in a certain way. Yet, the purpose of relating personally to God is undertaken with a view to achieving some further purpose. Moreover, this further purpose involves self-directed concerns such as a desire to overcome certain problems or to shed the weight of one's feelings of guilt.

But is it theologically acceptable to suppose that a person might exercise faith in God – that is, accept God's authority – as an intermediate purpose as she seeks to achieve some further, ultimate purpose that involves self-directed concerns? Certain writings of Augustine suggest a possible objection to such a scenario. Augustine affirmed that God created all the good things of this world, but he cautioned that we 'should love none of these things, nor think them desirable for their own sakes'.[28] He added that 'when you consider things beneath yourself to be admirable and desirable, what is this but to be cheated and misled by unreal goods?'[29] For Augustine, God constitutes the one ultimate good worth pursuing. After citing the biblical imperative to love God 'with all thy soul, with all thy heart, and with all thy mind',[30] he asked rhetorically how it cannot be concluded 'that our chief good which we must hasten to arrive at in preference to all other things is nothing else than God'.[31]

Preference for God above all other things, Augustine explained, has implications as to how we are to love other people. Augustine affirmed that 'we are commanded to love one another', but he pressed the question 'whether man is to be loved by man for his own sake, or for the sake of something else'.[32] His answer is that while 'God is to be loved for His own sake', 'every man is to be loved as a man for God's sake'.[33] Augustine even remarked that no one ought 'to have joy in himself, if you look at the matter clearly, because no one ought to love even himself for his own sake, but for the sake of Him who is the true object of enjoyment'.[34] In distinguishing how loving someone for his own sake differs from loving someone for the sake of something else, Augustine commented that, 'If it is for his own sake, we enjoy him; if it is for the sake of something else, we use him'.[35]

Returning now to the account of faith I have sketched, I have suggested that one might, in response to God's invitational statements, agree to relate to God in order to accomplish further goals having to do with one's own good. Does this amount, though, to 'using' God in the pursuit of other purposes – e.g. one's own well-being and happiness – that one considers to be a greater good than God himself? Drawing upon Augustine's writings, we might formulate the following objection to the account of faith I have sketched. 'The only proper, Christian response to God is one that is motivated by a love of God for God's own sake.[36] Thus, if some people do pursue the (intermediate) purpose of relating to God in order to achieve a further (ultimate) purpose, this further purpose must involve goals one has for God (e.g. that he receive due honour and glory) and not goals one has for oneself (e.g. that one receive comfort or blessing). Otherwise, one's motivation in pursuing a relationship with God will be the (inappropriate) motivation of self-love and not the (solely appropriate) motivation of love of God'.

In response to this objection I concede that, if the genuine exercise of Christian faith requires that one be motivated solely out of love of God for God's own sake, then any further ultimate purpose one pursues by means of exercising faith in God cannot involve self-directed concerns. However, such a requirement seems unwarranted. We can perhaps acknowledge the Christian understanding that the most mature of Christians in the heavenly realm, stirred by the beatific vision, may be solely motivated in their actions by an unadulterated love of God. At the same time, there is, I think, no good reason to suppose that a person whose motives fall short of full Christian maturity cannot still exercise genuine faith in God by accepting his authority as a means of achieving some further, self-directed purpose. In support of this claim we need look no further than the recorded words of Jesus, who, in urging others to respond to God, repeatedly appealed to the self-interested (though not self*ish*) motives of storing up treasures for oneself in heaven and avoiding the miseries of hell. Take, for example, Jesus's recorded teachings from the Sermon on the Mount. Why should I not judge others? Because 'in the same way as you judge others, you will be judged, and with the measure you use, it will be measured to you'.[37] Why should I consider myself blessed if persecuted by others because of Jesus? Because 'great is your reward? Because 'you will have no reward from your Father in heaven'.[39] Why should I not take undue pride in my own good works or give in to things like anger and lust? Because these are paths that can lead to hell. [40]

Of course, the Christian scriptures also describe Jesus as

encouraging people to love God and others in the soft of self-giving way in which he described God as loving us.[41] So we should not think that God's acceptance of less than fully mature Christian motives, in a person who begins to exercise faith in him, means that he is not at the same time intent on helping that person grow in her relationship with him and come to be motivated more and more by the kind of self-giving love representative of full Christian maturity. Still, the crucial point is that while unadulterated love for God may well be the mature Christian's motivation in relating to God, there seems no good reason to insist that this motivation must be the sole or ultimate motivation in everyone who genuinely accepts God's authority and thereby agrees to his invitation to a personal relationship.

All this is not to say that the exercise of Christian faith is compatible with *any* ultimate self-interested purpose one might seek to achieve. Suppose a person has as a goal the achievement of financial prosperity at the expense of others from another ethnic group he happens to dislike. Reading the Bible, he may selectively consider certain Old Testament passages involving Israel's achievements at the expense of other nations – while dismissing the possibility that such passages are part of a greater progressive revelation culminating in the teachings of Jesus Christ. He may make what he takes to be a positive response to these selected passages by asking God to bless his plans to swindle others from the ethnic group in question – just as, he reasons, God blessed Israel at the expense of other nations.

In such a case as this, the Christian theist will, I think, want to maintain that the person's response to God's statements (i.e., the selective Old Testament passages) does *not* establish a positive, personal relationship with the Christian God. For the person so misunderstands the character and purposes of God that a personal relationship simply is not possible. The phenomenon of people seeking to relate to the person they mistakenly take someone else to be is not uncommon. We interact on a daily basis with acquaintances, co-workers, and even close friends, who have incomplete or distorted understandings of who we really are. We realize that, strictly speaking, they are responding to whom they take us to be – rather than to who we really are. Sometimes we are willing to accept a personal relationship with them on these terms, interacting with them in ways that remain possible. At other times their misunderstanding of who we are makes a meaningful relationship impossible. To illustrate: a person may end a friendship by saying, 'If you think I would be interested in being your partner in this shady scheme, then you really do not know me after all'. Likewise, a person may break off communication with a co-worker by saying, 'There can be no meaningful conversation between us as long as you continue wrongly to interpret everything I say to you as an attempt to undermine your position with the company'. Returning to the example of the person who asks God to bless his financial plans, the Christian theist will surely want to maintain that God's purposes are so at odds with the purposes the person imagines God to have that a personal relationship built on the person's positive response to selected Old Testament passages is simply not possible. The person's own ultimate purposes in responding to these passages are thoroughly at odds with the purposes God is intent on pursuing and helping others pursue. He can accept God's authority as a means of achieving his own ultimate purposes only if he profoundly misconstrues the character of the person in whom he purports to put his faith. So there are limits to the kinds of ultimate purposes that are consistent with a person's decision to exercise Christian faith as a means to those purposes.

We have already concluded that the acceptance of God's authority as a means of accomplishing some other, self-interested purpose does not *ipso facto* signify a theologically objectionable motivation. At the same time, we should acknowledge in response to Augustine that the acceptance of God's authority as an intermediate purpose *can* signify just that. Augustine's comments serve as a warning against idolatry, which marks a failure to pay honour to that which has honour or virtue. Idolatry involves the pursuit of something less good than might otherwise be pursued and, importantly, involves the pursuit of something *at the expense of* a greater good.[42]

Suppose that a woman teaches her son the central elements of the Christian gospel message and encourages him to accept God's invitation of a personal relationship. If her ultimate goal involves her son's well-being, does her behaviour amount to idolatry? The answer, I think, is that it *might*. If her ultimate goal can be more precisely described in terms of desiring that her son receive the benefits that God promises to all who relate to him as Lord, then her actions *cannot* rightly be described as idolatrous. She desires that her son relate to God on the terms on which God, himself, extends an invitation to all people to enter into an everlasting relationship. It is true that her actions may be motivated largely by a love for her son – rather than by a love of God for his own sake. Again, though, Jesus repeatedly appealed to this kind of self-interested motivation in explaining why we should live our lives in accordance with God's will. While the mother's motivation perhaps is not indicative of full Christian maturity, it nonetheless does not denote an idolatrous attitude.

On the other hand, we can imagine a scenario in which the

mother's actions *do* amount to idolatry. We have assumed thus far that the mother's ultimate goal is that her son receive the eternal benefits of the relationship into which God invites him. However, let us suppose instead that the mother's ultimate goal is that her son be happy and comfortable here and now. (If this is her ultimate goal, full stop, then it is her goal irrespective of whether it is accomplished through her son living the Christian life.) As it happens, she believes that this ultimate goal can be achieved if her son leads a Christian life. This much we can deduce from her action of introducing her son to the gospel message. However, if she were to come to see the Christian life as demanding too much of her son in the here and now in terms of compromised popularity or financial hardship, she would not continue to work to ensure that her son led a life of Christian discipleship. For her ultimate goal is not compatible with her son following too closely Christ's example to 'deny himself and take up his cross'[43] as part of her son's relationship with God. Clearly, these are not the terms on which God extends an invitation to enter into a relationship where he is Lord. The mother's ordering of purposes – in addition to being imprudent from the Christian perspective – evinces an idolatrous commitment to prioritize the short-term happiness of her son over a commitment to see him relate to God as Lord.

In the end, Augustine has helped us to see that there can be a link between idolatry and acting from a motivation other than love of God for his own sake. However, as we have also seen, this link is by no means a necessary one.

Conclusion

In this chapter I have proposed the following as an account of what it is to put one's faith in someone else:

> Person *S* has faith in person *G* inasmuch as *S*, in response to *G*'s invitational statement(s) to *S*, accepts *G*'s authority in the areas to which this statement(s) indicates that *G*'s authority extends.

It has been my contention that, when people put their faith in God under this description, they relate to God personally on the terms on which, from the Christian perspective, God seeks to relate to them.

Of course, it would be quite implausible to suppose that people typically have as an articulated goal the acceptance of the authoritative claims that accompany God's invitational statements – even when they act in ways that in fact amount to accepting God's authoritative claims. It is much more plausible to suppose that people typically (at least in this life) respond positively to God as a means of achieving some other ultimate goal, such as freedom from

loneliness or troubles. In such a scenario, one's positive response to
God will constitute an intermediate purpose, which serves as a
means to other ultimate purposes. Yet, as we have seen, the positive
response to God's authority as an intermediate purpose seems
consistent with some exercise of Christian faith.

Notes

[1] Clement of Alexandria (c. 202) stated that faith 'is a voluntary [anticipation], the assent of piety . . . The exercise of faith directly becomes knowledge' (Bk 2, Ch. 2). See also Irenaeus c. 180: I, Ch. 10; Tertullian c. 200: II, I, Ch. 10; and Basil of Corsica 361: 59. All link faith with assent to the teachings handed down from the Apostles.

[2] See Aquinas 1265–73: II–II, iii, 3 and II–II, 2, ix, ad. 1; Peter Lombard 1145–51: Bk III, xxiii, 3; and Duns Scotus 1300–07: 419.

[3] See Luther 1520a: 368. Richard Swinburne (1981) provides an overview and comparison of these accounts of faith, which he respectively calls the Thomist view and the Lutheran view of faith. He concludes that the disagreement – which most notably occurred at the time of the Protestant Reformation – between advocates of these two views of faith was largely a semantic matter. And this despite the Council of Trent's declaration that 'If anyone shall say that justifying faith is nothing else than trust (*fiduciam*) in the divine mercy, which pardons our sins for Christ's sake, or that it is this trust alone by which we are justified, let him be anathema' (*Enchiridion Symbolorum* 1957: 822). Yet, despite the Catholic emphasis on love (which presumably was seen to be missing from the Lutheran account of faith as 'mere' trust), Luther (1522) did state that faith 'cannot do other than good at all times. It never waits to ask whether there is some good work to do. Rather, before the question is raised, it has done the deed and keeps on doing it. A man not active in this way is a man without faith' (288). Swinburne (1981) points out that 'if the Lutheran holds that to have faith a man must. . .be ready to do good works, that means that he must have, in the Catholic sense, Love' (114).

[4] See, e.g. Bonhoeffer 1937: 53–4 and Barth 1953: IV, i, 758.

[5] See, e.g. Aquinas 1265–73: II–II, iii, 1–2 and Barth 1953: IV, i, 777.

[6] Moltmann 1965; Muyskens 1979; and Pojman 1986: Ch. 16.

[7] Dulles 1994: 20.

[8] Cf. Brümmer (1993) for a similar observation about the use of 'love' in the Bible: 'Although the biblical authors use the *word* love in many contexts, they never provide a systematic development of the *concept* of love they are expressing by spelling out all its implications and presuppositions and its logical relations to related concepts' (31).

[9] Adams 1984: 16.

[10] In much of this section I follow Wolterstorff's (1995), *Divine Discourse*, an important work.

[11] Strictly speaking, God's producing a belief in me that he is asking something is not *ipso facto* God's asking. We get closer to the actual act of asking if we assume that (a) God produces in me the true belief that he is asking me to do something; (b) God produces in me the further belief that God intends me to recognize that the previous belief has been produced by him; and that (c) God intends that this recognition should be my reason for doing what is asked.

[12] Cf. Wolterstorff 1995: 38f.

[13] Lk. 10.16.

[14] Wolterstorff (1995) acknowledges that 'some of the discourse appropriated will itself be divine discourse; that will be true for those passages which are a record of prophetic utterance' (54).

[15] Wolterstorff 1995: 54.

[16] Often the conversations at dinner parties are laced with 'inside jokes', where one communicates things to one's spouse in the midst of communicating something else to other dinner guests.

[17] Of course, the canonization of scripture shows that the Christian tradition has seen the inspiration of scripture as carrying unique implications. But these unique implications are not what concern us here.

[18] If 'promising' is construed widely enough so that the statement, 'I promise that England will win the World Cup', constitutes a promise instead of an assertion, then the guarantee is not that one can ensure that the promise is realized but rather that one is in a position to know that the promise will be realized.

[19] Wolterstorff 1995: 35.

[20] It seems best not to describe the act of flipping blinkers as a promise, given that one needs the other person's permission to go back on a promise.

[21] Wolterstorff 1995: 83. Wolterstorff goes on to explain that such a speech-act can be 'undercut' when one has reason to think that it is 'malformed in such a way that the prima facie rights and responsibilities which accrue to speakers and hearers upon its performance do not, in this case, actually accrue to them' (88).

[22] Of course, there is a minimal sense in which almost any statement carries a claim to authority. Even a poet who purposefully writes from anonymity may hope that his readers recognize that the marks on the page they read come from a thoughtful person with typical human experiences.

[23] Though the columnist does invite her readers to *relate* to her in some way, it would probably be too strong to say that the columnist here invites her readers to enter into a *personal relationship* with her. For a personal relationship, as noted earlier, requires a mutual recognition of, and response to, the agency of the other person. And it is doubtful that the kind of mutuality that makes possible the interchange within a bona fide personal relationship can be present given that (a) the columnist does not know the specific individuals to whom she communicates her messages, and (b) she does not know whether and in what way her readers have responded to her messages and/or her authoritative claims accompanying her messages. Such potential obstacles to a bona fide personal relationship, though, do not surface when the discussion turns to an omniscient God issuing invitational statements.

[24] The fact that Gary's assertion serves as an invitation to enter into a personal relationship does not necessarily mean that the issuing of such an invitation was the sole, or even a primary, purpose he sought to achieve in making the assertion to Sue.

[25] Tillich 1948: 162. We can also note that Tillich did not share the traditional Christian assumption that God is a personal being, instead describing God as the 'Ground of Being'.

[26] Such kinds of decisions are not uncommon. A mother may find herself with a teenage son who responds to her commands as though she is a peer and not a parent. The mother may decide that she is willing to carry on in a less-than-ideal relationship with her live-in son in which he accepts her authority (merely) as a peer. Alternatively, she may threaten to kick her son out of the house, stating, 'You may continue to live here only if you're willing to obey my rules without question'.

[27] Mt. 11.28.

[28] Augustine 388: Ch. 21.

[29] Augustine 388: Ch. 21.

[30] Augustine 388: Ch. 11. Cf. Deut. 6.5; Mt. 22.37.

[31] Augustine 388: Ch. 11.

[32] Augustine 397: Bk I, Ch. 22.

[33] Augustine 397: Bk I, Ch. 27.

[34] Augustine 397: Bk I, Ch. 22. Augustine's rather extreme view here becomes more understandable when we take into account his Platonic background. For Platonists, having a property consists in participating in an ideal form. Thus, having the property

of goodness consists in participating in ideal goodness – i.e., God. On this
understanding of what goodness consists in, it would not make sense to love
ourselves as good or for our own sake. Taking the larger Christian tradition as a
whole, there has sometimes been disagreement over whether it is appropriate to love
ourselves for our own sakes (or others for their own sakes) and to respond positively
to God for the sake of our own well-being. Luther in 1515–16 distinguished his own
view on this matter from the view of John Duns Scotus and Gabriel Biel, censuring
those who 'regard themselves as holy and who love God with a covetous love, i.e., for
the sake of their own salvation and eternal rest and for the purpose of avoiding hell,
in other words: not for God's sake but for their own sake' (262). Luther's view seems
to be consistent with that of Eckhardt, whose alleged errors, as condemned by Pope
John XXII, included the proposition: 'In those men who do not seek after wealth, or
honours, or utility, or interior devotion, or sanctity, or reward, or the kingdom of
heaven, but renounce all these things even that which is theirs, God is honoured'
(*Enchiridion Symbolorum* 1957: 508). For further discussions on the disagreement
within the Christian tradition over the value of disinterested love of God, see Kirk
(1931: 451–66); Passmore (1970: 88–92); and Swinburne (1989: 134–6).

[35] Augustine 397: Bk I, Ch. 22.

[36] Cf. the *Westminster Shorter Catechism* (1648), which represents well the Christian
tradition in affirming that the 'chief end of man' is to be in a relationship with God
where we 'enjoy him for ever' (359).

[37] Mt. 7.1-2.

[38] Mt. 5.11-12.

[39] Mt. 6.1-4.

[40] Cf. Mt. 5.22; 5.27-30.

[41] Cf. Mt. 5.43-8; 22.37-9.

[42] For a fuller discussion on the notion of idolatry, see Adams (1999: 199–213).

[43] Mt. 16.24.

THE ELEMENT OF BELIEF IN FAITH

4.1 *The beliefs assumed in acts of faith*

Having identified faith in God as the acceptance of the authoritative claims of God that accompany his invitational statements, let us now consider the question of which beliefs we must assume a person to have if we are to talk about her accepting God's authority. We noted in section 1.2 that beliefs explain why a person attempts to achieve her purposes through a particular means, or action, instead of through some other means. In addition, we saw in section 1.6 that an analysis of what it means for someone to believe 'that p' may need to take into account the alternatives with which p is being contrasted. If we know that a man in the woods had the single purpose of taking a path out of the woods, and if we know that he chose to walk down a certain path when six different paths were available to him, then we can deduce that he believed that no other path provided a better chance for him to achieve his purpose of getting out of the woods. Similarly, if we know that a man has the single purpose of getting to heaven (we could substitute various purposes here), and if we know that he is accepting the authority of the Christian God, then we can deduce that he believes that no other action is more likely to achieve his purpose. Thus, in order to put one's faith in the Christian God, one must have the following belief: that there is no better way to achieve (at least one of) one's purposes than by accepting the Christian God's authority.[1] For simplicity's sake, we shall refer to this belief involving one's purposes as belief$_p$.

This belief$_p$ presupposes still other beliefs, prominent among them the belief that the invitational statements to which one is responding really are *God's* statements. Take the case of the man lost in the woods who believes that only one path – a man-made path – leads out of the woods. In order for him to choose which path he will take, he must first have beliefs about which paths *exist*. If he does not believe that a certain clearing in the undergrowth is actually a man-made path, then this clearing will not constitute for him a viable option as he considers which path to take as a means of accomplishing his purpose of getting out of the woods. Similarly, responding to God's invitational statements by accepting his authority constitutes an option for achieving one's purposes only if one believes that one has in fact received such invitational statements from God.

This belief that a certain statement comes from God is only one belief a person will need to hold if he is to form the further belief, belief$_p$. Other such needed beliefs – at least in cases where one arrives at the belief$_p$ through inference – will include the beliefs that God exists, that one is capable of receiving and remembering statements from God, and that God has certain authority-making features that might be accepted. The number and nature of all these needed beliefs will vary according to the reasons why a person comes to believe that accepting God's authority will best achieve her purposes. To illustrate: two people might each understand God to be communicating to her the message that her own financial debt will be eased if she asks for God's help. Further, each might come to conclude that asking for God's help – which is how one would go about accepting God's authority in this case – constitutes her best means of achieving her purpose of debt relief. One person in our example might form her conclusion because she believes God will probably increase her income. The other person might form her conclusion because she believes God may decrease her desire for expensive things. Thus, even among people who jointly conclude that a specific purpose is best achieved by responding in a specific way to a specific statement from God, the beliefs they need to hold in order to form this joint conclusion may vary.

The belief that a statement in question does indeed come from God will be a focus of our discussion for three reasons. First, as already mentioned, one must hold this belief if one is to go on to form the further belief, belief$_p$. Second, this belief itself entails a number of other beliefs – e.g. that God exists, that one is capable of receiving and remembering statements from God, and so forth – that are also requisite for anyone who forms a belief$_p$. Third, in explaining why it is that Christians, but not non-Christians, respond to certain statements by accepting God's authority, perhaps the most ready single explanation is that Christians believe that these statements come from God, whereas non-Christians do not. In other words, not holding the belief that certain statements (e.g. remarks attributed to Jesus in the New Testament) truly come from God seems to be a (if not *the*) principal impediment to someone's exercise of Christian faith. So, within our discussion of those beliefs one needs to hold in order to form a belief$_p$, we shall consider as primary the belief that a certain message(s) does indeed come from God. Let us call this latter belief a belief$_m$.

For a person who exercises Christian faith, with what degree of certainty will she need to believe that the statement(s) to which she is responding really does come from God? The answer is simply this:

she will need to believe with whatever degree of certainty is needed for her to recognize (i.e., believe) that the acceptance of God's authority is the best way to achieve her purposes. To see that the strength of the belief in question may vary among people of faith, consider again the case of the man seeking to take a path out of the woods. Perhaps the man thinks that the way out of the woods probably lies to the north and that paths that begin in a northward direction continue in a northward direction. Looking north, he sees no clear indication of a man-made path. He notices a small clearing in the undergrowth but is unsure whether this clearing is actually a man-made path. How sure about this clearing being a path will he need to be in order to believe that it represents his best chance of taking the right path out of the woods? Well, if he is wavering in his belief that the way out lies to the north, he probably will need to be very sure that the clearing is actually a man-made path. On the other hand, if he is absolutely convinced that the way out lies to the north, he may well follow the clearing despite being unsure whether the clearing is actually a path, reasoning, 'If the clearing really *is* a path, it will lead me northward and thus assuredly out of the woods'.

Consider now two people who are unsure as to whether the statements on which they are both reflecting really are God's statements. Let us suppose that the statements in question are Jesus's recorded statements on forgiveness. And let us suppose that each person has the similar (ultimate) purpose of softening her own anger. The first person may be far from certain that, even if the statements are assumed to be God's statements, responding to them will in fact help her achieve the purpose she is trying to achieve. Consequently, the person might need to be certain that Jesus's recorded statements truly constitute God's statements to her if she is even to consider responding to these statements as a way of achieving her purpose. In contrast, the second person may be absolutely convinced that if these aforementioned statements of Jesus really do constitute God's statements to her, then they hold the key to her struggle with anger. Accordingly, this person might well respond positively to these statements despite having serious doubts whether the statements really are God's statements to her. The general point is that there can be all sorts of other beliefs that contribute to one's conclusion about which course of action will best help one achieve one's purpose(s). The needed strength of one of these contributing beliefs will depend (among other things) on the nature and strength of other contributing beliefs one holds. Thus, to the question of how firmly one must, in order to exercise Christian faith, believe that a given statement really comes from God, the answer again is this: a person will need to believe with whatever strength is needed for her to conclude that there exists no better way of achieving her purpose(s) than by accepting God's authority in response to that statement.

4.2 *Kierkegaard's objection to lack of certainty*

This conclusion does not place the kind of emphasis on certainty of belief that is found in some accounts of faith within the Christian tradition. On Aquinas's account of faith, the faith of one person can be 'greater' than the faith of another in virtue of the firmness with which one's beliefs are held. After remarking that 'the act of faith proceeds both from the intellect and from the will', Aquinas stated: 'Consequently a man's faith may be described as being greater, in one way, on the part of his intellect, on account of its greater certitude and firmness, and, in another way, on the part of his will, on account of his greater promptitude, devotion, or confidence'.[2] Sometimes within the Christian tradition firmness of belief has been viewed as essential for *any* exercise of faith. The pronouncements of certain Church councils have required that all believers who make professions of faith state that they 'firmly believe' or 'steadfastly hold' the articles of faith as set forth by the Church.[3] Pope Innocent XI, in listing 'Various Errors on Moral Subjects', went so far as to condemn the notion that assent to faith is consistent with 'only the probable knowledge of revelation, even with the fear by which one fears lest God has not spoken'.[4]

If faith were a matter merely of belief, then the benefits of believing with certainty would be obvious. A firm belief would translate into a firm faith. However, on the account of faith outlined in Chapter 3, faith is not to be identified simply with the holding of beliefs. Of course, in our examination of faith we have recognized that the holding of particular beliefs is a necessary *prerequisite* to the exercise of faith. The question before us is whether the proper exercise of faith requires that one hold with *certainty* the beliefs requisite for faith.

In section 1.6 we discussed how probability assessments can explain why a person performs some action A in an attempt to achieve some purpose P – even when the person is far from certain that his attempt will succeed. Thus, a person may think that Brazil's chances of winning the World Cup are only around 0.3, and thus not actually believe the proposition 'Brazil will win the World Cup' to be true. Still, if the person believes Brazil's chances to be greater than those of any other team, this probability assessment is sufficient to explain her action of picking Brazil in an attempt to pick the World Cup winner for an office pool. So it would seem possible that a person might perform the action of exercising faith – that is, accepting God's authority – even though she is very much less than certain that such an action will in fact achieve her ultimate purpose(s) in performing this action. For what is needed by way of belief is simply the assessment that there is no better way to achieve this purpose(s).

At the same time, we should recognize that sometimes a person may not be sufficiently *motivated* to seek to achieve a purpose unless she believes that her chances of success are high. For example, a person might believe that her best chance to achieve her goal of losing weight is by following a particular diet programme whose list of permitted food items contains only those items she finds exceedingly bland and unattractive. Such might be the case that the person will first need to be absolutely certain that the diet programme will be successful in order for her then to muster the willpower to start it. These considerations should lead us to recognize that in individual cases it may be that a person will be motivated to exercise faith in God only if she has a certain level of confidence that in so doing she will achieve some ultimate purpose(s) she has. Still, the question before us is whether, in order to exercise genuine faith in God, one *must* in principle hold with certainty the beliefs requisite for faith. The considerations in this paragraph do not warrant such a conclusion.

We can acknowledge that the Christian theist might reasonably consider it *good* that all individuals who exercise faith be certain in their belief that they can best accomplish particular purposes of theirs by accepting God's authority. Perhaps, it could be argued, a person who is certain on this matter is less likely eventually to come to believe that these purposes of theirs are *not* best accomplished by accepting God's authority. Also, it could be argued that some persons, as they decide which of their various purposes they will attempt to achieve, are more likely to pursue those purposes that they believe they will most probably achieve. Thus, if such persons were to be certain that the acceptance of God's authority would indeed achieve a particular purpose of theirs, they might be more inclined to pursue this purpose than other purposes of theirs – purposes the achievement of which, by contrast, do not involve the acceptance of God's authority. Still, while these considerations might constitute reasons for thinking it *good* that people of faith be certain in those beliefs requisite for Christian faith, these considerations do not serve as a basis for insisting that Christian faith *necessitates* certainty of belief. For, again, one can exercise Christian faith – that is, accept God's authority – whether or not one holds with certainty those beliefs requisite for Christian faith.

One who insists that certainty of belief *is* requisite for any genuine exercise of Christian faith will need to argue that the very nature of a proper human-divine relationship necessitates us believing particular things about God with certainty. Perhaps the best-known proponent of such a view is Søren Kierkegaard. I shall consider his arguments along these lines, as well as the comments of Robert Adams, who picks up on Kierkegaard's arguments and offers his own explanation as to why religious faith calls for certainty of belief.

One of the recurring themes in Kierkegaard's writings involves the idea that because God is of infinite value to the individual, one must strive for God with an infinite passion. This infinite passion is possible, in his view, only under certain epistemic conditions:

> ... if I am in truth resolved to venture, in truth resolved to strive for the attainment of the highest good, the uncertainty must be there, and I must have room to move, so to speak. But the largest space I can obtain, where there is room for the most vehement gesture of the passion that embraces the infinite, is uncertainty of knowledge with respect to an eternal happiness.[5]

Kierkegaard speaks here of 'uncertainty of knowledge', and it might be thought that he construes infinite passion as a desire that works together with weak belief to produce the action of 'striving' for God. On this understanding, even though one very much doubts that one's efforts will be successful – because, for instance, one thinks it improbable that God exists – one still strives for God against the recognized odds because one desires so passionately to find the object of one's strivings.

While this understanding of Kierkegaard's idea of infinite passion seems consistent with certain passages in his writings, it does not fully account for all that Kierkegaard wants to say on the matter. Central to Kierkegaard's writings on the infinite passion of faith is his distinction between objectivity and subjectivity. Objective enquiry was for Kierkegaard a matter of dispassionate weighing of public evidence, the kind of search for an 'objective' grounding of one's beliefs characteristic of scientific enquiry. Kierkegaard urged that the temptation to replace 'passionate conviction' with these sorts of 'probabilities and guarantees' is for the believer 'a temptation to be resisted with all his strength'.[6] Instead of following automatically from the weighing of public evidence, the believer's firm religious belief ought to be the result of a subjective decision to believe.

> ... it behoves us to get rid of introductory guarantees of security, proofs from consequences, and the whole mob of public pawnbrokers and guarantors, so as to permit the absurd to stand out in all its clarity – in order that the individual may believe if he wills it: I merely say that it must be strenuous in the highest degree possible.[7]

We discussed at length in Chapter 2 the difficulties with the idea that one can acquire a belief simply by willing to have it – even if one wills it with the 'highest degree possible' of strenuousness. However, what concerns us here is the idea that there is something about the divine-human relationship that demands convictions on our part that are firmer than the probabilities associated with what Kierkegaard calls 'objective' enquiry.[8]

With this brief synopsis of Kierkegaard's understanding of what firm conviction is and how it is achieved, let us now turn to Robert Adams's discussion of firm conviction and religious belief. Adams begins by quoting a passage from Kierkegaard's *Concluding Unscientific Postscript* in which Kierkegaard seems to suggest that 'belief' is not true belief unless it is certain belief.

> What if instead of talking or dreaming about an absolute beginning, we talked about a leap. To be content with a 'mostly', and 'as good as', a 'you could almost say that', ... suffices merely to betray a kinship with Trop, who, little by little, reached the point of assuming that almost having passed his examinations, was the same as having passed them.[9]

In commenting on this passage Adams notes that

> There certainly have been scholars who have aspired to be in a position to say, 'Probably Jesus rose from the dead' – and philosophers who have been prepared to identify belief in general, and religious belief in particular, with an assignment of probabilities. Kierkegaard's central point, in this passage, is that that is not enough for religious faith. 'Probably Jesus rose from the dead' and 'Probably God is love' are not affirmations of faith. To get from this probability assignment to the simple affirmation of faith, 'Jesus rose from the dead', a transition is needed, which Kierkegaard calls a 'leap'.[10]

Adams grants that in some contexts probability assignment is appropriate. Consider the case of a financial adviser's beliefs about the future prices of a client's securities, or the case of a doctor's beliefs about the possible effects of various treatment alternatives for a patient. In contexts such as these, Adams states, 'a probability assignment is all the belief that is required of us'.[11] Adams then asserts that

> there are also contexts in which more conviction is demanded. 'Probably so', in answer to the question, 'Do you love me?' is not exactly an affirmation of love. In answer to 'Is the moral law binding on us?' it is apt to leave the impression that the respondent is insufficiently committed to morality ... Kierkegaard is surely right in placing religious faith in this category of beliefs for which 'probably' is not enough.[12]

Adams seems correct in pointing out that we do often look for a kind of 'definiteness' in others and ourselves in contexts such as a loving relationship and compliance with moral laws. However, it seems more plausible to suggest that what we typically want to urge in others is a definite *commitment* to a relationship or to moral laws rather than a definite *belief* that one loves another person or that the moral law is binding. After all, one could believe with certainty that a certain moral law is binding on all people; yet one could at the same time fail to adhere to the law due to, for instance, weakness of will. Adams, though, rejects the notion that the kind of commitment at issue here amounts simply to a resolution to perform acts consistent with love or with certain moral laws.

> 'Probably so' cannot be turned into an affirmation of faith by adding, 'And I have therefore decided to act resolutely on the assumption that it is so'. What may still be lacking in such a resolution is a deeply *felt* conviction that the proposition believed is true. There is a pattern of emotionality, as well as a pattern of voluntary actions, that belongs to a religious way of life. The ideal of religious faith therefore has an emotional aspect. Peace, joy, gratitude, and the freedom to love are supposed to flow from a confidently held conviction that God is good. In this faith one is to respond emotionally to the divine goodness in which one believes, rather than to the balance of the evidence that one sees for it and against it.[13]

It is possible to identify two lines of argument from this passage in support of the claim that the conviction needed for religious faith involves a 'pattern of emotionality' as well as probabilistic belief and actions. To see the first line of argument, consider Adams's contention that emotional states such as peace, joy and love 'are supposed to flow from a confidently held conviction that God is good'. The idea here seems to be that certain emotional states are fruits of believing with certainty that God is good. Assuming that this is true, we can grant that there are emotional benefits to believing with certainty in God's goodness. However, even if we also grant that belief in God's goodness constitutes one of the beliefs requisite for Christian faith, the question of which emotional benefits accrue to one who holds this belief with certainty is a different issue from the question of how firmly one needs to hold those beliefs requisite for faith if one is in fact to exercise genuine faith. Thus, this first line of argument, while interesting, is not directly relevant to our discussion of the certainty with which the person of Christian faith must hold those beliefs requisite for Christian faith.

Let us turn then to the second line of argument suggested by Adams's defence of the notion that religious commitment involves a 'pattern of emotionality'. Adams contends that, in religious faith, 'one is to respond emotionally to the divine goodness in which one believes'. The idea here seems to be that one's emotional response to God's goodness is what *motivates* the person of true religious faith. And it might be argued that such a motivation can indeed be the unwavering motivation for a person of faith only when that person's belief in God's goodness is unwavering. In considering what implications to draw from this line of argument, we can think back to our discussion in section 3.4, where it was suggested that love for God may well be the primary, if not sole, motivation behind the mature Christian's response to God. However, as we saw in that section, this suggested fact about full Christian maturity gives us insufficient grounds to insist that love for God must be the sole or primary motivation for everyone who exercises genuine Christian faith.

Taking both lines of argument together, it seems that Adams perhaps has in mind in his discussion the situation of the mature religious believer. Indeed, in the passage cited above he states that 'the ideal of religious faith' has an emotional aspect. However, this appeal to the emotions that characterize ideal religious faith does not support the claim that the genuine exercise of Christian faith – i.e. the genuine commitment to relate to God as Lord – is impossible if one lacks these emotions associated with firm and certain belief. Thus, we have found no support for Kierkegaard's claim that the nature of faith in the divine is such that one can exercise faith only when one holds the beliefs requisite for faith with certainty.

4.3 *Acceptance as a substitute for belief?*

In recent years some writers have sought to dispense with belief as a necessary component of an authentic exercise of Christian faith. The general idea is that a different propositional attitude – e.g. hope or acceptance – can, at least in some cases, serve as a viable substitute for belief. Such a suggestion would serve as a rejoinder against my explanation that a belief$_m$ and a belief$_p$ are necessary prerequisites for the exercise of Christian faith. So let us consider what I take to be a well-articulated example of this general line of argument: William Alston's proposal that acceptance can substitute for belief in an authentic exercise of Christian faith.

Before discussing the details of Alston's suggestion, we must first note that his use of the term 'acceptance' differs from my own use of 'acceptance', as outlined in the discussion in section 3.3 on the nature of faith. Alston's use of the term 'acceptance' is in keeping with Jonathan Cohen's use of the term. As we saw in section 1.2, Cohen's analysis of 'acceptance' centres on how acceptance differs from 'belief'. For Cohen, to accept 'that p' is 'to have or adopt a policy of deeming, positing, or postulating that p – that is, of going along with that proposition ... as a premiss in some or all contexts for one's own and others' proofs, argumentations, inferences, deliberations, etc.'[14] Belief, on the other hand, Cohen describes as 'a disposition to feel it true that p, whether or not one goes along with the proposition as a premiss'.[15] Alston follows Cohen in this distinction, adding that 'to accept that p is to "take it on board", to include it in one's repertoire of (supposed) facts on which one will rely in one's theoretical and practical reasoning and one's behavior'.[16]

Alston's contention is that 'accepting basic Christian doctrines can undergird a full-blown Christian commitment'.[17] In the same way that one's beliefs about Christian doctrines can serve as the basis of one's religious striving, Alston maintains that one's acceptance of these doctrines can also serve as a sufficient basis. He states that

> The person who *accepts* the doctrines is not necessarily inferior to the *believer* in commitment to the Christian life, or in the seriousness, faithfulness, or intensity with which she pursues it. The accepter may pray just as faithfully, worship God just as regularly, strive as earnestly to follow the way of life enjoined on us by Christ, look as pervasively on interpersonal relationships, vocation, and social issues through the lens of the Christian faith.[18]

Alston then points out that accepting a proposition, unlike forming a belief about it, 'is a voluntary act. I have effective voluntary control over my acceptances and abstentions therefrom.'[19]

While Alston's analysis of the beliefs involved in Christian faith is not directed at the specific beliefs, a belief$_m$ and a belief$_p$, his analysis is directly relevant to our larger project. One of Alston's chief goals in proposing acceptance as a substitute for belief is to carve out a role for voluntary actions in the exercise of Christian faith. His concern is that, if faith 'must contain certain propositional beliefs, and these are not within our voluntary control, how can anyone require us to have faith, and how can any merit attach to our doing so?'[20] The challenge to Christian theism we are outlining in Part 1 is, of course, very much in line with Alston's concern here. If Alston is correct that acceptance can substitute for belief in the exercise of Christian faith, then the challenge we are outlining disappears. Yet, on closer analysis, Alston's proposal does not obviate this challenge.

To see why this is so, we should keep in mind that acceptance is, for both Cohen and Alston, an *action* one performs. Indeed, Alston stresses this point repeatedly that acceptance 'is something one *does* at a particular time'.[21] As an action, it seems analysable in terms of 'beliefs + purposes' – a point we examined in section 1.2. Thus, even if we assume that a belief$_m$ and a belief$_p$ are not requisite for the exercise of Christian faith – assuming, instead, that acceptance of these corresponding propositions is sufficient – we can still ask why someone would accept these propositions. That is, we can still ask what purposes and *beliefs* one had that explain why one performed the act of accepting these propositions that are requisite for faith.

Perhaps an example will make the point clear. In his explanation of how acceptance can serve as the basis for genuine Christian faith, Alston offers various (hypothetical) examples of why a person might accept Christian doctrines – even though the person, after considering evidence both pro and con, does not find herself in a state of belief.

> ... perhaps she has been involved in the church from her early years, from a preskeptical time when she did fully believe, and she finds the involvement meeting deep needs and giving her life some meaning and structure. And so she is motivated to accept Christian doctrines as a basis for her thought about the world and for the way she leads her life. Or perhaps the person is drawn into the church from a condition of religious noninvolvement, and responds actively to the church's message, finding in the Christian life something that is deeply satisfying, but without, as yet, spontaneously feeling the doctrines to be true. Such a person will again be moved to *accept* the doctrines as something on which she will build her thought and action.[22]

So a person might be motivated to ensure that her 'deep needs' are met and that she experiences 'deep satisfaction'. These purposes are achieved by 'responding actively' to the Christian message – i.e., living the 'Christian life'. If we assume that the person's commitment to the Christian life is based on a belief about Christian doctrines, then, using the terminology of section 1.2, we could explain her action of living the Christian life in terms of (1) her ultimate *purpose* to have her deep needs met; and (2) her *belief* that this purpose is best achieved by practising the Christian way of life.

But could we equally explain her action in terms of (1) her purpose of having her deep needs met; and (2) her *acceptance* that this purpose is best achieved by practising the Christian life? The answer is 'no'. For this latter explanation is simply not a full explanation of her action. We will want to know *why* she would seek to achieve her purpose (of having her deep needs met) by performing the action of accepting as accurate the Christian account of the meaning of life. After all, there are a great many ways in which a person might try to achieve the purpose of having her deep needs met. Even within the confines of religion, there are any number of spiritual pathways to which a person might have been exposed and which thus present themselves as options for her acceptance. We will want to know why the person from Alston's example accepted the *Christian* way of life as a means of achieving her purpose of having her needs met. The answer must surely be that she *believed* (based on her positive experiences within the Church) that by accepting the Christian way of life she had the greatest chance to achieve her ultimate purpose of having her deep needs met. Thus, we might grant that, in order to exercise Christian faith, the person from Alston's example need not *believe* – but can instead choose to *accept* – the proposition, 'My purpose of having my deep needs met is best achieved by participating in the Christian way of life'. However, in order to accept this proposition she will still need to hold some *further* belief that this action of acceptance in some way[23] constitutes her best chance to achieve her ultimate purpose. In the end, we cannot escape the need to hold certain beliefs if one is to exercise Christian faith.

4.4 *The problematic notion of voluntary faith*

We come now to the place where we can press the objection against the Christian theist that is our chief concern in our overall discussion. One of the core doctrines of the Christian creeds involves the idea that each human will at some point be 'judged' by God. An individual's subsequent fate will then, from the Christian perspective, hinge on the kind of relationship one has with God through Jesus Christ. As stipulated earlier, those who have the kind of relationship with God that accomplishes the ends of the Christian religion are those who have put their 'faith in' God.

We saw in Chapter 2 that though a person may exhaust every resource in trying to acquire a given belief, there is no guarantee that his efforts will be successful. Given this involuntary understanding of belief, a looming question awaits the Christian theist who defends both the goodness of God and the possibility that God might judge some people to have failed to have put their faith in him. This question can be put to the Christian theist in the form of the following objection: in order for a person to put his faith in God, he must first have certain beliefs – in particular, a belief$_m$ and a belief$_p$. Given the involuntary nature of belief, the real possibility seems to exist that a person may involuntarily lack those beliefs requisite for faith. The Christian God, if indeed perfectly good, would not hold any person culpable for decisions or actions she did not freely perform; and God would not consign a person to suffer complete and final separation from himself for a non-culpable failure to put her faith in God. How, then, can the Christian theist hold that God will judge all people according to whether or not they put their faith in him – given the real possibility that a person's lack of faith may stem from an involuntary and therefore non-culpable failure to hold those beliefs requisite for faith?

In the Introduction, we noted that one obvious way of meeting this objection would be to deny that culpability does presuppose a voluntary action of some sort. However, we are proceeding on the assumption that culpability presupposes free and morally significant decisions. More specifically, culpability for a decision or action accrues only when one freely attempts to realize a desire at the expense of what one believes to be a moral obligation.

The Christian tradition seems widely to have assumed that among those morally significant decisions a person makes are decisions whether or not to hold certain Christian beliefs. Origen remarked that, if the word of God does not change some people's nature, 'the cause must be held to lie in their own will, which is reluctant to accept the belief that the God over all things is a just Judge of all the deeds done during life'.[24] Augustine cited St Paul as an example of one who 'refused to believe' but was turned by Christ into a 'willing believer'.[25] Kierkegaard, in reference to those religious beliefs central to Christian commitment, commented that an individual 'may believe if he wills it'.[26] And Vatican II, following Aquinas,[27] described the person of faith as one who is 'freely assenting to the truth revealed by [God]'.[28]

Contrary to what the Christian tradition seemingly has often wanted to affirm about the possibility of voluntarily holding religious beliefs, we concluded in Chapter 2 that a person (often, at the very least) cannot in fact hold a belief simply by willing to hold it. Of course, a person may choose to seek to acquire (indirectly) a belief. Again, though, there is no guarantee that one's efforts to acquire a belief will be successful. Thus, it will not do for the Christian theist to defend the goodness of God's final judgment by pointing to the decision 'to believe' as the common decision for which all people who lack Christian faith are morally culpable.

Conclusion

Our discussions thus far have led us to consider an apparent problem for the Christian theist who defends the Christian teaching that all people will at some point be judged according to whether they have put their faith in God. We have seen that such faith amounts to the 'acceptance of God's authority' in response to God's 'invitational statements'. We have also identified two beliefs that are requisite for Christian faith: a belief that some message comes from God (a belief$_m$); and a belief that there exists no better way to achieve a purpose one has than to accept God's authority in response to this message (a belief$_p$). Given our conclusions about the involuntary nature of belief, the real possibility seems to exist that a person could make all the decisions he was morally obligated to make and still fail to hold those beliefs requisite for Christian faith. How then can the Christian theist deny the possibility that some people suffer final separation from God for a lack of faith toward which they did not voluntarily contribute? In what follows I shall explore whether there is a plausible line of response the Christian theist might offer to this objection such that would enable her to affirm both that God is perfectly good and that God does in fact judge all people according to whether they have put their faith in him.

Notes

[1] Strictly speaking, we will want to say that the belief in question will be that there is no better way to achieve one's purposes than by accepting *what one takes to be* the Christian God's authority. At the same time, this distinction becomes somewhat mooted when we consider our discussion from section 3.3 that to have faith in another person requires that one's recognition of that person's authoritative claims correspond to a certain degree to the authoritative claims that person seeks to make.

[2] Aquinas 1265–73: II–II, v, 4. Others in the Christian tradition who have stressed the importance of firmness of assent include Tertullian, Clement of Alexandria, Gregory Nazianzen, and Bonaventure.

[3] Cf. Fourth Lateran Council and Council of Trent, *Enchiridion Symbolorum* 1957: 428, 994.

[4] *Enchiridion Symbolorum* 1957: 1171.

[5] Kierkegaard 1846: 381–2.

[6] Kierkegaard 1846: 15.

[7] Kierkegaard 1846: 190.

[8] Kierkegaard clearly held that a firm and certain belief is the only appropriate response to the divine object of faith that is so infinitely worth having. Yet, he did not explain precisely *why* a proper, personal relationship with God can only be established through this kind of response. He did, however, provide more detailed arguments on the separate question of why one cannot arrive at the kind of firm and certain belief needed for religious faith if one bases one's belief on the 'objective' weighing of public evidence. For a discussion of these arguments, see Adams (1976) and Evans (1998: 11–13, 106–10).

[9] Kierkegaard 1846: 105.

[10] Adams 1987: 43–4.

[11] Adams 1987: 44.

[12] Adams 1987: 44.

[13] Adams 1987: 46.

[14] Cohen 1989: 368.

[15] Cohen 1989: 368.

[16] Alston 1996: 8.

[17] Alston 1996: 9.

[18] Alston 1996: 17.

[19] Alston 1996: 11.

[20] Alston 1996: 25.

[21] Alston 1996: 8.

[22] Alston 1996: 17.

[23] Either the acceptance of the proposition in question makes possible some further actions through which the person attains the deep satisfaction that is her ultimate purpose, or the acceptance itself of the proposition (that is, the decision itself to pursue these further actions) provides (at least some of) the deep satisfaction.

[24] Origen c. 248: Bk III, Ch. 69.

[25] Augustine 428: Ch. 4 [II].

[26] Kierkegaard 1846: 190.

[27] Cf. Aquinas 1265–73: II–II, i, 4; II–II, ii, 9; II–II, v, 2.

[28] *The Documents of Vatican II* 1966: 113.

PART 2

5

SPIRITUAL BLINDNESS AND UNBELIEF

In much of Part 2 I wish to explore the question of why not everyone holds the beliefs requisite for Christian faith. A natural enough short answer to this question would seem to be: because some people simply do not find their evidence as on balance supporting such beliefs. Before proceeding further, however, I wish to consider two challenges to this working assumption about why a person might not hold Christian beliefs. In the next section I shall consider Alvin Plantinga's proposal that a person's Christian beliefs might not be based on evidence. Then, in the following section, I shall consider Kierkegaard's understanding that one's Christian beliefs should only be based on a particular kind of evidence.

5.1 Can the beliefs requisite for Christian faith rest on no evidence at all?

We concluded in section 1.5 that, in cases where a belief is formed on the basis of evidence (i.e. on the basis of other beliefs one holds), a person's belief will be the conclusion to which he sees (consciously or unconsciously) the evidence as pointing. Of course, basic beliefs (if the foundationalist is right in positing their existence) would constitute a notable exception to this link between beliefs and evidence. Basic beliefs have typically been characterized within so-called 'classical foundationalism' as what one takes as apparently self-evident truths or apparent deliverances of perception and the senses. Recently, however, self-described 'Calvinist' or 'Reformed' epistemologists – including Alvin Plantinga, Nicholas Wolterstorff, William Alston and George Mavrodes – have challenged the assumption that basicality should include only these types of beliefs.[1] The most notable element of this challenge has been Plantinga's proposal that Christian beliefs might also properly be described as basic.

Plantinga uses the term 'Christian belief' to denote both general theistic beliefs (e.g. that God is an all-knowing, all-powerful, wholly loving being) and uniquely Christian beliefs (e.g. that we humans are mired in rebellion and sin and that we can be delivered from this state through the sacrificial death and resurrection of Jesus Christ).[2]

As we shall soon see, Plantinga's discussion of Christian belief includes the belief that a particular speech act is in fact a word from the Lord. Thus, his proposal that Christian belief can be formed in a basic way is relevant to our discussion of whether a belief$_m$ is linked with one's assessment of evidence. If a belief$_m$ can in fact be formed (and sustained) in a basic way, then we will need to rethink our working assumption that the holding of a belief$_m$ is dependent on one's assessment of the evidence for and against the truth of that belief$_m$.

Plantinga traces the roots of his proposal for the basicality of Christian belief back to the writings of Calvin and (in a more recent appeal)[3] Aquinas. Specifically, he notes that both these theologians concurred that there exists in humans a kind of natural knowledge of God – a theme Calvin developed by appealing to the idea of a *sensus divinitatis*. Plantinga understands this idea along the following lines: 'God has implanted in us a sense of divinity, or a tendency to form beliefs about him. This tendency to form Christian beliefs is realized under certain conditions – and as the Holy Spirit 'witnesses' to us, or 'instigates' the realization of this tendency – and is realized in a way that does not require the assessment of evidence.'

We shall soon examine some of the specifics of Plantinga's general claim. But let us first look briefly at his appeal to Calvin and Aquinas.

Calvin's writings on the formation of Christian beliefs do seem in keeping with Plantinga's claim that these beliefs can be formed in a way independent of evidence assessment.

> Let it therefore be held as fixed, that those who are inwardly taught by the Holy Spirit acquiesce implicitly in Scripture; that Scripture carrying its own evidence along with it, deigns not to submit to proofs and arguments, but owes the full conviction with which we ought to receive it to the testimony of the Spirit. Enlightened by him, we no longer believe, either on our own judgment or that of others, that the Scriptures are from God; but, in a way superior to human judgment, feel perfectly assured ... that it came to us, by the instrumentality of men, from the very mouth of God. We ask not for proofs or probabilities on which to rest our judgment, but we subject our intellect and judgment to it as too transcendent for us to estimate.[4]

Calvin does not elaborate on exactly how the Holy Spirit 'testifies' to people, but he seems clear on the point that the Christian beliefs resulting from such testimony do not (or at least should not) involve any human assessments of evidence for what is believed: 'our conviction of the truth of Scripture must be derived from a higher source than human conjectures, judgments, or reasons; namely, the secret testimony of the Spirit'.[5] Thus Plantinga seems within his rights in tracing his proposal of the basicality of Christian belief back to Calvin.

Things are not so clear, however, when we turn to Aquinas. In examining Aquinas's writings on the formation of Christian beliefs, we can begin with his remarks on how people form general, theistic beliefs. Aquinas did state that 'To know that God exists in a general and confused way is implanted in us by nature.'[6] At the same time, he also acknowledged that people do sometimes form certain general, theistic beliefs on the basis of a reasoned inference from evidence. He remarked that, as men see 'that natural things are arranged in a certain order, – since there cannot be order without a cause of order – men, for the most part, perceive that there is one who arranges in order the things that we see'.[7] Still, as Nicholas Wolterstorff notes, Aquinas held that reasoned arguments are incapable of grounding the more specific beliefs constitutive of Christian faith – e.g. doctrinal beliefs involving the Incarnation and the Trinity. And we can note that Aquinas acknowledged that 'the existence of God and other like truths about God, which can be known by natural reason, are not articles of faith but are preambles to the articles'.[8] Thus, having acknowledged that people sometimes do use inference in moving from the evidence of an ordered world to the conclusion that an orderer exists, Aquinas explained that this evidence does not settle the issue of 'who or of what kind' of being this orderer is, or 'whether there be but one' orderer of nature.[9]

As for the formation of those more specific beliefs that constitute the Christian articles of faith, Aquinas did appeal to the witness of the Holy Spirit. He remarked that the act of assenting to divine truth occurs as one is 'moved by the grace of God'.[10] But would Aquinas have allowed, with Plantinga, that the Christian's religious beliefs might involve no assessment of evidence? Such an interpretation of Aquinas does seem possible, but the matter is not clear. Consider Aquinas's understanding of how the Holy Spirit might be the 'internal cause' of a person coming to hold Christian beliefs.

As regards ... man's assent to the things which are of faith, we may observe a twofold cause, one of external inducement, such as seeing a miracle, or being persuaded by someone to embrace the faith: neither of which is a sufficient cause, since of those who see the same miracle, or who hear the same sermon, some believe, and some do not. Hence we must assert another internal cause, which moves man inwardly to assent to matters of faith.[11]

Now, it may be that, for Aquinas, miracles and reasoned arguments are simply the *occasions* on which God moves one inwardly to form beliefs in a basic way. Such a scenario would be entirely consistent with Plantinga's description of Christian beliefs formed in a basic way. However, it also seems possible to interpret Aquinas here as holding that the formation of Christian beliefs involves one being moved to recognize – through reasoned inference – that the divine character of a purportedly miraculous event points to the truth of an accompanying, purportedly divine message.[12] In the end, it seems unclear whether Aquinas would have allowed that Christian beliefs might properly be formed in a basic way without any assessment of evidence and without reasoned inference. Plantinga's appeal to the Christian tradition on this matter appears on safer grounds when restricted to the Calvinist tradition.

Turning now to some of the specifics of Plantinga's proposal that Christian belief be rightly considered basic, we can note that he provides examples of beliefs that are (typically, at least) formed in a basic way. These examples include one's belief in other minds when one interacts with others; one's belief that another person is angry, depressed or delighted when one witnesses the person's facial expressions; and one's belief that God exists when one views a nature scene. None of these instances of belief formation is basic under the criteria of classical foundationalism. Yet Plantinga is adamant that, in standard cases, these beliefs are formed in a basic way:

> It isn't that one beholds the night sky, notes that it is grand, and concludes that there must be such a person as God: an argument like that would be ridiculously weak ... It is rather that, upon the perception of the night sky or the mountain vista or the tiny flower, these beliefs just arise within us. They are *occasioned* by the circumstances; they are not conclusions from them.[13]

In accordance with God's design, Plantinga affirms, Christian beliefs are triggered in certain circumstances by the *sensus divinitatis*. He notes that the 'deliverances of the *sensus divinitatis* are not quick and *sotto voce* inferences from the circumstances that trigger its operation'.[14] Instead, one simply finds oneself with Christian beliefs.

Plantinga acknowledges that a Christian's religious beliefs *could* be accepted on the basis of other propositions she believes:

> A believer could reason as follows: I have strong historical and archaeological evidence for the reliability of the Bible (or the church, or my parents, or some other authority); the Bible teaches the great things of the gospel; so probably these things are true. A believer *could* reason in this way, and perhaps some believers do reason this way.[15]

Still, Plantinga wants to defend a model of Christian belief in which beliefs are formed without a reasoned assessment of evidence. He comments that, when the Christian hears the gospel preached or encounters a scriptural teaching, 'What is said simply seems right; it seems compelling; one finds oneself saying, "Yes, that's right, that's the truth of the matter; this is indeed the word of the Lord" '.[16]

An objector might point out that the Christian, in coming to such a conclusion, might be making *unconscious* inferences from other (conscious or unconscious) beliefs she holds. If her conclusion is in fact based entirely on other beliefs she holds, then her conclusion does not, of course, constitute a basic belief. It seems impossible to adjudicate between conflicting descriptions here of how the Christian might reach the conclusion in question. For there is no phenomenological distinction between a belief formed in a basic way and a belief formed by way of unconscious inference.

But let us grant that Plantinga is correct in his assertion that Christian beliefs are (typically, at least) formed in a basic way. The question still looms as to whether such beliefs can be *sustained* in a basic way. To see why a belief formed in a basic way may cease to be sustained in a basic way, we need to consider the role of *defeaters*. Supposing that a person forms a belief$_m$ in a basic way, her belief is still subject to defeaters in the form of evidence: e.g. that the existence of evil makes God's existence improbable; that her belief$_m$ is widely disputed by others within her religious tradition; or that other theists from different religious traditions might plausibly lay claim to basically formed religious beliefs that are incompatible with her own beliefs. Noting the widespread exposure in modern times to so many potential defeaters, Philip Quinn concludes that 'many, perhaps most, intellectually sophisticated adult theists in our culture are seldom, if ever, in conditions which are right for propositions like ['God is speaking to me'] to be properly basic for them'.[17]

Quinn is interested in the question of whether religious beliefs can be *properly* basic, where 'properly' denotes justification or warrant. However, we are interested here in the non-normative question of whether people *do* hold religious beliefs in a basic way – not the question of whether people *should*, or are justified, in so doing. Still, it is possible to consider Quinn's line of argument as a possible defeater for the claim that people hold religious beliefs in a basic way; and we shall do just that.

Plantinga's response to Quinn's line of argument is that defeaters 'depend on and are relative to the rest of your noetic structure, the rest of what you know and believe'.[18] Thus, for a person with a firmly held (basic) religious belief, forceful contrary evidence may still not be enough to uproot his belief. The question remains, though, whether the very *consideration* of a potential defeater of one's basic belief does not change the status of that belief from basic to non-basic. Let us look at another example Plantinga uses as an analogue of Christian belief. His claim is that

> the *sensus divinitatis* resembles perception, memory, and a priori belief. Consider the first. I look out into the backyard; I see that the coral tiger lilies are in bloom. I don't note that I am being appeared to [in] a certain complicated way (that my experience is of a certain complicated character) and then make an argument from my being appeared to in that way to the conclusion that in fact there are coral tiger lilies in bloom there.[19]

Elaborating on the analogy between basic Christian belief and perception, Plantinga considers the possibility that one might respond to the question 'Why do you believe that you see a tree?'

> by citing a proposition about my experience [viz., that I seem to see a tree]. But does it follow that I believe the proposition *I see a tree* (call it 'T') on the basis of that experiential proposition? I should think not. Surely it does not follow that at t, the time of the query, I believed T on the basis of the experiential proposition. At t perhaps I did not even *believe* the experiential proposition; I may have been concentrating on the tree rather than on my experience; and surely it is not possible that at time t I accept a belief B on the basis of a belief A if at t I do not even believe A.[20]

Plantinga seems correct in pointing out that when one looks out of the window and forms a basic belief that there is a tree in the yard, one's focus will be on the *tree* – as opposed to one's *experience* of seeing a tree. And Plantinga is correct in pointing out that 'even if I believe something in the basic way, it doesn't follow that I wouldn't cite various other propositions in response to your question, "Why do you believe p? What is your reason for believing p?" '[21] Still, when one considers potential defeaters of a basic belief one holds, does one's focus remain solely on the *content* of what was initially believed, or does one's focus shift to one's *experience* of forming the belief?

It seems difficult to deny the latter when we consider cases where one's basic belief *is* in fact defeated. In the example of believing a tree to be in the yard, decisively defeating evidence might be a subsequently formed belief that one merely dreamt of looking out the window or that one has recently taken a hallucinatory drug, or following from Carl Ginet's example, that fake trees made of cardboard have recently been erected in the yard. In such cases, the belief 'that there is a tree in the yard' is defeated because of new evidence one acquires (in the form of new beliefs). This new evidence is taken to be decisive in that one comes to believe that one's total

evidence now supports the falsity of what was once believed –
namely, 'that there is a tree in the yard'.

What I wish to draw attention to is that when one acquires
potentially belief-defeating evidence and comes to reflect on one's
total evidence, part of that evidence will be the belief 'that I had an
experience of (apparently) seeing a tree'. It is *this* belief about one's
experience that is part of one's total evidence as one reflects on
whether one's initial belief 'that there is a tree in the yard' is in fact
true. Thus, if Quinn is correct about the near inevitability that an
adult in our culture today will come across potential defeaters to
religious beliefs such as a belief$_m$, then such beliefs – even if *formed*
in a basic way – will nonetheless not in standard cases be *sustained* in
a basic way. For, even if the potentially defeating evidence one
considers does not in fact defeat one's initial, basically formed
belief, the mere consideration of evidence means that one's initial
belief is no longer a basic one.

Take, for example, a person who forms religious beliefs in a basic
way and then comes to consider the hypothesis that religious beliefs
are in fact false and are the product of wish-fulfilment. Although the
religious beliefs may have been formed without the evidential
support of other beliefs the person holds, they will be sustained
(partly) on the basis of her further belief that she is not a delusional
person whose religious beliefs in the past have all turned out to be
false. We thus conclude that the notion of basic beliefs does not
undermine our working assumption that whether a person (or, at
least, an adult in our culture today) holds a belief$_m$ is a matter of
how she assesses the evidence for and against the truth of that
belief$_m$.

5.2 *Must the beliefs requisite for Christian faith rest on evidence only of a certain kind?*

In the previous section we saw how evidence assessment *does*
inevitably play a role in the holding of Christian beliefs such as a
belief$_m$. It was John Locke's contention that a reasoned evaluation
of evidence *should* always be one's basis for holding a belief that a
particular message comes from God. In commenting on a person
who receives what she considers to be a possible direct revelation
from God, Locke asks: 'How shall anyone distinguish between the
delusions of Satan, and the inspiration of the Holy Ghost?' He is
clear in his answer:

> God when he makes the Prophet does not unmake the Man. He leaves all
> his Faculties in their natural State, to enable him to judge of his
> Inspirations, whether they be of divine Original or no ... If he would

have us assent to the Truth of any Proposition, he either evidences that Truth by the usual Methods of natural Reason, or else makes it known to be a Truth, which he would have us assent to, by his Authority, and convinces us that it is from him, by some Marks which Reason cannot be mistaken in. *Reason* must be our last Judge and Guide in every Thing.[22]

Against Locke's assertion that reason should be the Christian theist's 'final judge', those in the Christian tradition commonly called fideists insist that faith must be 'above' reason, instead of the other way round.

Søren Kierkegaard, perhaps the most recognizable fideist in the Christian tradition, rejected the role Locke assigned reason in the formation of Christian beliefs.[23] But did Kierkegaard really reject any and all appeals to reasoned evidence evaluation in the forming and maintaining of Christian beliefs such as a belief$_m$?

Against such a conclusion C. Stephen Evans points out that 'Kierkegaard, in writing about the case of a Danish pastor deposed for claiming to have had a special revelation, offers criteria for recognizing a genuine revelation'.[24]

Evans's reference is to Adolph Adler, a priest who claimed to have received a personal revelation from Jesus Christ and who was deposed by the Church on grounds of mental instability.[25] Kierkegaard issued a number of criticisms of Adler; and Evans identifies as implicit in these criticisms three general criteria for recognizing a genuine revelation.

First, Kierkegaard noted that, unlike Adler, one who has been entrusted with a genuine revelation will, in announcing this revelation to others, appeal only to 'having divine authority' and not to his own 'genius'.[26] Second, a bearer of genuine revelation will not make use of 'influence and powerful connections' to ensure that his revelation 'is victorious over people's opinions and judgments'.[27] (While these first two criteria involve the *bearer* of a revelation – rather than the *revelation itself* – Kierkegaard is presumably working with the assumption that God would not entrust a genuine revelation to someone who would fail to meet these criteria.) Third, Kierkegaard maintained that a genuine revelation will maintain the look of a paradox: 'However long it is proclaimed in the world, it remains essentially just as new, just as paradoxical'.[28]

All three criteria are essentially 'negative' in character in that they are not sufficient for demonstrating that a purported revelation is indeed genuine. While it is possible to use the criteria to show that a purported revelation is *not* genuine, the criteria by themselves do not establish that a purported revelation *is* in fact genuine. At best they allow one to conclude that a purported revelation might well be genuine.

Turning to the question of whether Kierkegaard allowed for any sort of 'positive' criteria in assessing evidence for a belief$_m$, his stated position as discussed in section 4.2 would appear to be 'no'. In that previous section, we examined the sharp distinction Kierkegaard made between *objective* evidence assessment (which shows central Christian doctrines to be improbable at best) and *subjective* belief that those central doctrines are true (a belief which the believer acquires through a strenuous exertion of the will). However, Evans seems right in commenting that Kierkegaard's talk of objective improbability turns out in the end to be a criticism of a particular perspective that gives rise to conclusions of subjective improbability.

> Climacus [the pseudonymous author of Kierkegaard's *Philosophical Fragments*] says that the believer must firmly hold to the notion that the incarnation is a paradox and is therefore improbable. However, since the believer thinks the incarnation has actually occurred, he cannot believe that the objective probability of the event is low, since the objective probability of an event that has occurred is 1. The meaning must be that the believer understands the event as one that will appear improbable to someone who holds certain beliefs. For example, someone such as Hume who believes that miraculous events are in general improbable, will certainly make the same judgment about the idea of a divine incarnation ... This conclusion corresponds perfectly with Climacus' own contention that the paradoxicalness of the paradox is a function of sin, which creates the 'absolute qualitative distance' between God and human beings.[29]

In section 1.5 we noted that where one's belief 'that *p*' occurs in the context of evaluating evidence, this belief will be the conclusion to which one takes the balance of one's total evidence to point. Thus, if Kierkegaard (or anyone else) believes e.g. that God became incarnate in Jesus or that a particular message comes from God, then he could not at the same time assert that *his own* assessment of the evidence has led him to think that these things are not true. Moreover, Kierkegaard surely would not want to posit that God – who *ex hypothesi* has complete access to and appreciation of the evidence we see only dimly – finds the evidence telling against these things being true. It seems, then, that Kierkegaard's position turns out to be that central Christian doctrines seem improbable to those who evaluate evidence *from a certain perspective*.

Kierkegaard's writings are marked by a criticism of the rationalists of his time (most notably Hegel) as being woefully over-optimistic in their attempts to ascertain metaphysical truths through a reasoned evaluation of only those facts that stand up to scientific enquiry. His repeated references to 'objectivity' seem in fact to be references to the (subjective) perspective of many of the rationalist thinkers of his day. Still, if this line of analysis is correct, then we might ask why Kierkegaard does not simply claim that, from a general Christian perspective, certain specific doctrines *do* come to appear to be probable. Evans offers the following response to this question:

> The answer surely lies in the fact that Christianity assumes that human beings are in fact sinners. This perspective is in fact the perspective that every human being occupies, at least prior to faith. And since the transition from sin to faith is not, for Climacus, a one-time event, but a transition that must continually be renewed, it remains necessary for the believer to define the content of her faith polemically, as that which necessarily is in opposition to the thinking of sinful human beings.[30]

So we have seen that Kierkegaard's criticism of 'objective enquiry' ultimately amounts to criticism of a certain type of subjective enquiry commonly practised by his rationalistic contemporaries. And we have seen that, inasmuch as the Christian holds a belief$_m$, her perspective is that the evidence points to the truth of what she believes. We might now ask why the subjective evidence assessment of the authentic Christian should be preferred to the subjective evidence assessment of the rationalist whom Kierkegaard criticizes.

Leaving aside the issue of differences in the *way* evidence is assessed, I wish here to explore the suggestion in Kierkegaard's writings that an assessment of only a *certain kind* of evidence can serve as the proper basis for Christian beliefs. Specifically, I have in mind Kierkegaard's insistence that the only proper basis for Christian beliefs is divine authority.

To be sure, there have been numerous theologians within the Christian tradition who have appealed to God's authority as the basis for Christian beliefs. Regarding this appeal to divine authority, Scott MacDonald notes that 'The tradition is rooted in Augustine who distinguished faith from another sort of belief – what he called understanding (*intellectus*) – on the basis of its epistemic grounds. According to him, faith is belief based on authority whereas understanding is belief based on reason'.[31] Aquinas, following Augustine, stated that 'The faith of which we are speaking, does not assent to anything, except because it is revealed by God. Hence the mean on which faith is based is the Divine Truth'.[32] Similarly, the First Vatican Council declared that 'it is necessary to divine faith that revealed truth be believed because of the authority of God who reveals it'.[33]

Kierkegaard's primary reason for insisting that the Christian's beliefs be based on God's authority seems to involve a concern that the Christian believer exhibit trusting obedience toward God. In defence of the notion that trusting obedience is possible only when one forms beliefs based on God's authority, Kierkegaard offers a number of illustrations. He mentions a king's decree,[34] a father's command[35] and a police officer's directions.[36] In each case, if a person concludes that she should follow the instructions given her simply because they strike her as sound, then her beliefs that she should follow the instructions – along with her subsequent following of these instructions – are not formed in a way that exhibits trusting obedience. Kierkegaard remarks:

> If a son were to say, 'I obey my father not because he is my father but because he is a genius, or because his commands are always profound and brilliant,' this filial obedience is affected. The son emphasizes something altogether wrong, emphasizes the brilliance, the profundity in a command ... and on that basis he simply cannot obey him, because his critical attitude with regard to whether the command is profound and brilliant undermines the obedience.[37]

Restating Kierkegaard's line of argument here, we might say that there are two distinct reasons why a son might form the belief that he should act in accordance with his father's commands. First, his belief might be based on a further belief that the commands are wise and profound. Second, his belief might be based on the further belief that the father possesses the authority to issue a command with the proper expectation that it be obeyed. Kierkegaard submits that only in the latter case is the basis for belief consistent with the formation of the doctrinal beliefs of the authentic Christian.

The two cases have a common feature in that, in each case, the son forms the belief 'that I, the son, should act in accordance with what my father has commanded'. The two cases differ in that they have *different evidential bases* (viz. the belief 'that the commands are profound' vs the belief 'that the father possesses the authority to issue the command') for the formation of this belief. Thus, it seems that Kierkegaard's insistence that Christian beliefs be formed in the proper way amounts to an insistence that only evidence of a certain kind – namely, the evidence of another person's authority – constitutes a proper basis for Christian beliefs.

Let us turn now to consider the specific religious belief, belief$_m$. How should we assess the claim that a person would fail to exhibit the proper response to God's message to her if she came to believe on evidence other than that of God's authority that that message did in fact come from God? At this point, we must be precise about that which reason is supposed to help us discover. John Locke, who advocated the kind of reasoned evaluation of evidence to which Kierkegaard objected, was clear to state that the role of reason in evaluating purported revelations is not to provide reasons independent of God's authority for thinking a purported revelation profound or true: 'Whatever God hath revealed is certainly true: no doubt can be made of it. This is the proper object of faith: but whether it be a divine revelation or no, reason must judge.'[38] Thus, whether or not reasoned evidence assessment is inconsistent with a proper response to God will depend on what conclusions one attempts to reach by means of such evidence assessment. As Evans observes:

> A distinction should be made between critical questions about the content of what is revealed and critical questions about the credentials of the source. It is true that I do not obey my parents if I only obey an order they have given me when I have independently decided that the action commanded would be a good one. However, suppose I receive an order that purports to be from my parents, but one that I have reason to doubt really comes from them? In that case, reflection on the order does not necessarily stem from lack of trust in the parents. If I look at the signature with care to see if it looks genuine, or reflect on whether or not this order is consistent with other orders I have received from them, then this may be because I desire to obey them, not because I am rebellious or insubordinate. Similarly, reflection on whether a revelation is really from God is not necessarily a symptom of a desire to evade God's authority.[39]

Kierkegaard rightly notes the importance of a proper recognition of, and response to, the divine authority that lies behind any divine message. And his concern about the (in)compatibility of evidence assessment with acceptance of divine authority seems a legitimate one. His concern is mitigated, however, when we distinguish the different ways in which one might come to the conclusion that a purportedly divine message contains true or profound information. If one forms the conclusion solely on the basis of evidence for the message's content being true – irrespective of where the message originated – then one's assessment of evidence does indeed seem incongruous with an acceptance of divine authority. However, if one forms the conclusion in question because one sees the evidence as showing that the message originates from God, whose messages are always true, then one's assessment of evidence is entirely consistent with a proper recognition of, and response to, divine authority.

Not only is assessment of evidence (beyond the evidence of God's authority) *consistent* with recognition of divine authority, it is also *necessary* for such recognition. To see why this is so, suppose that a person believes that she has received a message – in the form of information about where her obligations lie – intended for her and sent by God. Suppose that she believes this information to be true and that the basis for her belief is God's authority (that is, because it is God who gave the message). Now, in order to believe the information on God's authority, she must already believe that God has certain authority-making features, such as having a set of true beliefs about where people's obligations lie and being committed not to lie to them about these.[40] Why would she believe *these* facts about God? If we claim that God has communicated these facts about himself to her and that she believes them to be true on God's authority, then we assume her to have still other beliefs about God's authority-making features – such as a knowledge that he is not mistaken in his beliefs of where people's obligations lie and a commitment not to lie about himself. And why would she believe that God has *these* further authority-making features? If we claim that the basis of her beliefs on these matters is God's authority, then we carry on the discussion *ad infinitum*.

Not all regresses, of course, are problematic. Yet the kind of regress under consideration here cannot be epistemically sustained. For, if the evidence of another's authority is the only evidence one can consider, then in order for one to hold any belief on another's authority, one would need to reason through an infinite number of beliefs about that person's authority-making features. And this seems an epistemic impossibility. (Plus, there is the additional implausibility of asserting that the other person conveys an infinite number of messages regarding his own authority-making features.) At some point a person's evidence for believing that God has a certain authority-making feature must be 'outside' evidence – i.e. evidence that is not accepted simply on the basis of God's authority. In the case we considered, outside evidence might include a priori arguments that God, if he exists, does not lie and does possess complete knowledge of his created creatures' obligations. (Alternatively, following Plantinga, we might allow for the possibility that a person could, without assessing evidence, form (in a basic way) the belief that God has certain authority-making features. However, in the previous section we noted the near inevitability that a normal adult in our society, even if he *forms* a religious belief in a basic way, will come to consider evidence in the course of *sustaining* that belief.)

Before moving on we should note that the appeal to outside evidence in recognizing another person's authority is entirely consistent with the account of faith outlined in Chapter 3. We noted in that chapter that faith in another person becomes possible only when one responds to the authoritative claims that lie behind what we termed 'invitational statements' – as opposed to responding merely to the statements themselves. To illustrate this distinction, we considered the case of an advice columnist who makes invitational statements (in the form of relationship advice) to her readers with the desire that her readers' recognition of her authority as a PhD in psychology with clinical experience be (part of) the readers' reason for responding in a positive way to her advice. If the

columnist's readers put their faith in her, one of the things they will
need to believe is that having a PhD in psychology and having 20
years of clinical experience help to make one an authority on
relationships. The readers, though, will not hold this belief on the
advice columnist's authority. Instead, they will have outside
evidence that having a PhD with 20 years of experience confers
on a person certain authority-making features. Despite having
outside evidence as to *why* the advice columnist *is* an authority, the
readers are still accepting her authority when they respond
positively to her authoritative claims. Similarly, our depiction of
Christian faith as the acceptance of God's authority is in no way
undermined by the recognition that some of the beliefs requisite for
Christian faith (e.g. a belief$_m$) are themselves not believed simply on
God's authority.

5.3 *The notion of spiritual blindness*

We began this chapter by noting that it seems natural to suppose
that the reason nonbelievers do not hold the beliefs requisite for
Christian faith (particularly, a belief$_m$) is that they do not believe
that their evidence supports such beliefs. Having found in the
writings of Plantinga and Kierkegaard insufficient reason to
abandon this working assumption, let us now explore the question
of why someone might not believe with the Christian tradition that
certain messages – which Christians have thought to be essential to
their faith – do in fact come from God.[41] To put the question
differently: why might someone – contrary to the judgments of
Christian theists – fail to see the available evidence as pointing to the
probable truth of certain beliefs$_m$? I wish in this section to explore
the idea that a person who fails to hold with the Christian theist
certain beliefs$_m$ may fail to do so on account of his own 'spiritual
blindness'.

I should emphasize at the outset that in this section – as well as in
Chapter 6 to follow – I shall not seek to advance any empirical claim
about how prevalent the phenomenon of spiritual blindness is in our
world. That is, I shall not put forward any particular view as to the
extent to which spiritual blindness does account for the failure of
actual nonbelievers to form Christian beliefs. Rather, my aim is
simply to provide an account of what it would mean for a person to
wilfully (and culpably) 'blind' himself to some spiritual truth.

The idea that character flaws can prevent one from acquiring
certain kinds of beliefs or knowledge is hardly novel. Aristotle
linked vice with the destruction of one's practical wisdom.

Pericles and men like him have practical wisdom ... because they can see what is good for themselves and what is good for men in general ... but the man who has been ruined by pleasure or pain forth with fails to see ... that for the sake of this or because of this he ought to choose to do whatever he chooses and does.[42]

While Aristotle appealed in more general terms to the connection between epistemic shortcomings and corrupted character, writers within the Christian tradition have often used this purported connection in explaining why not all people form the more specific beliefs requisite for Christian faith. Bonaventure maintained that the failure to hold an unwavering belief that God exists stems 'from a defect in the knower rather than from a deficiency in the object known'.[43] John Henry Newman remarked that there exist good arguments for the Christian faith, which are capable of convincing anyone who 'fairly studies' their premises.[44] Newman also noted that 'It is almost a proverb, that persons believe what they wish to be true ... [People] readily believe reports unfavourable to persons they dislike, or confirmations of theories of their own'.[45] William James went so far as to state that 'As a rule we disbelieve all facts and theories for which we have no use. Clifford's cosmic emotions find no use for Christian feelings. Huxley belabors the bishops because there is no use for sacerdotalism in his scheme of life'.[46] The comments of Newman and James go beyond merely pointing to some general character flaw that keeps one from forming Christian beliefs. Their point is roughly this: a person who fails to see his evidence as indicating that a certain proposition is true may fail to do so because of some sort of negative demeanour toward the possibility that that proposition is true.

Perhaps the two best-known articulators within the Christian tradition of this line of thought are John Calvin and Jonathan Edwards. Both authors take their cues from Romans 1.18-20, where St Paul writes that

The wrath of God is being revealed from heaven against all the godlessness and wickedness of men who suppress the truth by their wickedness, since what may be known about God is plain to them, because God has made it plain to them. For since the creation of the world God's invisible qualities – his eternal power and divine nature – have been clearly seen, being understood from what has been made, so that men are without excuse.

Both Calvin and Edwards insisted that the world provides ample evidence to support those beliefs requisite for Christian faith. Edwards maintained that God gave humans an understanding of the divine, eternal things that concern them. As to central, Christian doctrines, Edwards concluded that 'if men have not respect to

[them] as real and certain things, it cannot be for want of sufficient evidence of their truth'.[47]

Calvin likewise asserted that God 'has been pleased ... to manifest his perfections in the whole structure of the universe, and daily place himself in our view, that we cannot open our eyes without being compelled to behold him'.[48] Given this overwhelming nature of the evidence for theism, and given Calvin's understanding that God has instilled in all humans a tendency to see his hand at work in the world, Calvin concluded that, even in the most corrupt of humans, 'the conviction that there is some Deity continues to exist, like a plant which can never be completely eradicated'.[49]

Although Calvin here seems to suggest that some beliefs requisite for Christian faith are held by *all* people (e.g. the beliefs that God exists and that he created this world), he maintained that human corruption prevents many of us from seeing other Christian truths that we 'are desirous not to know'.[50]

> ... how can the idea of God enter your mind without instantly giving rise to the thought, that since you are his workmanship, you are bound, by the very law of creation, to submit to his authority? – that your life is due to him? – that whatever you do ought to have reference to him? If so, it undoubtedly follows that your life is sadly corrupted.[51]

Following Calvin, Edwards asserted that 'The mind of man is naturally full of enmity against the doctrines of the gospel; which is a disadvantage to those arguments that prove their truth, and causes them to lose their force upon the mind'.[52] As Nicholas Wolterstorff summarizes, 'characteristic of the Reformed tradition' in which Calvin and Edwards feature prominently is the view that 'cases of unbelief' stem not so much from insufficient available evidence, but rather from '*resistance* to the available evidence'.[53]

It seems obvious enough from everyday observations that people's desires can impact upon what they come to believe. As we observe, for instance, how sports fanatics tend to evaluate referees' performances or how parents tend to evaluate their children's athletic potential, it is not difficult to reach Francis Bacon's general conclusion that 'what a man would rather was true, that he the more readily believes'.[54] But how exactly can one's desires affect one's beliefs? And, if we are to think of people as morally culpable for being in a spiritually blind state where their desires affect their beliefs, what morally significant choices of theirs might we point to as culpably leading to their being in this state? To answer these questions we will need to examine the psychological literature in some detail. Our next chapter will be devoted to doing just that.

Conclusion

We began this chapter by asking why someone might not form certain beliefs requisite for Christian faith – particularly a belief$_m$. After considering possible objections from Plantinga and Kierkegaard, we retained the straightforward answer that a person simply might not see the balance of his evidence as pointing to the truth of these beliefs. In explaining why some people might not believe with the Christian theist that the available evidence points to the truth of certain Christian affirmations, we have noted the explanation from some Christian writers that those who do not believe are spiritually 'blinded' to the truth. As we examine how we might make sense of the idea of being spiritually blinded, we turn now to explore the psychological literature on the effects one's desires can have on what one believes.

Notes

[1] For a good introduction to these authors' critiques of classical foundationalism, see Plantinga and Wolterstorff (1983).

[2] Cf. Plantinga 2000: vii.

[3] For a time Plantinga interpreted Aquinas as an advocate of just the kind of evidentialism to which he objects (cf. Plantinga 1983: 40–8). See Plantinga (2000: 82) for an explanation of his interpretive reversal.

[4] Calvin 1559: I, vii, 5.

[5] Calvin 1559: I, vii, 4.

[6] Aquinas 1265–73: I, ii, 1, ad. 1. Cf. Aquinas 1261–64: Bk III, Ch. 38.

[7] Aquinas 1261–64: Bk III, Ch. 38.

[8] Aquinas 1265–73: I, ii, 2, ad. 1.

[9] Aquinas 1261–64: Bk I, Ch. 38.

[10] Aquinas 1265–73: II–II, ii, 9.

[11] Aquinas 1265–73: II–II, vi, 1.

[12] Regarding the kind of evidence that miracles provide, Aquinas noted elsewhere that 'a visible work that can be from God alone, proves the teacher of truth to be invisibly inspired' (1261–64: Bk I, Ch. 6).

[13] Plantinga 2000: 175.

[14] Plantinga 2000: 175.

[15] Plantinga 2000: 250.

[16] Cf. Plantinga 2000: 250.

[17] Quinn 1985: 481.

[18] Plantinga 2000: 360.

[19] Plantinga 2000: 175.

[20] Plantinga 1983: 51.

[21] Plantinga 2000: 176.

[22] Locke 1690: IV, xix, §14.

[23] In section 4.2 we briefly looked at some of Kierkegaard's reasons for resisting an objective evidential basis for Christian commitment.

[24] Evans 2000: 48.

[25] Cf. Evans 1998: 88 and Evans 2000: 54.

[26] Kierkegaard 1846–47: 177.

[27] Kierkegaard 1846–47: 186.

[28] Kierkegaard 1846–47: 176. In listing these criteria, I do not mean either to endorse or to offer a critique of them. I list them merely to demonstrate that Kierkegaard did allow a role for reason in judging whether or not a given message truly comes from God.

[29] Evans 1990: 481. Quotation is taken from Kierkegaard (1844: 46–7).

[30] Evans 1990: 481.

[31] MacDonald 1993: 56. Cf. Augustine 389–91: XXIV, 45.

[32] Aquinas 1265–73: II–II, i, 1.

[33] *Enchiridion Symbolorum* 1957: 1811. Cf. 1789.

[34] Kierkegaard 1846–47: 178.

[35] Kierkegaard 1846–47: 185.

[36] Kierkegaard 1846–47: 180.

[37] Kierkegaard 1846–47: 185.

[38] Locke 1690: IV, xviii, §10. Locke himself defined faith as 'the Assent to any Proposition, not thus made out by the Deductions of Reason; but upon the Credit of the Proposer, as coming from GOD' (IV, xviii, §2).

[39] Evans 1998: 89–90.

[40] We assume here that God's message involves an already existing obligation that the person has. If we suppose that God's message is a command which itself established an obligation, then the person in question would not need to have the further beliefs about God we have listed. After all, a command is not the kind of thing which might be a lie or about which the issuer of the command might be mistaken.

[41] The Christian tradition, of course, has had disagreements over which messages should be attributed to God (e.g. the inclusion of certain material in the Christian canon) and over the meaning of these messages (e.g. the implications for episcopal authority stemming from Jesus's statement to Peter that 'on this rock I will build my church' (Mt. 16.18)). Still, the religious communities stemming from the twelve apostles have held certain common, central beliefs about what God has communicated to humankind – e.g., that God created this world and that God has chosen to reconcile sinful people to himself through the atoning work of Jesus Christ.

[42] Aristotle n.d.: IV, 1140^b.

[43] Bonaventure 1254–57: q. I, i, 1.2.3.

[44] Newman 1853: 27.

[45] Newman 1872: 189.

[46] James 1896: 10.

[47] Edwards 1758: 157.

[48] Calvin 1559: I, v, 1.

[49] Calvin 1559: I, iv, 4.

[50] Calvin 1559: I, iii, 2. For a discussion of what the reprobate do and do not believe, see I, ii, 1.

[51] Calvin 1559: I, ii, 2.

[52] Edwards 1746: 307.

[53] Wolterstorff 1981: 145.

[54] Bacon 1620: Bk I, §xlix. Strictly speaking, Bacon's conclusion does not seem to be universally true. Fear, for example, may lead a child to believe that there are monsters lurking under his bed – and this despite his desire that all monsters be kept well away from him. Still, the concept of spiritual blindness does involve the idea that one is 'blinded' to what one desires not to see.

SELF-DECEPTION AND WILFUL CHOICES

6.1 *Hot and cold motivations*

Francis Bacon anticipated the research findings of modern-day psychologists in commenting that 'in innumerable ways, and those sometimes imperceptible, the affection tinges and infects the Intellect'.[1] Often, the uncomfortable nature of a belief provides the key to understanding how one's desires affect the formation of that belief. A mother who very much wants it to be the case that her son is innocent of the crime for which he has been arrested might well come to believe in her son's innocence despite contrary evidence that others consider fairly conclusive. Similarly, a husband might believe his wife's attestations of faithfulness despite contrary evidence that more neutral observers find overwhelming. In each case, the uncomfortable nature of a particular belief 'that p' leads the person very much to desire that p not be true; and this desire in turn seems somehow to affect the formation of the person's belief 'that p'.

A belief may be uncomfortable or undesirable for any number of reasons. Sometimes a person may wish for something to be false simply because someone she dislikes is committed to it being true. For example, a person who is in unhealthy competition with a work colleague may wish that her colleague's hypotheses be proved wrong; and a person who dislikes a politician may want the politician's proposals to prove embarrassingly ineffective. In each case the person wants things to be a certain way; and certain beliefs (e.g. that her colleague is right and that the politician has good ideas) may therefore be uncomfortable for her. David Pears has pointed out that some beliefs may be uncomfortable because they stand in the way of a person performing certain actions – including akratic (weak-willed) ones – that he wants to perform. Suppose, for example, that a man at a party desires to have more drinks – but judges it best, because he must drive home, to stop at the two drinks he has already had. Pears remarks that the man 'might tell himself, against the weight of his evidence, that it is not dangerous to drive home after six measures of whisky, or he might forget, under the influence of his wish, how many drinks he had already taken'.[2] Here the man is resistant to holding a belief because the belief makes a desired action more difficult. In the end, we can imagine any number of scenarios in which a person might be motivated to hold (or not to hold) a particular belief.

In instances where certain desires do affect the formation or continued holding of one's beliefs, it will sometimes be the case that one is unaware that one has these desires. The man from a previous example who believes his wife's attestations of faithfulness may see his own belief as characteristic of the charitable way he judges other people – when in truth his belief stems from a desire to avoid the public embarrassment of a divorce. As other examples, we might cite a wife who does not see that her affair is really an attempt to punish her husband; a son who does not see that his rebellion is really an attempt to get his parents to listen; and a daughter who does not see that her eating disorder is really an attempt to gain some control over her life. Psychotherapists commonly help people make these types of discoveries, which often are discoveries about why one performs the actions one performs. Put another way, they are often discoveries about the purposes one seeks to achieve. And so, among those beliefs affected by desires we should include beliefs as to what one's purposes in acting truly are.

Even when one *is* aware that one has a certain desire, one may still not be aware that that desire plays a causal role in one's own actions and in what one believes. A university student may be very aware of her own desire that her parents love her and may believe that her parents, who are both physicians, would undoubtedly love her were she to follow in their steps as a physician. However, as Alfred Mele has pointed out, given that a person can be mistaken about her actual purposes in acting, we can suppose that this desire leads her to enter medical school without also supposing that she *believes* that this desire has anything at all to do with her decision.[3]

There is nothing too difficult in understanding examples of this kind. Greater ambiguity lies in cases where a person either believes or suspects that his desires *might* be affecting his actions and beliefs. Consider the case of a sports fanatic who strongly believes that the majority of a referee's bad decisions are going against the team he is supporting. Upon seeing that the opposing team's fans are expressing similar outrage at the referee's decisions, the fan may come to think that perhaps his own desire for his team to win is influencing his evaluation of the referee. If the sports fan comes to believe that his original belief about the referee stemmed from his own bias toward the prospects of his team winning, then this recognition will tend strongly to undermine his original belief – and this for the reasons discussed in section 2.2 where we considered the case of one who comes to believe that his belief 'that *p*' was acquired through an unreliable means. But what if the sports fan merely suspects that his general biases *might* be affecting his specific belief about the referee? It seems clear that such a suspicion would still *tend* to some extent toward undermining his original belief, though it seems difficult to say more here with much exactness. Still, the general point remains that desiring p to be the case can affect whether one comes and/or continues to believe that p is the case – even though one is not aware that one's desire is having this effect or that one even has this desire.

Instances where one's desires affect the formation of one's beliefs sometimes fall under the description of irrationality, in that one's desires may keep one from meeting correct and/or one's own standards of evidence assessment and proper reasoning. Because such irrationality involves one's desires, we might refer to it generally as 'motivated' irrationality, or irrationality generated through 'hot' mechanisms. At the same time, it is important to note how one's beliefs can be affected by *un*motivated irrationality, or irrationality stemming from 'cold' mechanisms. So-called perversions of reason are cognitive failures of some kind, though they do not stem from wanting things to be a certain way.

Among the common kinds of unmotivated irrationality is what Daniel Kahneman and Amos Tversky term the 'availability heuristic'.[4] According to the availability heuristic, 'subjective probability is evaluated by the difficulty of retrieval and construction of instances'.[5] Because it is easier for most people to think of words starting with 'k' than to think of words that have 'k' as the third letter, people may sometimes tend toward believing that there exist more words of the former sort than words of the latter sort.[6] Another source of unmotivated irrationality identified by Kahneman and Tversky is the 'representativeness heuristic'. A person may be asked whether the births of six children in a family are less likely to have the gender sequence of BBBGGG than the sequence of GBBGBG. According to Kahneman and Tversky's experiments, persons asked show on the whole a tendency to judge the first gender sequence a less likely scenario than the second.[7] Because the first sequence can seem less 'representative' of the random process by which gender is determined, some people will accordingly see this first sequence as less likely to occur.

Yet another source of unmotivated irrationality involves the undue weight we can give to certain evidence if that evidence is in some way especially vivid to us. Richard Nisbett and Lee Ross identify three main ways in which information (which is potential evidence for a given conclusion) can strike us as especially vivid. First, some information can carry more emotional interest with us than other information. If one is told that 'Jack skidded off an icy road and demolished a parked car', and if the parked car happens to

belong to a stranger, then we may to a certain extent be inclined to
think that Jack was an unlucky victim of the icy road. But if the car
is one's own or belongs to a close friend or relative, then we may be
more inclined to conclude that Jack was careless or that he was
driving too fast.[8] Second, information may be especially vivid to us
if it is particularly concrete. Nisbett and Ross point out that the
information that 'Jack was killed by a semitrailer that rolled over his
car and crushed his skull' is more vivid and image-provoking than
the information that 'Jack sustained fatal injuries in an auto
accident'.[9] As such, this information is more likely to be recognized
and recalled as evidence for conclusions such as that speed limits
should be lowered on motorways. The third source of vividness that
Nisbett and Ross identify involves the temporal, spatial and sensory
proximity of the information. Nisbett and Ross explain:

> The news that a bank in one's neighborhood has been robbed just an
> hour ago is more vivid than the news that a bank on the other side of
> town was robbed last week. The former bank robbery, accordingly, is
> likely to have a greater impact on one's views of the seriousness of the
> crime problem in one's city or the need for stiffer prison sentences for
> bank robbers.[10]

This list of 'cold' mechanisms is by no means exhaustive. Yet it does
allow us to imagine any number of examples where one's beliefs are
affected by perversions of reason.

Sometimes the line between 'cold' explanations and 'hot' explanations will not be altogether clear. In testing a favoured hypothesis
people will often tend to recognize confirming evidence more readily
than dis-confirming evidence. If this 'confirmation bias' stems
simply from the fact that people tend to see more easily that which
they expect to see, then it is cold mechanisms that will be affecting
the formation of a person's beliefs. If, however, this 'confirmation
bias' is the result of a person's desire that her initial hypothesis be
proved right, then a hot explanation is in order. Where both hot and
cold mechanisms are at work, it may be impossible to discern
precisely what influence on belief formation any one mechanism is
having.

Within hot explanations of the link between desires and belief
formation, an understanding of cold mechanisms can help us
explain how it is that desiring something to be the case can lead to
one's believing that something is the case. Taking as an example the
mother who desires that her son be innocent of the crime of which
he is accused, we might suppose that her desire leads to feelings of
great emotional comfort when she considers evidence in favour of
her son's innocence. Though this evidence she considers might not
be particularly good evidence – even by her own standards – the

evidence might be especially vivid to her by virtue of her emotional reaction to it. Being vivid evidence, it might through cold mechanisms be given undue weight. Also, the emotional comfort the mother finds in contemplating this evidence might lead her frequently to do so, which would naturally tend to make this evidence more available to her as she considers various pieces of evidence for and against her son's guilt. Further, if her desire leads her to form the belief that her son is in fact innocent, then her belief will constitute a sort of initial hypothesis for her. As such, she may tend to recognize evidence in favour of her son's innocence more readily than contrary evidence – and this on the cold explanation that one sees more easily that which one expects to see.

Given that spiritual blindness involves a desire for things to be a certain way, a person cannot rightly be described as blinding himself to some spiritual truth if his failure to believe that truth stems purely from cold mechanisms.[11] At the same time, the presence of a hot motivation that something be a certain way does not by itself establish culpability – even when this motivation keeps one from holding some Christian belief that one otherwise would hold. As stipulated in the Introduction, one of our working assumptions is that culpability only arises when one decides to act in violation of what one believes to be a moral obligation. Thus, if the Christian theist is rightly to assign moral culpability for being in a state of spiritual blindness, she will need to point to some decision the spiritually blind person makes that contributes to his being in this state.

It is certainly in keeping with many Christian writers that people can and sometimes do play an active role in 'blinding' themselves to the truth of certain Christian beliefs. Aquinas, for example, maintained that sometimes 'ignorance is directly and essentially voluntary, as when a man is purposely ignorant that he may sin more freely'.[12] And Joseph Butler, in his aptly titled sermon, 'Upon Self-Deceit', asserted that 'It is as easy to close the eyes of the mind, as those of the body: and the former is more frequently done with wilfulness, and yet not attended to, than the latter'.[13] In exploring what it would mean for a person to perform the intentional action of 'wilfully blinding himself' to the truth of some matter, we shall need to examine in some detail the notion of self-deception. And as we seek to identify what sort of intentional actions might contribute to self-deception, the first thing we must recognize is that the notion of literal self-deception is deeply paradoxical, if not incoherent.

6.2 *The paradox of self-deception*

Raphael Demos, in his essay, 'Lying to Oneself', compares self-deception to failing to notice a headache when one goes to the cinema and becomes engrossed in an exciting film.[14] Demos states that 'the person who lies to himself, because of yielding to impulse, fails to notice or ignores what he knows to be the case'.[15] This description of lying to oneself, though, seems to contain a crucial equivocation with respect to whether lying to oneself involves intentional actions. Demos remarks that one who lies to himself 'fails to notice' or 'ignores' what he knows to be the case. However, as M.R. Haight points out, 'failing to notice is prima facie not deliberate'; whereas ' "Ignore" means "*choose* not to notice" ... If I ignore a headache, I deliberately turn my thoughts to other things.'[16] The notion of lying seems clearly to involve the deliberate attempt to mislead someone. The same goes for the broader notion of attempting to deceive someone about the truth of some matter. Thus, as we examine the idea of self-deception, we will want to keep clear the distinction between things we deliberately do and things that merely happen to us.

There is nothing odd about the idea that a person may lie to himself. A novice archer may tell himself that he will certainly win a forthcoming competition against archers of far greater skill; and an airline passenger may tell himself in the midst of a turbulent flight that he has already landed and is back safely at home with his loved ones. What *does* seem questionable is the further suggestion that one might be successful in getting oneself to believe one's own lies. As Kant remarked, 'a lie requires a second person whom one intends to deceive, and intentionally to deceive oneself seems to contain a contradiction'.[17] As to the exact nature of the (at least apparent) contradiction here, we might begin by asking whether it is possible for a person to hold contradictory beliefs. In order for self-deception to occur in a strict literal sense, one would have to believe some proposition in one's role as deceiver and at the same time believe the negation of that proposition in one's role as deceived. But is it possible for a person to be in such a state?

We should note that one who defends the possibility of literal self-deception need not go so far as to claim both that the self-deceiver has a particular belief and that the self-deceiver does *not* have that particular belief. That is, the defender need not claim that '*S* believes *p*' and that '~*S* believes *p*'. This would be to claim a blatant contradiction. Instead, the defender of literal self-deception need only claim that, in addition to believing a certain proposition, the self-deceiver *also* believes that that proposition is not true. That is, the defender need only claim that '*S* believes *p*' and that

'*S* believes ~*p*'. And it does seem entirely possible for a person to hold such opposing beliefs. A man may move from the northern hemisphere to the southern hemisphere and explain to his son that the water where they now live drains clockwise. The same man also may have the peculiar habit – perhaps stemming from a concern for dishwashing ultra-efficiency – of stacking certain cooking utensils to soak in the kitchen sink in a precise way. Specifically, he may always place the colander in the sink at a certain angle with the intent that, when the sink plug is pulled, the counterclockwise flow of draining water will push through the bottom of the colander, thereby tending to clean the colander ever so slightly more efficiently than if it had been left to soak in the sink in a different position. After his move to the southern hemisphere, the man may continue to place the colander in the same position in the sink – with the continued expectation that the water will move in a counterclockwise manner. Of course, when he does so, he forgets the very lesson he has taught his son. It is entirely possible that he might even explain to his son (while reflecting on the matter) the direction of draining water in the two hemispheres at the very same time that he is (without such reflection) stacking dishes. In such a case, we might say of the man that he believes that the water in his new house does not flow in a counterclockwise manner (as evidenced by the instruction he gives his son) and at the same time believes that the water in his new house does indeed flow in a counterclockwise manner (as evidenced by his stacking of dishes).

Still, literal self-deception seems to require more than merely that a person believe a certain proposition while unaware that she also believes a contradictory proposition. The notion of continued, successful deception requires that a person *maintain an awareness* (in her role as deceiver) of the falsity of that which she believes (in her role as deceived). As Sartre argued with respect to self-deception:

> I must know in my capacity as deceiver the truth which is hidden from me in my capacity as the one deceived. Better yet I must know the truth very exactly *in order* to conceal it more carefully – and this not at two moments, which at a pinch would allow us to re-establish a semblance of duality – but in the unitary structure of a single project.[18]

It seems impossible that a person could continue to hold opposing beliefs (in her roles as both deceiver and deceived) if she is simultaneously aware that she holds them and understands that they contradict one another. Thus, defenders of literal self-deception have commonly wanted to posit some theory of 'systems' within persons, where the differing beliefs of the deceiver and deceived belong to different systems.

Following Freud, such theories generally assign the role of

deceiver to an unconscious system that censors uncomfortable beliefs from consciousness. According to Freud, such censoring of uncomfortable beliefs stems from the common impulse to move from 'unpleasure' to 'pleasure'.[19] As discussed in section 1.1, when one finds that the world conflicts with one's desires, a typical reaction will be to attempt to change the world in order to satisfy one's desires. Thus, if I desire that the coffee-pot next door be full for my use later this afternoon, and if I find that the coffee-pot is now in fact empty, I may attempt to make coffee. As Freud rightly pointed out, though, a person is not always able to change the world in such a way that all her desires are satisfied. Consequently, Freud maintained, a 'secondary', unconscious system may act to censor information from one's 'primary', conscious system so that one is not aware of the discord between one's wishes and the way the world is.[20] Such censorship may take the general form of a repression of one's true desires or a repression of certain beliefs about the way the world is.

Freud seems entirely correct in his claims that a person can be aware of a certain belief he holds while at the same time unaware – even upon first-person reflection – of a conflicting belief he also holds. Against Descartes' overly optimistic claim that 'there is nothing which is easier for me to know than my own mind',[21] Freud provided abundant examples of cases where one's public behaviour belies those beliefs and desires one sincerely avows as having.[22] And just as we can infer others' beliefs and desires from their public behaviour, Freud reasoned that we can infer about ourselves 'the existence of psychical acts which lack consciousness' by reflecting on phenomena like dreams and slips of the tongue that are out of character with the mental lives of which we are aware:[23] 'all the acts and manifestations which I notice in myself and do not know how to link up with the rest of my mental life must be judged as if they belonged to someone else: they are to be explained by a mental life ascribed to this other person'.[24] Yet, while Freud seems rightly to have pointed to the existence of unconscious beliefs and other mental states, his claims regarding the intentional actions performed by unconscious, secondary systems within humans are more controversial. As David Pears points out, in any viable theory of systems 'it must be possible for an element to belong to one system within a person and to pass information about itself to another system within him and yet not belong to that other system'.[25] In the case of a censor operating within an unconscious secondary system, we must suppose that this secondary system has access to the mental activity of the conscious primary system. Otherwise, the secondary system could not identify which uncomfortable beliefs and desires needed to be repressed from consciousness – or when such repression was needed. With respect to the primary system's access to the secondary system's mental activity, it will of course be necessary that a number of things remain hidden if literal self-deception is to occur. Most obviously, the suppressed uncomfortable belief or desire must remain hidden. Furthermore, the process of censorship, or deception, must also remain hidden. For the attempt at successful deception of almost any kind would clearly be undermined if the (would-be) deceived understands what the deceiver is attempting to do.[26]

There certainly are documented cases in the psychological literature where an asymmetrical flow of information between multiple, dissociated 'personalities' makes self-deception possible. In Thigpen and Cleckley's well-discussed account of 'Evelyn Lancaster', for example, the personality 'Eve Black' – who knew the thoughts of the personality 'Eve White' – could cause 'Eve White' to experience hallucinations and could erase certain beliefs from the memory of 'Eve White'. 'Eve White', on the other hand, was not aware that the personality 'Eve Black' even existed. Literal self-deception, then, does seem possible in certain extreme cases of dissociated personalities.[27] It seems a rather speculative thesis, though, to make the further claim that, in most individuals, an unconscious mental system can purposefully and successfully act to deceive one's primary conscious system. For it seems difficult to imagine how we might conclusively either confirm or disprove such a thesis.

But let us grant that Freud's theory of systems does show that literal self-deception can occur within most individuals. There is still the question of just how often we need to appeal to the notion of literal self-deception to explain human behaviour. Alfred Mele argues that, in the vast majority of cases we typically associate with self-deceptive behaviour, people do not act with the intention of literally deceiving themselves.[28] Consider the mother who believes in her son's innocence despite contrary evidence that the neutral observer finds overwhelming. If she selectively attends to evidence with the result that she is 'blinded' to the truth about her son, is her behaviour best explained by supposing that she (at some level) believed that her son was guilty and then pursued the purpose of deceiving herself? Mele argues that it is more plausible to think that the mother's purpose in selectively attending to evidence is simply to avoid unpleasant thoughts.[29] Mele compares self-deception to akratic action on this point:

> When an agent acts incontinently he acts intentionally; but that he act incontinently typically is not part of his intention. He does not aim at acting incontinently; this is not part of the action-plan that he wants to

put into effect. Although, against his better judgment, he intentionally eats the sweet before him, he is not (at least characteristically) intending at the time to act incontinently.[30]

So, we might imagine that a given person has a desire that *p* be the case. We might further suppose that she is fully aware that she has this desire. We might even suppose that this desire motivates her to perform the intentional action of manipulating data in some manner – with the result that she comes to believe that *p* is the case. Mele's point is that it is a mistake to think that this scenario warrants the conclusion that her *intention* in acting was to deceive herself into believing something she knew was not the case. Put another way, on Mele's account, one's motivation is simply a desire for things to *be* a certain way – rather than the desire that one *believe* that things are a certain way.

In the end, we should acknowledge that it is *possible* to interpret instances of self-deceptive manipulation of data along Freudian lines. However, it is just as possible to explain self-deceptive behaviour – where a person's desires cause her to manipulate data with the result that she believes what she desires to believe – without appealing to Freud's more speculative thesis involving the intentional, deceptive actions of an unconscious mental system.

If we construe self-deceptive behaviour along these more conservative lines, we might ask just how appropriate the term 'self-deception' really is. Purposeful, interpersonal deception clearly involves the intention of one party to lead another party to believe something that the first party knows not to be the case. This description, of course, accords well with a Freudian account of literal self-deception, where one's unconscious system acts with the intention that one's conscious system believe something that one's unconscious system knows not to be true. However, on the more conservative – and, it seems to me, more plausible – account of self-deceptive behaviour, one does not simultaneously hold contradictory beliefs. If, in the vast majority of cases we typically associate with self-deceptive behaviour, one does not actually act with the intention of deceiving oneself, then is the term 'self-deception' misleading?

Even if the term is a bit misleading in a strict sense, there are conceptual reasons why we might want to retain the term 'self-deception' in describing certain kinds of human behaviour. Despite the dissimilarities between interpersonal deception and our more conservative account of self-deceptive behaviour, there remain some central points of correlation. In both cases a person's desire motivates her intentionally to manipulate data. Also, in both cases the manipulation of data may lead to some person[31] believing something that, *ceteris paribus*, he would not otherwise believe. And this resultant belief, in both cases, helps to satisfy the initial desire that motivated the manipulation of data.[32]

So let us keep the term 'self-deception' and specify that, in our discussions, it will refer to a process the result of which is that one is 'blind' to some truth one would otherwise recognize. This process begins with some desire, or 'hot' motivation, that things in the world be a certain way. Acting on this desire, one performs the intentional action of manipulating data – with the result that one fails to see something one would otherwise have seen: namely, that one's evidence on balance points to the truth of some proposition. Even though one might not act with the intention literally to deceive oneself, it nonetheless seems appropriate to describe this process as wilful self-deception. For in this process one is motivated by the uncomfortable nature of some proposition to perform some act that contributes to one's own failure to see that proposition as probably true.

Having sketched an account of what 'self-deception' amounts to, we now need to examine in more detail what kinds of decisions might contribute to the self-deceptive process. It is to this question that we now turn.

6.3 *Self-deceptive strategies*

We can begin our examination by categorizing self-deceptive strategies as being one of two types. First, there are ways in which a person can bias her own interpretation of information she is considering. Second, there are ways in which a person can influence which pieces of information are available to her for further consideration. As an example of the first type, we might imagine a scenario where Tom is hopelessly in love with Tina. Tina has consistently declined Tom's invitations to dinner and has indicated to Tom that she doesn't much care for his general demeanour. Tom's friends may tell him what should be obvious for all to see: Tina simply is not interested in Tom. Yet, because of Tom's desire that Tina love him, he may continue to interpret her behaviour as coming from one who very much *is* interested but who is 'playing hard to get' as a way of encouraging his attention.[33] Tom has the same information that his friends have; and we can suppose that, were it not for his strong desire, Tom would reach the same conclusion that his friends have reached. However, his strong desire has clearly affected his interpretation of the data he is considering.

Similarly, we might suppose that a mother is told that her teenage son has been arrested for drug distribution. The mother acknowledges that the arrest *is* evidence that her son is guilty, but there is also the evidence that he was a kind, innocent, naïve boy just a few short years ago – certainly not the kind of boy who would turn to a life of crime in just a few years.[34] When the mother considers the evidence for and against her son's guilt, she may be repeatedly drawn to mental images of her son doing things from previous years such as blowing out birthday candles and playing in the garden. If the mother did not have such a strong desire for her son to be innocent, she would readily dismiss this evidence as not particularly good evidence. However, because the evidence of the mental pictures is so comforting and thus vivid to her, it is not difficult to imagine that she might come to give this evidence undue weight and subsequently conclude that her son must be innocent.

We might expand on the example of the mother to turn our discussion to the second type of self-deceptive strategy: namely, the influencing of which pieces of evidence are available for one's further consideration. We can imagine that the mother's mental images of her son during happier times provide a great deal of emotional comfort. Subsequently, she may find these mental pictures dominating her thoughts whenever she considers the question of her son's guilt. Given that her focus on these mental pictures comes at the expense of possible reflection on contrary evidence, her consideration of evidence becomes (unbeknown to her) selective. And the selective consideration of evidence is an obvious enough means by which the process of self-deception might occur.

To cite another example, we might imagine a literary historian who publishes a book claiming that Shakespeare did not write many of the works attributed to him. We imagine that his book sparks a host of responses in the form of articles from other historians. Because the historian very much wants his original thesis to be correct, he may specifically look for all the articles he can find by historians he suspects will be sympathetic to his own position. Conversely, he may read only a sampling of articles by those of his fellow historians whom he suspects will not receive his position with much charity. Thus, as the historian investigates further his original hypothesis, his consideration of evidence will be selective and therefore biased. Moreover, we might imagine that in reading through the articles he does survey, the historian adopts the following practice. When he comes to a passage supporting his original thesis, he says to himself, 'Yes! That's right', and he then rereads the passage. However, when he comes across data contradicting his own hypothesis, he typically reads quickly further along, hoping that the author will eventually offer a rebuttal to this data. As a result of this pattern of reading, the historian might well remember small and detailed pieces of supporting evidence – despite failing to remember more obvious and compelling contrary evidence.

In discussing how a person might influence which pieces of evidence are available for her further consideration, we have thus far focused on how one might gather and attend to certain evidence at the expense of gathering and attending to contrary evidence. In addition to restricting in this way the flow of evidence against a given conclusion, humans also seem quite capable of *generating* evidence supportive of a given conclusion. Suppose that Jane has a disagreement and subsequent unpleasant verbal exchange with a shop assistant one day. When she reflects on the event, she may be resistant to the idea that she is in any way to blame for the angry escalation of words. Inasmuch as her desire to be the innocent party colours her interpretation of the words that were actually spoken, she might be described as considering evidence in a biased manner. However, after repeated reflection upon the event, she may come to consider evidence that was *not* part of the actual exchange that took place. As she rehearses the scene again and again in her mind – playing, of course, both the role of herself and the shop assistant – her own lines become more and more innocuous as the shop assistant's lines become more and more acerbic. Her original statement, 'I need to return this', eventually becomes 'I wonder if I could return this'. The shop assistant's original statement, 'Do you have a receipt?', eventually becomes 'Well, where's your receipt?' Also, the tone of what is spoken changes, so that the shop assistant's tone of voice becomes more and more rude. Given that Jane is now considering evidence that she herself generated, it is not surprising that she would reach the conclusion that she is in no way to blame for the argument. And if the shop assistant reflects on events in a corresponding manner, then it would not be surprising if he were to reach a completely opposite conclusion. In everyday parlance we might say of Jane that she has 'convinced herself' that she was in the right.

Another prominent method by which one can generate evidence involves the notion of pretending. A miserly man might yet wish he were a charitable person – or, at least, wish that others would view him as a charitable person. Such a man might then decide to act as a charitable person would act. He might say 'Hear, hear!' when speeches are made about helping the poor, and he might adopt phrases that he has heard fêted philanthropists use. By pretending in this way to be a charitable person, the miserly man might actually come to believe that he is more charitable than is actually the case. As Daryl Bem has argued, 'Individuals come to "know" their own attitudes, emotions, and other internal states partially by inferring them from observations of their own overt behaviour and/or the

circumstances in which this behaviour occurs'.[35] In support of the
thesis that people do sometimes infer their own mental states from
their own public behaviour, we can note how subjects under post-
hypnotic suggestion commonly misidentify their true motives in
acting. Freud describes an experiment he witnessed in which a
hypnotized subject was ordered to open an umbrella five minutes
after awaking.[36] The subject carried out the instruction and was
then asked why he was acting in this way. Freud reports that
'instead of saying that he has no idea', the subject felt 'compelled to
invent some obviously unsatisfactory reason'.[37] Specifically, the
subject claimed he wanted to make sure the umbrella was in good
working order – a motive we would find natural to attribute to
someone else we observed opening an umbrella indoors. It would
seem, then, that the subject's understanding of his own motives
stemmed from observing his own public behaviour.

Of course, this case is one in which the subject does not have first-
person access to his own mental states. It might be thought that
when a person *is* aware through introspection that he has been
pretending in some matter, this awareness must surely overshadow
any third-person inferences about his own mental states he might
make from observing his own behaviour. To a large extent it does
perhaps initially seem implausible to argue otherwise. Yet, experiments have shown that people do tend to infer mental states from a
person's behaviour even when they know that the person is 'acting
the part'. Edward Jones and Victor Harris document cases where
subjects are shown essays advocating certain political positions.[38]
The subjects are told that the essay-writers fell into a 'no choice'
category in that their positions were determined by someone else
(e.g. a debate coach). Also, the subjects were told that the essay-
writers had access to stock arguments that had been prepared by
others.[39] Despite the knowledge that the essay-writers came from a
'no choice' category, the subjects still tended to infer a mild
correlation between the positions taken in the essays and the essay-
writers' true beliefs on the subject. (Perhaps more obvious examples
of this phenomenon can be found in the common practice of
attributing real-life beliefs and attitudes to actors in line with the
beliefs and attitudes of the characters we see them portray.)

In addition to the ways in which our beliefs about ourselves can
be influenced by our own observations of our own pretending,
Daniel Gilbert and Joel Cooper point out that pretending can have
far-reaching effects by virtue of the fact that it is a strategy that
involves other people.[40] Given that our conceptions of ourselves
hinge largely on our perception of how others perceive us, Gilbert
and Cooper note that 'the targets of our self-presentations may
reciprocally convince us of the validity of their impressions'.[41] The

two cite a number of studies in support of the links in this 'self-presentational feedback loop', and they maintain that the complex nature of social interaction can blur the distinction in our own minds of where our pretending ends and our true attitudes begin: 'If our behaviour is shaped by subtle social forces, we may fail to recognize these as the true causes of our actions, concluding that we do indeed possess the dispositions we were once merely pretending to possess'.[42] In the end, the social aspect of pretending does seem to allow for a kind of 'feedback loop' through which a good deal of far-ranging self-deception can occur. We end this section, then, having identified a number of different ways in which a person's decisions can contribute to her failure to form beliefs she would otherwise have formed.

6.4 *Moral responsibility for self-deception*

Having outlined some of the kinds of decisions that can contribute to a self-deceptive process, let us now consider the extent to which one can be morally responsible for making such decisions. Some of the examples of self-deception from the previous section provide obvious ways in which one might make decisions for which one is morally responsible. Pretending that something is so and rehearsing scenes in one's mind are two obvious possibilities. If one believes that it is wrong to pretend to be charitable or to rehearse repeatedly in one's mind someone's blameworthy behaviour, then to do so would be to perform an act for which one is morally culpable.

But what of Tom, who misinterprets Tina's refusal of his advances as an attempt to 'play hard to get'? Or what of the mother who believes that her son is innocent? In these examples the person in question manipulates data in such a way that they came to believe something that perhaps we are inclined to think they really should not believe. But before we can talk about moral responsibility for the self-deceptive process in either case, we must first identify a decision the person makes for which they might be morally responsible. Yet, in each case it is not readily apparent that any *decision* led to the failure to believe some truth that should have been obvious.

Now, we might suppose that in each case the subject had moments when the truth began to dawn on him or her. It is common enough to have doubts creep to mind as to whether that which one believes might really be false after all. If we imagine this to be the case in the examples under consideration, we might imagine that the subjects wilfully chose to ignore such doubts when they arose, turning their thoughts instead to other matters.

Even if we assume that the subjects in our examples did not make choices of this kind, it would be too quick a move to conclude that no choices by the subjects whatsoever were involved in the self-deceptive process. For there might have been any number of other, more subtle decisions made by the subjects that contributed to their own deception. Take the case of Tom, who misinterprets Tina's refusal of his romantic advances. If Tom does not experience any nagging doubts about the accuracy of his own interpretation, it might nonetheless occur to him to ask certain questions. For example, he might think to ask his friends whether they agree with his interpretation. He might also think to reflect on whether his romantic desires have previously led to mistaken conclusions regarding the attitudes of women he has approached in the past. The choice not to pursue such questions might well amount to a choice that contributes to his own deception. And if Tom believes that he might have an obligation to ask such questions, then he would be morally culpable for a refusal to pursue the matter.

If we suppose that no such questions occur to Tom, we might ask why this is so. Perhaps Tom is simply not in the habit of asking such questions, and it therefore does not occur to him to ask them. We might then ask how Tom came to have this particular habit (of not asking). If the habit owes its development in part to past refusals to pursue such questions when they occurred to him, then the contributing factors in his current deception *do* include choices he has made. Indeed, it seems possible to imagine any number of decisions Tom could have made in the past that might be part of the process of self-deception that led to his current beliefs about Tina's hidden motives in refusing his advances. And if Tom believed at these earlier points that it might be wrong for him not to ask such questions, then the conditions for moral culpability are again met. In the end, there may be any number of morally significant decisions Tom makes that contribute to his failure to see the truth about Tina.

Let us turn now to consider the specific question of how someone might be morally responsible for a failure to see that a purportedly divine communication really is authentic. We should note first that there are any number of reasons why a person might be motivated to engage in self-deceptive behaviour in such a matter. That is, the belief 'that a purportedly divine statement is (or might be) true' might be uncomfortable for any number of reasons. One might have invested time and energy in trying to disprove the existence of God and therefore desire that one's initial hypothesis be proved right. One might dislike certain religious proponents and desire that they be proved wrong in their beliefs. Perhaps the most potentially powerful motivation is that the purportedly divine communication has implications as to what one's moral obligations might be.

Take, for instance, the affirmations in Christian scripture as to

Jesus's divinity and to what directives he issued. Jesus's recorded directives may be uncomfortable to an individual largely because they preclude various actions she desires to perform. Thus it is not difficult to see how one might be motivated actively to resist the conclusion that Jesus was in fact divine and that he did not make the statements attributed to him in the gospels. Given that the motivation to avoid uncomfortable moral obligations seems potentially the most powerful motivation for self-deceptive behaviour in this area, let us focus our remaining discussion on this motivation.

An active resistance to what one believes to be one's moral obligations may take any number of forms. An obvious example is a decision to perform some action that one believes God has identified as wrong. Another slightly less obvious example is the decision wilfully to turn one's attention away from the question of whether it is possible that God may in fact have identified that action as wrong. There are also much less obvious examples of resisting what one believes are, or might be, one's moral obligations. Take, for instance, the various ways in which one might resist the truth about oneself. C.R. Snyder, in discussing strategies of excuse-making,[43] observes that a person whose behaviour does not meet her own personal standards may engage in a 'reframing performance strategy', where she works to diminish the extent of her failure. Thus, if a person finds that her behaviour conflicts with what she believes or suspects to be the truth about God's commands, she may remind herself and others that her behaviour does not really hurt anyone or that her 'sin' is not one of the more serious ones. Alternatively, Snyder points out, a person may engage in a 'transformed responsibility strategy', where she acknowledges her failure but downplays her responsibility for it. She may, for instance, take a 'consensus-raising approach' by reminding herself and others that everyone fails in this manner; or she may perhaps take a 'consistency-lowering approach' by seeking to explain her failure as a temporary and uncharacteristic lapse.

There may be no end to the ways in which one can seek to avoid the conclusion that one's own behaviour falls short of what one believes God has, or may have, commanded or encouraged. We may sabotage the efforts of friends so that our own behaviour appears good by comparison.[44] We may seek to avoid conclusions about our own behaviour and motives by taking performance-inhibiting drugs such as alcohol so as to handicap our own performances and thereby create a ready-made, external explanation for our moral failings.[45] We may even in certain cases embrace the diagnosis of a mental or physical illness, because the conclusion 'I'm unwell' is more comfortable than the conclusion 'I'm wilfully engaged in unacceptable behaviour'.[46] Instances of resisting the truth about oneself in manners such as these constitute subtle ways one might resist moral conclusions such as: 'God may want me to act in a certain way, and I may be in the wrong if I act in another way'. By engaging in subtle, yet active, resistance to this proposition, one may, as we have seen, contribute to a self-deceptive process whereby one fails to believe that this proposition (and others like it) are true.

The forms of resistance to the possible truth that one may have certain moral obligations may indeed be innumerable and ever so subtle. Resistance to such possible truths may even be couched within an overt claim to be seeking after the truth in these matters. The gospel accounts of Jesus's life record a time when an expert in the law asked Jesus what must be done to inherit eternal life. According to St Luke,[47] when Jesus asked the man how he read the Jewish law on the matter, the man responded, ' "Love the Lord your God with all your heart and with all your soul and with all your strength and with all your mind";[48] and, "Love your neighbour as yourself" '.[49] Jesus replies that he has answered correctly and states, 'Do this and you will live.' St Luke then comments that the man 'wanted to justify himself, so he asked Jesus, "And who is my neighbour?" ' Luke's comment seems to convey the idea that the man's final question, though expressed as a search for further truths about his obligations, actually stemmed from a desire to resist the truth he did know: namely that he should act in loving, self-giving ways to those around him.

Thomas Morris's comments on another recorded exchange Jesus had with a religious authority suggest that Jesus may have been all too aware of the different motives people can have as they profess to search for moral truths. The gospel of John records a time when Nicodemus, a member of the Jewish ruling council, approached Jesus and said, 'Rabbi, we know you are a teacher who has come from God. For no one could perform the miraculous signs you are doing if God were not with him.'[50] As Nicodemus's comments stand, they represent a solid example of *modus tollens* deduction. However, as Morris points out, we do not find Jesus 'congratulating him on his independence of mind, his theological astuteness, and his rigor in reasoning'.[51] Instead, we find Jesus offering the following, seemingly non-responsive 'answer': 'I tell you the truth, no one can see the kingdom of God unless he is born again.' Morris comments on this exchange as follows:

> There are two ways to respond to a remark. Every question, every argument, every conversational statement embodies assumptions, is made from a perspective, and implicitly lays down rules for a proper response, for an appropriate answer. If you accept the assumption, endorse the perspective, and find the rules appropriate, you can play the

game launched by the question or comment and answer or otherwise respond to it on its own terms. Or you can change the game being played ... The name of the game for Nicodemus, it seems, was satisfying intellectual curiosity. He had changed his mind. But Jesus wanted him to change his life. So Jesus didn't play the game according to Nicodemus's rules. He did not encourage his theologizing. He did not praise his intellectual acumen. He challenged him to be 'born again' – an odd and extreme metaphor for a necessary and extreme change of heart.[52]

Again, then, resistance to the truth about where one's moral obligations may lie may be subtly couched within a more public search for moral truths.[53]

If we turn now to consider the specific question of how someone might be morally responsible for a failure to see some truth about God (e.g. that God has communicated a certain message), we can begin by noting the Christian explanation of why people form beliefs that certain actions are wrong. The Christian tradition has wanted to affirm that our ability to make moral judgments is the result of deliberate divine planning. More specifically, it has wanted to affirm that one's conscience, especially when properly tuned, yields moral beliefs that are somehow 'put there' by God through the activity of the Holy Spirit. It is Jesus who is recorded in the gospel of John as clarifying the Holy Spirit's role as the one who 'will convict the world of guilt in regard to sin and righteousness and judgment'.[54]

In section 3.2 we discussed some of the ways God might communicate to humans, noting that God could perform speech acts without actually performing the physical acts of inscribing words or uttering sentences. If certain moral beliefs, or intuitions, or 'promptings', do come from God, then the Christian theist can plausibly describe them in terms of divine communication. When one chooses, then, to follow the urge of a desire at the expense of such a moral leading, one actively resists a message that comes from God (whether or not one recognizes that one's moral intuition is in fact a message from God). We have already explored some of the many ways in which one's active resistance to some proposition p can lead to one's failure to see that p is true. Thus, it is not difficult to imagine how a person's active resistance to the truth of a certain moral belief, or divine message, can contribute to a self-deceptive process whereby one fails to believe that that message (or similar messages) does in fact come from God and is thus an accurate picture of where one's moral obligations really lie.[55]

I want now to offer a general characterization for those intentional actions one might perform that contribute to a self-deceptive process whereby one is 'blinded' to some moral truth.

Such actions, to use the language I adopted in Chapter 3, amount to *failures to accept the truth*.[56] More precisely, they constitute failures to accept, or respond positively to, the truth as one sees it. A person may intentionally act against her moral beliefs, which, again, can be construed as divine communication. In so doing, she performs an action for which she is morally culpable and which contributes to a process whereby she may become a person unable to recognize certain spiritual truths – e.g. that a particular message comes from God and accurately identifies where her moral obligations lie. By contrast, if a person does *not* resist, but instead responds positively to, moral truths as she sees them, then she can in no way be described as engaging in wilful spiritual blindness. For if such a person fails for some reason to recognize certain spiritual truths, it will not be because she contributed to this process by performing acts for which she is morally culpable.

In support of this characterization of wilful spiritual blindness as a refusal to accept the truth, we might look to the writings of St Paul. In introducing the notion of spiritual blindness in section 5.3, we noted Paul's declaration that 'what may be known about God' is 'clearly seen' by those who do not 'suppress the truth by their wickedness'.[57] Paul goes on in this passage to cite one's stance toward truth in identifying that which humans do to incur God's judgment. He writes that 'for those who are self-seeking and who *reject the truth* and follow evil, there will be wrath and anger'.[58] I take the account of spiritual blindness outlined in this chapter as a plausible spelling-out of Paul's general insight here.[59]

At this point we may want to say a bit more about precisely what it is for which the spiritually blind person is said to be culpable. On a preliminary note, we should acknowledge that there may be cases where a person is simply blind to spiritual matters – such as recognizing divine communication – in much the same way that a colour-blind person cannot recognize the colour green. That is to say, there may be people who, given their genetic make-up and social upbringing, simply cannot recognize an instance of divine communication. Our concern in this chapter, however, is with *wilful* spiritual blindness. And so let us consider the question of whether the person who actively resists moral truths can rightly be held culpable for being in a state of spiritual blindness.

Our working assumption has been that moral culpability only arises when one decides to act so as to realize one's desires at the expense of acting in accordance with what one believes to be one's moral obligation. On these conditions for moral culpability, it seems that a person could only be held morally culpable for being in a state of spiritual blindness if she believed she had a moral obligation to avoid such a state of spiritual blindness. Yet, it is clearly implausible to think that people, when they perform those wilful actions that set in motion a self-deceptive process, typically have in mind the goal of allowing themselves to be blinded to some spiritual truth. So, with respect to those who do wilfully resist the truth about God with the result that they fail to see that God has issued a given statement, are they morally culpable for being in a state of spiritual blindness? While they may be culpable for their wilful acts that *lead* to their state of spiritual blindness, is it appropriate to describe them as culpable for being in that state itself?

Plausible arguments seem to exist for answering 'yes' and for answering 'no' to this question. If one were to answer 'yes', one might do so on the grounds that a strict interpretation of the conditions I have outlined for moral culpability would be too restrictive. After all, if a landowner continually refuses to pay his workers the fair wage he thinks he ought to pay them, and if this pattern of behaviour results in his eventual failure to see that there is anything actually wrong with this practice, it may seem only natural to blame the landowner for failing to see that he ought to pay a fair wage. Perhaps the feeling here is that, although the landowner did not set out to 'blind himself' to the existence of certain obligations he has toward his workers, there exists such a tight connection between the character-forming actions he performed and the character he ended up with that to be culpable of the former is to be culpable of the latter. To conclude otherwise would be to hold a person culpable for performing greedy acts and at the same time *not* culpable for being a greedy person.

If one were to answer 'no' to the question before us, one might emphasize the point that the best anyone is capable of doing is simply that which they believe to be right. Thus, if it honestly never occurs to the landowner that his selfish acts might shape his character such that he becomes blinded to the wrongfulness of them, then he is not to blame for his failure to believe that his payment of low wages to workers is wrong. Of course, he may be culpable for many things – things that in fact led to his failure to form this particular moral belief. But his failure to hold this particular moral belief is not, strictly speaking, one of the decisions for which he can rightly be held culpable.

In the end, the issue of how the question before us should be settled will not affect our overall discussion in any crucial way. For all parties here at least can agree that the person who engages in what we have termed 'wilful spiritual blindness' is culpable for performing those actions that initiate a self-deceptive process whereby one fails to believe some truth about God. And this point is all we need to establish at this stage of our discussion. In Chapter 8 we shall explore the further question of the criteria God might use in determining whether to accept an ongoing eternal relationship with someone. We shall see in this section that it is those actions that *lead* to spiritual blindness – as opposed to the state of spiritual blindness *per se* – that the Christian theist will want to point to in explaining how a person might culpably fail to exercise saving faith. At the current stage of our investigation of the Christian theist's response to the objection set forth in Part 1, we need only note that one can, in many ways, voluntarily resist the truth about God with the result that one fails to hold certain beliefs about God – most notably a belief$_m$.

6.5 *The extent of our resistance to perceived moral truths*

Before moving on, we might ask just how endemic is the failure to accept moral truths. St Paul certainly represents the Christian tradition well in quoting the psalmist on these matters: 'There is no one righteous, not even one; there is no one who understands, no one who seeks God.'[60] Of course, it is not that uncommon to hear people *profess* – presumably honestly – that they seek to follow the truth wherever the truth lies. Yet, John Locke, for one, was pessimistic about the actual motives of most who make such professions:

> There is no body in the Commonwealth of Learning, who does not profess himself a lover of Truth: and there is not a rational Creature that would not take it amiss to be thought otherwise of. And yet for all this one may truly say, there are very few lovers of Truth for Truths sake, even amongst those, who perswade themselves that they are so.[61]

Locke's pessimism seems evidenced by the all-too-typical conclusions two parties make when the parties have conflicting interests. We have already discussed how sports fans supporting opposing teams in a given match will usually have opposite views as to which team received the short end of the majority of the referee's poor decisions. Members of the general public who watch an election debate will often be asked afterwards to identify the candidate who won the debate. Opinions tend to differ wildly, but they do tend to differ squarely along party lines. If we learn that a group of college housemates are set to have a discussion about whose turn it is to do the washing up, it will not be difficult to predict that they may well have wildly different accounts of who has taken the most turns at washing up in the last month. And if we learn that two men are due to testify in court about a disagreement in which they came to blows with one another, we would expect them to offer starkly different accounts as to who was the instigator of and aggressor in the altercation. In all these cases, the parties might sincerely avow that they have 'set aside their own biases' and are seeing things as they really are. Yet, the very nature of self-deception is such that, when one is self-deceived, one does not – by definition – recognize how it is happening.

It seems reasonable to expect greater tendencies toward self-deception in instances where there is greater interest that things be a certain way. Thus, there may be more motivation for a mother self-deceptively to resist the possibility that her son is a drug-dealer than for a nominal sports fan to resist the possibility that the local team has received unfair treatment from a referee. When we consider the directives that the Christian tradition affirms as coming from God, we can see that they deal with issues that people commonly care very deeply about. These directives involve such sensitive areas as one's vocational choices, sexual practices and financial habits. It seems plausible, then, for the Christian theist to argue that matters of religion comprise perhaps the foremost set of issues about which people potentially have the most motivation to engage in self-deceptive behaviour.

The Christian theist's line of argument here as I have outlined it is not designed to show that certain purported directives from God really *are* authentic. Rather, it is an *ad hominem* argument that those who do not believe that certain directives come from God have reason to suspect that their lack of belief is the end result of a self-deceptive process. Similar lines of argument have, of course, been erected against Christian theists. David Hume raised the question of why humans ever launched a 'first enquiry' into an 'invisible intelligent power', and he provided the following answer:

> Not speculative curiosity, surely, or the pure love of truth. That motive is too refined for such gross apprehensions; ... No passions, therefore, can be supposed to work upon such barbarians, but the ordinary affections of human life; the anxious concern for happiness, the dread of future misery, the terror of death, the thirst of revenge, the appetite for food and other necessities. Agitated by hopes and fears of this nature, especially the latter, men scrutinize with a trembling curiosity, the course of future causes, and examine the various and contrary events of human life. And in this disordered scene, with eyes still more disordered and astonished, they see the first obscure traces of divinity.[62]

Feuerbach stated more succinctly that 'The fundamental dogmas of Christianity' are 'realized wishes'.[63] Explaining 'God' as a human projection,[64] Feuerbach observed that 'God is the Love that satisfies our wishes, our emotional wants; he is himself the realized wish of the heart'.[65] Perhaps the most thorough discussion along these lines still belongs to Freud:

These [religious beliefs], which are given out as teachings, are not precipitates of experience or end-results of thinking: they are illusions, fulfilments of the oldest, strongest and most urgent wishes of mankind. The secret of their strength lies in the strength of those wishes. As we already know, the terrifying impressions of helplessness in childhood aroused the need for protection – of protection through love – which was provided by the father; and the recognition that this helplessness lasts throughout life made it necessary to cling to the existence of a father, but this time a more powerful one. Thus the benevolent rule of a divine Providence allays our fear of the dangers of life; the establishment of a moral world-order ensures the fulfilment of the demands of justice, which have so often remained unfulfilled in human civilization; and the prolongation of earthly existence in a future life provides the local and temporal framework in which these wish-fulfilments shall take place.[66]

Freud's *ad hominem* response to the Christian theist is to note the 'very striking fact' that the theist's belief about how things are 'is exactly as we are bound to wish' things to be.[67]

There is no need to attempt to adjudicate here between *ad hominem* arguments. Perhaps both parties are right with respect to some people. That is, perhaps it is the case that the beliefs both of some theists and of some atheists are formed as a result of their wishing things to be a certain way. Perhaps it is even the case that some theists engage in self-deceptive and culpable behaviour leading to their religious beliefs. For example, in the hypothetical case given in section 3.4 of the man who believes that God blesses people's efforts to oppress certain ethnic groups, perhaps the man's own racist behaviour and subsequently hardened attitudes has led him to believe that such a God exists.

Again, I have not put forward any particular view as to the extent to which the unbelief of actual non-theists in our world *does* stem from culpable, self-deceptive behaviour. Rather, I have merely outlined the conditions that would need to be met in order for a person rightly to be described as culpable for her failure to hold certain Christian beliefs. At this point in our discussion we need only note that the *ad hominem* arguments of non-theists such as Feuerbach and Freud do not undermine the force of the theist's *ad hominem* argument. If the Christian God does exist and has in fact issued directives as to how we should live our lives, then our failures to recognize these divine directives as such may well stem from our desires to live our lives in ways that conflict with these directives.

Before concluding this section, we might ask the following question: if a person does not believe that certain directives or other purportedly divine messages come from God, is there a way for him to check to ensure that his lack of belief does not stem from a resistance at some level to perceived moral truths? There may be reason to be somewhat pessimistic on the general matter of self-knowledge of one's moral attitudes and motivations. Nietzsche commented that actions we take to be virtuous and indicative of 'love of neighbour' can actually stem from such attitudes as fear of neighbour,[68] timidity[69] and sloth.[70] Kant remarked that

> It is indeed sometimes the case that after the keenest self-examination we can find nothing except the moral ground of duty that could have been strong enough to move us to this or that good action and to such great sacrifice. But there cannot with certainty be at all inferred from this that some secret impulse of self-love, merely appearing as the idea of duty, was not the actual determining cause of the will. We like to flatter ourselves with the false claim to a more noble motive; but in fact we can never even by the strictest examination, completely plumb the depths of the secret incentives of our actions.[71]

More recently, psychological studies have shown that self-reflection does not necessarily increase the correlation between one's true attitudes and one's self-report of one's true attitudes. In fact, self-reflection may in some cases actually make one *less* likely to identify correctly one's own motives and reasons for acting.[72] Of course, this is not to say that self-reflection can *never* help one to achieve a more accurate understanding of one's own attitudes toward perceived facts. It seems clear from experience that we do sometimes gain a better understanding of ourselves through self-reflection. Again, though, the nature of self-deception is such that, if one's biases really are affecting one's beliefs, one is by definition unaware of the manner in which one's beliefs are being affected.

With respect to identifying one's own biases against possible divine directives on any given matter, perhaps the best a person can do is to ask himself: '*If* I believed that God had issued such and such a directive for me to act in such and such a manner, would I be willing to follow this directive?' Put another way, it seems that a person can best check his own resistance to spiritually significant truths by asking himself if he is willing to accept the truth about God wherever the truth may lie. Such self-reflection may yet not result in accurate self-understanding of all the subtle ways one is resisting the truth. But it does seem the most forthright way of at least trying through self-examination to guard against self-deception.

Conclusion

In this chapter we have discussed how one might be morally culpable for a failure to recognize certain truths about God – e.g.

that a particular message comes from him and accurately identifies where one's moral obligations lie. When one considers the possibility of such a truth, one may find the possibility uncomfortable. Perhaps, for instance, the message speaks of a moral obligation that conflicts with certain behaviours in which one desires to engage. Motivated by a desire that the content of the message be false, one may engage in intentional actions that one believes to be wrong and that contribute to a self-deceptive process the result of which is that one fails to believe what one otherwise would have believed: namely, that a given message does in fact come from God and does accurately identify where one's moral obligations lie. In such a scenario, one can rightly be described as being morally culpable for those actions that result in one being 'blinded' to some spiritual truth.

Notes

[1] Bacon 1620: Bk I, §xlix.

[2] Pears 1984: 12.

[3] Cf. Mele (1987) for examples: 154–5.

[4] See Kahneman and Tversky 1972 and 1973.

[5] Kahneman and Tversky 1972: 452.

[6] See Kahneman and Tversky 1973: 211–12.

[7] Cf. Kahneman and Tversky 1972: 432.

[8] Nisbett and Ross 1980: 46. Cf. Walster 1966.

[9] Nisbett and Ross 1980: 47.

[10] Nisbett and Ross 1980: 49–50.

[11] I do not wish to deny that there may be religiously significant issues related to cold mechanisms. For instance, it may for religious reasons be a good thing – or indeed obligatory – that a person seek to eliminate or guard against perversions of reason. However, our concern here is with one's motivated resistance to certain beliefs.

[12] Aquinas 1265–73: I–II, lxxvi, 4.

[13] Butler 1729: 133.

[14] Demos 1960: 593.

[15] Demos 1960: 594.

[16] Haight 1980: 5.

[17] Kant 1797: 94.

[18] Sartre 1943: 49.

[19] See Freud 1900: V, 598.

[20] See Freud 1900: V, 598–603.

[21] Descartes 1642: 157.

[22] See Freud 1901.

[23] Freud 1915: 170. For a thorough discussion of the ways in which suppressed information can sometimes escape censorship, see Freud (1901).

[24] Freud 1915: 169.

[25] Pears 1984: 40.

[26] As Pears (1984: 71) notes, the defender of literal self-deception need not go so far as to insist that one cannot be conscious of the wish itself that motivates the process of self-deception resulting in a conscious, comforting belief. What needs to be hidden

from consciousness – apropos our findings in section 2.2 – is the realization that the wish *is causing* one to hold this conscious, comforting belief.

[27] Though one might argue that such cases do not describe one 'mental system' deceiving another 'mental system' within the same human self – but rather describe one 'self' deceiving another 'self' within the same human body. Cf. Rovane (1998), whose account of personal identity centres on having a rational point of view.

[28] See Mele (1987), especially Ch. 9.

[29] See Mele 1987: 129–30.

[30] Mele 1987: 124.

[31] In the case of self-deception, this 'person' is, of course, oneself.

[32] In addition to these conceptual reasons, there are also social reasons why people might resist abandoning the term 'self-deception' in everyday use. Kenneth Gergen (1985: 239) observes of the concept of self-deception that

> Like perhaps no other integer within contemporary discourse, it enables the individual to be held responsible for his or her actions, but simultaneously holds the person blameless. The individual is responsible inasmuch as he or she voluntarily originates the action in question, but is forgiven to the degree that the voluntary system was misled, influenced, or otherwise constrained by mental events obscured from consciousness.

(See also Haight 1980: Ch. 9.) As an example, a mother might tend to embrace the notion of literal self-deception as a way of being lenient to her son, whose criminal activity she describes as mitigated by the fact that he believed that his activity was not that bad. Such a description allows her to avoid the painful conclusion that her son possesses a truly bad character. At the same time, the mother can still maintain a certain disciplinarian resolve by asserting that her son really should have known better. The notion of literal self-deception also provides a way for individuals, themselves, to save face. For instance, a man who does not want to admit that he cannot stop drinking after a few drinks may tell his wife after a party that he must have deceived himself into thinking at some point that he had had fewer drinks than he actually did have.

[33] Cf. Mele (1987: 125–6) for examples.

[34] Cf. Mele (1987: 115–6) for an example.

[35] Bem 1972: 2.

[36] See Freud 1915–17: XVI, 277.

[37] Freud 1900: IV, 148.

[38] See Jones and Harris 1967. Cf. Jones 1979.

[39] This was to counter the possible conclusion by the subjects that essay-writers who argue skilfully in favour of a political position are familiar with that position and probably have experience of arguing for that position – and therefore probably agree with at least parts of that position.

[40] See Gilbert and Cooper (1985), especially 81f.

[41] Gilbert and Cooper 1985: 83.

[42] Gilbert and Cooper 1985: 84. As Gilbert and Cooper use the term, 'dispositions' are synonymous with propositional attitudes.

[43] See Snyder (1985), especially 36–42.

[44] Cf. Tesser and Smith 1980.

[45] Cf. Jones and Berglas 1978.

[46] Cf. Snyder, Higgins and Stucky (1983), especially 220f.; and Wilson, Snyder and Perkins (1983).

[47] See Lk. 10.25-9.

[48] Cf. Deut. 6.5.

[49] Cf. Lev. 19.18.

[50] See Jn 3.1-3 (cf. 3.4-21).

[51] Morris 1992: 106.

[52] Morris 1992: 107.

[53] Cf. 2 Tim. 3.7, which makes reference to those who are 'always learning but never able to acknowledge the truth'.

[54] Jn 16.8. Cf. Jn 14.26.

[55] Again, there may be various reasons why a person would want to resist the possibility that God exists and has communicated a given message. For sake of simplicity, we are focusing on the reason that a given message might outline obligations one has that conflict with certain courses of action one desires to pursue.

[56] I use the term 'accept' here in a less technical sense than in the Chapter 3 discussion involving one's response to invitational statements. The sense of 'accept' here is a general one, synonymous with 'positively respond to'.

[57] Rom. 1.18-20.

[58] Rom. 2.8 (emphasis added).

[59] Cf. 2 Thess. 2.10, which speaks of those who 'perish because they refused to love the truth and so be saved.'

[60] Rom. 3.10-1. Cf. Pss 14.1–3 and 53.1-3.

[61] Locke 1690: IV, xix, 1.

[62] Hume 1777: 28. Hume evinces his own deistic understanding of God in stating that 'Were men led into the apprehension of invisible, intelligent power by a contemplation of the works of nature, they could never possibly entertain any conception but of one single being, who bestowed existence and order on this vast machine, and adjusted its parts, according to one regular plan or connected system' (26).

[63] Feuerbach 1841: 140.

[64] Cf. Feuerbach 1841: 118.

[65] Feuerbach 1841: 121.

[66] Freud 1927: 30–1.

[67] Freud 1927: 33.

[68] Nietzsche 1886: ¶201.

[69] Nietzsche 1886: ¶197–8.

[70] Nietzsche 1892: III, ¶12.18.

[71] Kant 1785: II, §407.

[72] See Wilson 1985: 104–9.

7

INCULPABLE NONBELIEF AND DIVINE HIDDENNESS

To summarize where we are in our overall discussion: we are exploring in Part 2 whether the Christian theist can offer an adequate rebuttal to the objection outlined at the end of Part 1. This objection was that the Christian affirmation of God's perfect goodness is inconsistent with the Christian claim that only those who put their faith in God will enjoy the benefits of an ongoing eternal relationship with God. For, the real possibility exists that some people will not have an opportunity to choose to put their faith in God because they involuntarily fail to hold those beliefs requisite for any kind of personal relationship with God.

Thus far in Part 2 the Christian theist's apologetic work has been preliminary. We have not seen the Christian theist as yet seek to defend God's goodness in the face of the objection pending against her. We have merely explored the question of why someone might not hold the beliefs requisite for Christian faith – particularly, a belief$_m$. We have seen that the person who does not hold Christian beliefs simply does not see his evidence as pointing to the probable truth of these beliefs. And we have seen that there are various and subtle voluntary actions one might perform – actions for which one would be morally culpable – which can lead to one's failure to see that one's evidence supports the probable truth of these beliefs.

Again, we have not yet explored how the Christian theist might use the discussion in the past two chapters to defend God's goodness in the face of the objection outlined in Part 1. For example, a person's culpable contribution to self-deception has not been offered as justification for God's decision not to accept an ongoing relationship with that person. In our final two chapters, however, we shall turn our attention to how the Christian theist might explicitly seek to defend God's goodness in the face of the objection pending against her. The final form of this defence will not become clear until Chapter 8. But before then, we shall explore in this chapter whether the Christian theist has the resources to address another, related objection to her affirmation that God is perfectly good.

To see the importance of this other, related objection, let us suppose for the moment that the Christian theist is able adequately to rebut the objection outlined in Part 1. That is, let us suppose that God's goodness is not ultimately undermined by the fact that someone might involuntarily fail to hold those beliefs requisite for saving faith. To anticipate our discussion in Chapter 8, let us suppose that the Christian theist can defend God's goodness by plausibly arguing that the person who involuntarily fails to hold Christian beliefs can nonetheless attain eternal life in heaven. Even if this much is plausibly shown, the Christian theist may still be asked to defend God's goodness in the face of the fact that involuntary nonbelief occurs *at all*. Put another way, even if involuntary nonbelief in this life does not prevent one from being reconciled to God in the next life, it is still the case that involuntary nonbelief prevents one from being reconciled to God in *this* life. Thus, before exploring the effects of involuntary nonbelief on one's eternal fate, let us explore how the Christian theist might seek to reconcile God's goodness with the effects of involuntary nonbelief on one's earthly life.

To see why the earthly effects of involuntary nonbelief potentially undermine God's goodness, let us consider a line of argument put forward by J.L. Schellenberg. Schellenberg summarizes his argument as follows:

> A perfectly loving God would desire a reciprocal personal relationship always to obtain between himself and every human being capable of it. But a logically necessary condition of such Divine–human reciprocity is human belief in Divine existence. Hence a perfectly loving God would have reason to ensure that everyone capable of such belief (or at any rate, everyone capable who was not disposed to resist it) was in possession of evidence sufficient to bring it about that such belief was formed. But the evidence actually available is not of this sort ... The most obvious indication that it is not is that inculpable ... nonbelief actually occurs. Hence we can argue from the weakness of theistic evidence ... or more specifically, from the reasonableness of nonbelief, to the nonexistence of a perfectly loving God. But God, if he exists, is perfectly loving. Hence we can argue from the reasonableness of nonbelief to the nonexistence of God.[1]

We can put Schellenberg's line of argument in the following form:

(1) A perfectly loving God would desire a reciprocal relationship always to obtain between himself and every human capable of it.

(2) But a logically necessary condition of such a relationship is belief in God's existence.

(3) Hence, a loving God would bring it about that those not

resistant to the truth are in possession of sufficient evidence showing that God exists. (From (1) and (2))

(4)   Yet the available evidence is not of this sort, as evidenced by inculpable nonbelief.

(5)   Hence, a perfectly loving God does not exist. (From (3) and (4))

In this chapter I shall discuss how certain Christian writers have sought to account for the fact that God remains to some extent 'hidden' from us in this world. I shall then explore whether the Christian theist has adequate resources for offering an adequate rebuttal to the type of objection Schellenberg raises.

7.1 *Does inculpable nonbelief really occur?*

One possible response to Schellenberg would be to pick up on the discussions in the previous two chapters and claim that *whenever* a person fails to hold the beliefs requisite for theistic faith, he does so as a result of wilful spiritual blindness. Such a response would amount to challenging premise (4) in Schellenberg's line of argument. It is this kind of challenge to the notion of inculpable nonbelief that John Calvin seemed to offer in his discussion of spiritual blindness. As noted in section 5.3, Calvin seemed to suggest that all people have at least *some* beliefs about God. He maintained that

> a sense of Deity is indelibly engraven on the human heart. And that this belief is naturally engendered in all, and thoroughly fixed as it were in our very bones ... [T]his is not a doctrine which is first learned at school, but one ... which nature herself allows no individual to forget, though many, with all their might, strive to do so.[2]

At the same time, Calvin pointed to human sin in explaining why all people do not hold those further religious beliefs essential to a proper relationship with God, such as the belief that we are bound to submit to God's authority. As noted earlier, Calvin put it to his readers that for those who do not form such further religious beliefs, 'it undoubtedly follows that your life is sadly corrupted'.[3]

Calvin is not alone in maintaining that beliefs essential to a relationship with God would inevitably follow from a life that was free from sin. Tertullian wrote that

> the soul, be it cabined and cribbed by the body, be it confined by evil nurture, be it robbed of its strength by lusts and desires, be it enslaved to false gods, – none the less, when it recovers its senses, as after surfeit, as after sleep, as after some illness, when it recaptures its proper health, the soul names God.[4]

More recently Mark R. Talbot has argued that from the Christian
perspective it is entirely appropriate to assert the contrary-to-fact
conditional: 'Everybody would believe in God, if it weren't for sin'.[5]
Talbot goes so far as to claim that 'Even unbelievers have some
reason to think this is true'.[6] He defends this last claim by pointing
to Christians who testify that only at their conversions did they
recognize that sin had made them resistant to seeing certain truths
about God. Talbot then contends that even unbelievers can
recognize this testimony as evidence for the original contrary-to-
fact conditional that all people would be theists, were it not for sin.
     Is it plausible to suggest that *all* cases of theistic nonbelief stem
from morally culpable, self-deceptive acts? Schellenberg certainly
thinks otherwise and stresses the importance of a subject's conduct
'in other epistemic contexts'.

> Has he shown himself to be honest, a lover of truth? Does he resist his
> wants when his head tells him he ought not to give in to them? We may
> also have reason to believe that S *desires* to have a well-justified belief
> that G or that not-G. If this is clearly so in some particular case, then
> (unless there is strong evidence to the contrary) we may surely conclude
> that S is not self-deceived in arriving at [nonbelief].[7]

Schellenberg's point here in support of inculpable nonbelief is that,
if a nonbeliever has shown himself to be an earnest seeker of truth in
non-religious contexts, then we have no reason to suppose that he is
wilfully (and culpably) 'blinding' himself to the truth in religious
contexts.
     In response, the Christian theist might point out that there are
different reasons why a person might seek to hold true, well-justified
beliefs. A person might seek to do so because he desires to fulfil his
obligations toward his creator and wants to make sure he knows of
all such obligations he has. If this is the case, then the person can
indeed hardly be accused of self-deceptive resistance to the truth
about God. On the other hand, a person may in some instance seek
to hold true, well-justified beliefs simply out of a general desire to
know lots of facts or because he likes to think of himself as an
eminently rational person. If this is the case, then it is far from clear
that the person who seeks after truth in non-religious matters will
probably also be open to the truth on religious matters.
     If God does exist and seek to relate to us as Lord, then his
commands may fix for us any number of obligations – obligations,
as noted earlier, that may reach into such important and personal
areas as one's finances and sexual behaviour. Given that the kind of
behavioural implications stemming from religious questions seem
(at least potentially) far greater than with any other question, it
seems unclear just how reliable one's attitude toward the truth in

non-religious contexts will be in predicting one's attitude toward religious truths. For religious questions have implications for areas of life in which all people have heavy personal interest; and the greater one's personal interest in a subject matter, the more impetus there is for self-deception.

Despite this possible response by the Christian theist, Talbot's contrary-to-fact conditional ultimately seems unpromising as a challenge to the kind of objection Schellenberg raises. First, even if we suppose that without sin all people would form certain general beliefs about God – such as the belief 'that God exists' – it surely remains implausible to think that without sin all people would form the beliefs requisite for specifically *Christian* faith. A person who has never heard the gospel message about Jesus Christ represents an obvious example where it is more than sin that prevents one from forming Christian beliefs. Second, even if we grant that all people's failures to form Christian beliefs *do* stem somehow from sin, the Christian theist will still need to say more if she is to rebut the charge that nonbelief undermines God's perfect goodness. Thomas Morris explains:

> Human-defectiveness theories ... still fall short of what is needed. For any such accounts, as typically developed, may explain why we do not see the ordinary handiwork of God in creation and in his normal providential governing of the world as manifesting him, or why we don't experience his indwelling presence spiritually in any sort of regular or continuous way, but they do not offer any explanation of why God does not do more extraordinary, dramatic miracles to demonstrate his existence and governance.[8]

Thus, even if we grant that some sort of spiritual blindness is affecting the way in which a person assesses the evidence available to her, and even if we grant that without this spiritual blindness she would form the beliefs requisite for Christian faith, we will still want to know why God has not provided *more* positive evidence for her consideration.

This last point can serve to make Schellenberg's original line of argument even stronger. Premise (3) in Schellenberg's original line of argument was this:

(3) Hence, a loving God would bring it about that those not resistant to the truth are in possession of sufficient evidence showing that God exists. (From (1) and (2))

However, even if all nonbelievers are 'resistant to the truth' about God in that they resist the evidence they *do* have, we can still ask why a perfectly loving God would not do more to *overcome* this resistance by providing *more* evidence for them to consider. Thus, we might change premise (3) of Schellenberg's argument to the even more forceful

(3)' Hence, a loving God would bring it about that those not resistant to the truth *(to the extent that no amount of evidence would convince them)* are in possession of sufficient evidence showing that God exists. (From (1) and (2))

With this adjusted understanding of Schellenberg's third premise, we are free to remove the reference to inculpable nonbelief from his fourth premise. Thus,

(4) Yet the available evidence is not of this sort, as evidenced by inculpable nonbelief.

becomes simply:

(4)' Yet the available evidence is not of this sort.

With this amended line of argument, premise (4)' remains a challenge to the Christian theist even if Calvin and Talbot are correct in maintaining that inculpable nonbelief does not occur. For, even if all people *are* culpable for their failure to believe on the evidence available to them, the Christian theist may still be asked to explain why a loving God would not provide the kind of evidence that would surely convince even the most resistant toward the truth.

Would it be possible for God to provide evidence of this sort? In David Hume's *Dialogues Concerning Natural Religion*, the character Cleanthes imagines how God might seek to remove doubts that he exists and has communicated messages to humankind:

Suppose ... that an articulate voice were heard in the clouds, much louder and more melodious than any which human art could ever reach; suppose that this voice were extended in the same instant over all nations and spoke to each nation in its own language and dialect; suppose that the words delivered not only contain a just sense and meaning, but convey some instruction altogether worthy of a benevolent Being superior to mankind – could you possibly hesitate a moment concerning the cause of this voice, and must you not instantly ascribe it to some design or purpose?[9]

Cleanthes goes on to remark that a person who objects to theism may still reject this conclusion, reasoning that the 'voice' may well be the product of 'some accidental whistling of the winds'.[10] It seems more plausible, though, to suppose that most non-theists *would* form theistic beliefs upon witnessing such a dramatic event. N.R. Hanson, who argued against the existence of God, reflected on the possibility of a dramatic theophany in which a 'radiant Zeus-like figure, towering above us like a hundred Everests' exclaims for every man, woman, and child to hear: 'I have had quite enough of your too-clever logic-chopping and word-watching in matters of theology. Be assured, N.R. Hanson, that I most certainly exist'. Hanson continued, 'Please do not dismiss this example as a playful, irreverent Disney-oid contrivance. The conceptual point here is that *if* such a remarkable event were to transpire, *I* for one should certainly be convinced that God does exist'.[11] So, if God *does* exist and *has* issued statements to us to which he wants us to respond, then why has God not provided the kind of evidence that would, at least in most people's cases, remove all doubt about these facts? For surely there are many nonbelievers like Hanson who are not resistant to the truth about God to the extent that they would fail to hold the beliefs requisite for theistic faith if there were evidence of the sort Hanson describes. Is there some reason why God remains (at least to some degree) hidden?

7.2 *Historical responses to divine hiddenness*

Butler

Joseph Butler, in a sermon aptly titled 'Upon the Ignorance of Man', remarked that humans should not expect to understand the ways of God – including God's reasons for remaining partially hidden:

> And as the works of God, and his scheme of government, are above our capacities thoroughly to comprehend: so there possibly may be reasons which originally make it fit that many things should be concealed from us ... The Almighty may cast 'clouds and darkness round about him', for reasons and purposes of which we have not the least glimpse or conception.[12]

Butler held that some facts about God are clearly evidenced, remarking that 'it is as certain that God made the world, as it is certain that effects must have a cause'.[13] But as for the specifics of God's governance of the world, he maintained that the 'wisest and most knowing cannot comprehend the works of God, the methods and designs of his providence in the creation and government of the world'.[14] Drawing from Butler's line of argument, the Christian theist might be inclined to argue that God may well have good reasons for not providing us with greater evidence that, for instance, a purportedly divine message does in fact come from him. Yet, given our relative ignorance of the way God governs the world, so this line of argument would go, we should not be surprised that God's good reasons remain inscrutable to us.

Implicit in Butler's remarks seems to be the acknowledgment that,

from the human perspective, divine hiddenness may not appear to
be characteristic of a perfect world. After all, if God does exist, and
if the holding of true beliefs about God is a good thing, then it may
seem a natural enough judgment that a world with clear evidence in
support of these beliefs would be better than a world with religious
ambiguity. Butler's response is that we are not in a position to make
such a judgment.

> it is thought necessary to be thoroughly acquainted with the whole of a
> scheme ... in order to judge of the goodness or badness of it ... From our
> ignorance of the constitution of things, and the scheme of Providence in
> the government of the world; from the reference the several parts have to
> each other, and to the whole; and from our not being able to see the end
> and the whole; it follows, that however perfect things are, they must even
> necessarily appear to us otherwise, less perfect than they are.[15]

So, whatever bad effects might be associated with divine hiddenness,
it may yet contribute toward some greater good. At the same time,
given our very limited understanding of the ways in which the world
is connected and managed by God, we should not expect to
understand what these further good things are and why divine
hiddenness makes them possible. In short, Butler's main assertion is
that we are in a poor epistemic position to ascertain what good
reasons God might have for remaining (to some extent) hidden from
us.

In response to the contention that God's good reasons for
remaining hidden are inscrutable, Schellenberg comments as
follows: 'It is to be expected, perhaps, that a God would know of
kinds of goodness that are impossible for us to understand. But why
should this lead us to suppose that evils like that of the
reasonableness of nonbelief ... in fact *serve* such goods if God
exists?'[16] These comments seem telling against the adequacy of any
appeal to inscrutability as a means of rebutting Schellenberg's
original line of argument. Schellenberg's original argument gives us
reason to think that divine hiddenness precludes certain good things
– specifically the good things associated with a reciprocal relationship with God. If the Christian theist's response is merely that we
cannot grasp the ways of God, then the Christian theist will have to
concede that, as far as we know, it is just as likely that divine
hiddenness does *not* serve some further good as it is that divine
hiddenness *does* serve some further good. (Additionally, one might
press the point that, if we look for a further good and do not find
one, then we have prima facie reason for thinking that it does not
exist.) So, on the one hand we have a specific reason – apropos
Schellenberg's line of argument – to think that God's perfect
goodness *is* undermined by divine hiddenness. On the other hand we

have the contention – stemming from Butler's comments – that at best it is as likely as not that divine hiddenness is linked with some further good. This position hardly seems a comfortable one for the Christian theist.

Pascal

Other Christian writers have been more optimistic about the possibility of identifying what God's good reasons might be for remaining hidden. Blaise Pascal in his *Pensées* makes repeated references to human pride in addressing the question of why God does not do more to remove the religious ambiguity in the world. Pride, of course, plays a central role in the Christian tradition's explanation of what keeps humans from the kind of personal relationship with God for which they were created. Martin Luther remarked that justification before God is only possible when humility overcomes pride.[17] And Peter Lombard commented that 'pride is the root of evil, and the beginning of all sin'.[18] The aspect of human pride at issue here might be described in general terms as assuming a role that belongs only to God. John Wesley defined pride as 'idolatry; it is ascribing to ourselves what is due to God alone'.[19] In the case of Adam's fall, which serves in the Christian tradition as a prototype for all human sins, pride is displayed (at least in the view of Wesley and many other Christian theologians) as Adam comes to regard his own opinion more highly than God's opinion with respect to where his own best interests lie.[20] Accordingly, Butler remarked that 'Religion consists in submission and resignation to the Divine will'.[21] And Augustine pronounced that '[sinful] things are done whenever Thou art forsaken, O Fountain of Life, who art the only and true Creator and Ruler of the universe, and by a self-willed pride any one false thing is selected therefrom and loved'.[22] Pride is seen as the beginning of all sin because it is pride that leads us to dismiss what God has commended in deference to our own planned course of action.

Pascal identified pride as a fundamental impediment to our relationship with God; and he noted that God has taken steps to hold human pride in check. 'God wishes to move the will rather than the mind. Perfect clarity would help the mind and harm the will. Humble their pride'.[23] At first glance this passage may appear somewhat enigmatic. However, whatever else Pascal might be suggesting here, it seems clear that 'perfect clarity' works against certain aims God has for humanity. It also seems clear that God's aim of keeping human pride in check is somehow hindered by perfect clarity. Pascal goes on to explain this connection between pride and perfect clarity as follows:

If there were no obscurity man would not feel his corruption: if there were no light man could not hope for a cure. Thus it is not only right but useful for us that God should be partly concealed and partly revealed, since it is equally dangerous for man to know God without knowing his own wretchedness as to know his wretchedness without knowing God.[24]

As evidence that knowledge about God is harmful to the person who does not have an accompanying recognition of her absolute need for God, Pascal points to the 'arrogance of the philosophers, who have known God but not known their own wretchedness'.[25] Pascal's point here seems to run along the lines of: 'If the evidence for Christian beliefs were overwhelming, then people with prideful tendencies would come to form these beliefs. An acquisition of said beliefs in such people would actually lead them away from God, for it would bolster their confidence in their own mental abilities and thus serve to enhance their prideful commitment to self-sufficiency'.

Of course, Pascal did not suggest that God should provide *no* evidence in support of Christian beliefs. He noted the 'equal danger' of one coming 'to know his wretchedness without knowing God', and as evidence pointed to 'the despair of the atheists, who know their own wretchedness without knowing their Redeemer'.[26] Pascal's contention is that our religiously ambiguous world leads (or at least, tends to lead)[27] to the formation of Christian beliefs only in those who would benefit from having these beliefs:

> Thus wishing to appear openly to those who seek him with all their heart and hidden from those who shun him with all their heart, he has qualified our knowledge of him by giving signs which can be seen by those who seek him and not by those who do not. 'There is enough light for those who desire only to see, and enough darkness for those of a contrary disposition'.[28]

So, God has provided *some* evidence for Christian beliefs so that those who humbly seek him will come to see the truth about him. But God has not provided *more* evidence than he has because greater evidence would tend to lead to theistic beliefs among those in whom such beliefs would foster pride.

Against Pascal's defence of divine hiddenness Schellenberg offers several criticisms. First, he wonders whether evidence in the form of religious experiences really *is* likely to foster pride: 'Religious experience has its own distinctive psychological effects, and arrogance is not very naturally construed as one of them. Feelings of gratitude, joy, reassurance, astonishment, guilt, or dismay seem more likely'.[29] In response, though, the Christian theist may suggest that there is in fact some reason to think that religious experiences may often lend themselves to pride. Children and adults alike often queue for hours just to glimpse someone famous. An autograph of a sports star will often constitute a child's most prized possession and will trump almost any other child's claim to playground bragging rights. It is rare to find an adult who will not 'drop a name' if he has an appropriate name to drop. Indeed, many people's self-described claim to fame is simply to have accidentally crossed paths with someone famous. So, it does not seem implausible to suggest that one who experiences a direct encounter with the divine might well be tempted to take unwarranted pride in her experience.

Schellenberg offers a further criticism of Pascal that serves as a possible rejoinder to the Christian theist's line of response here:

> … part of what God might communicate to us through religious experience is *the very message of wretchedness and corruption* that Pascal suggests a Divine disclosure would inhibit. Religious experiences, it can be argued, are not all likely to provoke an arrogant response, inasmuch as they would awaken in us a sense of our wretchedness and corruption (a state *incompatible* with arrogance).[30]

But is it really the case that a recognition through religious experience of one's own corruption is incompatible with an arrogant response to that recognition? In C.S. Lewis's collection of fictional letters from Screwtape – a 'senior devil' who offers written counsel to his apprentice nephew in the art of temptation – we find the following instructions:

> All virtues are less formidable to us once the man is aware that he has them, but this is specially true of humility. Catch him at the moment when he is really poor in spirit and smuggle into his mind the gratifying reflection, 'By Jove! I'm being humble', and almost immediately pride – pride at his own humility – will appear. If he awakes to the danger and tries to smother this new form of pride, make him proud of his attempt – and so on, through as many stages as you please.[31]

When we consider the varied and subtle forms pride might take, it does not seem at all clear to what extent (if any) a divine message of one's own corruption would mitigate any tendency for that encounter with the divine to become a source of pride in one already tending toward prideful attitudes.

Schellenberg does offer, however, one objection to Pascal's line of argument that seems quite forceful. In reference to Pascal's construal of divine hiddenness as a divinely given impetus to seek God with humility, Schellenberg remarks:

> All these arguments suggest is that God has a reason for withholding good evidence from those humans whose present actions and motives are such as to prevent them from responding to it appropriately. No reason is

suggested for withholding evidence from those who do not fall into this category – from those, for example, who *have* felt their corruption and the emptiness of life without God and who have begun to search for God with proper motives.[32]

Are there people who search for God with humility and do not find him?

Perhaps the proponent of Schellenberg's line of argument will point to the testimonies of *believers* here. The Old Testament records the psalmist David crying out at one point, 'O my God, I cry out by day, but you do not answer, by night, and am not silent'.[33] In a similar vein, we find the prophet Isaiah avowing, 'Truly you are a God who hides himself, O God and Saviour of Israel'.[34] St Augustine is among many professing Christians who have wished that God would reveal himself more clearly: 'So speak that I may hear. Behold, Lord, the ears of my heart are before Thee; open Thou them, and "say unto my soul, I am thy salvation". When I hear, may I run and lay hold on Thee. Hide not Thy face from me. Let me die, lest I die, if only I may see Thy face'.[35] And St Anselm offers this poignant lament:

> Never have I seen You, Lord my God, I do not know Your face. What shall he do, most high Lord, what shall this exile do, far away from You as he is? What shall Your servant do, tormented by love of You and yet cast off 'far from Your face'? He yearns to see You and Your countenance is too far away from him. He desires to come close to You, and Your dwelling place is inaccessible; he longs to find You and does not know where you are; he is eager to seek You out and he does not know Your countenance. Lord, You are my God and my Lord, and never have I seen You. You have created me and re-create me, and you have given me all the good things I possess, and still I do not know You. In fine, I was made in order to see You, and I have not yet accomplished what I was made for.[36]

Granted, these cries are from believers; and our main concern is with the lack of evidence available to earnestly seeking *non*believers. Still, these testimonies do seem to illustrate the lack of any strict correlation between the extent to which one searches for truths about God and the extent to which one finds clear evidence in support of these truths.

Interestingly, although we have noted Pascal's contention that 'there is enough light' for those who seek God with proper humility, he seemed at one point in his *Pensées* to acknowledge that some earnestly seeking people may yet find God hidden to such an extent that they fail to hold theistic beliefs:

> amongst those who are not convinced, I make an absolute distinction

between those who strive with all their might to learn and those who live without troubling themselves or thinking about it. I can feel nothing but compassion for those who sincerely lament their doubt, who regard it as the ultimate misfortune, and who, sparing no effort to escape from it, make their search their principal and most serious business.[37]

Even if we accept Pascal's earlier contention that God remains hidden so as not to encourage undue human pride, is there a reason why a perfectly loving God would remain (to some extent) hidden from nonbelievers who *do* earnestly seek him with humility?

It might be thought that, even though *some* nonbelievers may be searching for God with humility, God must still maintain religious ambiguity in the world if he is to keep in check the pride of certain *other* nonbelievers who are *not* humble. Taking up Pascal's line of reasoning as to why God remains hidden, Thomas Morris writes:

> Were God to reveal himself to people improperly prepared to come to know and love him, such revelation would be more of a curse than a blessing. In order to allow us to develop to the point at which a knowledge of him would be the extraordinarily positive thing it can potentially be, God must govern his public manifestation in accordance with the needs of the least developed of his human creatures.[38]

Morris's point may well hold if we think of public manifestations of the divine as the only kind of evidence for Christian beliefs. However, when we consider the possibility of *private* religious experiences, we are still left with the question of why God does not ensure that all people who earnestly search for the truth about him come to see their evidence as clearly supporting those beliefs requisite for Christian faith.

Swinburne

Richard Swinburne has taken up this question and has argued that God does have good reasons for withholding overwhelming evidence of his existence from people – even from people who seek him with humility. Swinburne begins with the assumptions that (1) people desire to be liked by others – and would especially desire to be liked by God, if he exists; and (2) people have a desire for their own future well-being, which is in God's hands if there is indeed a God who allocates a fate to people in an afterlife. It is natural for one to believe, Swinburne continues, that, if God does exist, these desires will be realized if one acts well. Given a deep and certain awareness of God's presence, Swinburne points out that one would have to have remarkably strong desires to do wrong in order for serious moral decisions to be possible. For, as discussed in the

Introduction, a moral decision arises when one's desires tempt one to act contrary to what one believes to be morally right. And if the balance of one's desires does not seriously tempt one to act contrary to one's moral beliefs – as Swinburne imagines that they typically would not, given (a) one's desires to be liked by God and to secure future well-being, and (b) one's unwavering belief that by acting well God will ensure that these desires are realized – then one would not face moral decisions.

In order to provide people with moral choices, Swinburne acknowledges that God *could* have provided overwhelming evidence for theism and also given us a much more malicious nature, so that we lacked natural affection for our fellows. Because people would then have such a strong desire not to act in accordance with what they believed to be morally right, they would still – even with firm and certain theistic beliefs – have the opportunity to make moral choices. Alternatively (and preferably), God could have – and in fact has – made the evidence of his existence less than compelling. By doing so, he makes it possible for us to be 'naturally good people who still have a free choice between right and wrong'.[39] For, where there is uncertainty about the existence of God, there is uncertainty that one's desires to be liked by God and to secure a favourable afterlife will be met by doing what is morally right. Thus, these desires will not incline one so strongly to do what is morally right; and one will subsequently not need such strong and malicious desires to do wrong in order to be tempted to do so.[40]

Regarding the value of moral choices, Swinburne observes that we 'regard as blessed and honour those who freely do the good when they overcome the temptation to do instead the bad or less good'.[41] At the same time, Swinburne acknowledges that in addition to valuing good moral choices performed in the face of temptation to do otherwise, we also value 'the willingly generous action, the naturally honest, spontaneously loving action'.[42] And certainly the freedom to perform good actions without the impediment of contrary desires is a good thing. But is it more valuable than the freedom to perform the kind of difficult moral choices that can reshape a person's moral character? Swinburne admits that he has 'no easy algorithm for working out which kind of free will is best to have'.[43] Yet, his main point is simply that there is a trade-off between the two admittedly good kinds of freedom. Having freedom in one sense clearly precludes having freedom in the other sense. Swinburne concludes that it is no bad thing that God gives us the freedom to perform or reject the good for a time in this world, and then grants us the other kind of freedom (for a comparatively much longer time) in an afterlife.[44]

There are various responses to Swinburne's argument one might offer in an attempt to show that abundant theistic evidence would *not* in fact preclude moral choices. First, while it is true that people will desire a favourable afterlife if they believe one exists, one might point out that people can be very imprudent, putting off greater future goods for more immediate, short-term pleasures. And if short-term pleasures are not enough to tempt an unwavering believer to forsake his desire for a favourable afterlife, then he might still be tempted to put off performing the right acts he believes will help secure this favourable afterlife. Thus, he may decide upon a plan of sowing his wild oats for the time being, with the idea of asking for forgiveness and changing his lifestyle sometime later in life before he dies. Another source of temptation one might point to for the unwavering believer involves self-deceptive techniques to mitigate the badness of his acts. As discussed in section 6.4, a person may convince himself that his acts are not that bad or that everybody performs bad acts such as these. In this way, he may self-deceptively come to believe that the bad acts he desires to perform will not significantly undermine God's approval or his chances of a favourable afterlife. Finally, one might note that certain desires can have considerably more strength in a passionate moment than when a person is dispassionately reflecting – in what Butler termed 'a cool hour' – on his reasons for acting. A person may unwaveringly believe that God exists and may in a cool hour consistently have as his strongest desires the desires for divine approval and for a favourable afterlife – both of which he believes will be afforded to him if he acts rightly. The same person may nonetheless succumb to a desire to impress his peers during a spirited boys' night out or to sexual urges during a meeting with a woman he knows to be romantically off-limits. Surely unwavering believers, one might argue, can still succumb in the heat of the moment to temptations that they reflectively consider to be of much less value than the good goals their heated actions compromise.

Swinburne's general rejoinder to scenarios such as these is that the levels of self-deception and imprudence must be quite extreme if one is to perform bad actions despite holding firm and unwavering theistic beliefs. Inclinations toward such extreme imprudence or self-deception would, of course, be highly undesirable things. And so we find ourselves again with the following trade-off between theistic evidence and bad desires: in order for moral choices to present themselves, a person who possesses overwhelming theistic evidence and unwavering theistic beliefs must possess very strong inclinations to perform bad actions if he is to wrestle with moral choices. It is better, so we have seen Swinburne argue, that there be a certain amount of theistic ambiguity in our world so that moral choices can present themselves without us having to possess such strong inclinations to perform bad actions.

Whether or not abundant theistic evidence would *always* necessitate very strong inclinations toward the bad in order for moral choices to present themselves, Swinburne has at the very least shown that divine hiddenness represents *a* way in which God might provide moral probation and choice for people in this world. Yet, Schellenberg has a general objection to the idea that God would use the intellectual probation associated with divine hiddenness as a means of making moral probation and choice possible. He argues that there are *other* ways in which God could make moral probation and choice possible – ways available *within* a believer's ongoing relationship with God. As an example, Schellenberg points to the intellectual challenges afforded by a 'dark night of the soul', where God intends 'the believer to be troubled by questions that shake her confidence and motivate her to examine more closely the content of her belief'.[45] Thus, even if some sort of intellectual probation *were* necessary for moral probation, this intellectual probation would not have to come in the form of God remaining hidden to such an extent that earnest seekers could still fail to believe that God even exists.

7.3 *To what extent is a lack of evidence for theism a bad thing?*

Schellenberg moves from the superfluity of this kind of intellectual probation to the conclusion that a perfectly loving God would not use this kind of intellectual probation as a means of providing moral probation and choice. His reasons involve the negative effects associated with nonbelief:

> now, in the midst of earthly pain and conflict, is when we require Divine guidance, support, consolation, and forgiveness ... I suggest that there is indeed reason to suppose that a being who did not seek to relate himself to us explicitly in this life – who elected to remain exclusive, distant, hidden, even in the absence of any culpable activity on our part – would not be properly viewed as perfectly loving.[46]

But does a lack of theistic belief preclude one from receiving such things as divine guidance and consolation? A message one recognizes as coming from God is certainly one obvious way in which God might provide guidance. But there are also less obvious ways – consistent with God remaining hidden. It is quite conceivable that God could regulate a nonbeliever's desires so that she wants to do what God judges it best for her to do. God could also see to it that she comes to believe that a certain course of action is best or right or will most likely realize the desires she has.

As far as providing consolation and support, God could well

regenerate a nonbeliever's emotions so that she came to experience such things as joy, peace and relief from feelings of guilt. In support of the idea that God does this very thing, perhaps the Christian theist would see as evidence the positive feelings that even nonbelievers experience when giving to others, or the way in which even nonbelievers experience an easing of conscience when they admit past wrongdoings. It is true that *some* forms of support and guidance are not available to a nonbeliever. For example, a nonbeliever cannot experience the comforting thought that a loving and powerful God is aware of her problems and is working to help overcome them in his perfect timing.[47] Still, there seem to be a number of ways in which a nonbeliever might yet receive divine support and guidance in the midst of earthly pain and conflict.

Even so, Schellenberg points out that divine guidance and support are not the only things of value within a divine–human relationship:

> 'God seeks to be personally related to us'. In claiming that this proposition is essential to any adequate explication of 'God loves human beings', I am claiming that God, if loving, seeks *explicit, reciprocal* relationship with us, involving not only such things as Divine guidance, support, and forgiveness, but also human trust, obedience, and worship.[48]

The Christian theist will, I think, have to concede that a lack of theistic belief does preclude one from having with God the kind of explicit relationship of which things like worship are a part. Given that the Christian religion commends above all else an explicit personal relationship with God, one might put to the Christian theist the objection that the Christian God, if he really existed, would at all costs remove obstacles that stood in the way of such relationships with himself.

In responding to this objection the Christian theist might begin by stressing the point that true beliefs about God do not *automatically* lead a person into an explicit and positive personal relationship with God. Rather, true beliefs about God provide the *opportunity* for a person to respond positively to God and thereby (with perhaps other conditions also being met) enter into an explicit and positive personal relationship with him. Correspondingly, true beliefs about God also provide the opportunity for a person to respond *negatively* to God and thereby move further away from a positive relationship with him. The gospel of Matthew records Jesus denouncing certain cities that remained unrepentant in the face of miracles he performed in them:

> Woe to you, Korazin! Woe to you, Bethsaida! If the miracles that were

performed in you had been performed in Tyre and Sidon, they would have repented long ago in sackcloth and ashes. But I tell you, it will be more bearable for Tyre and Sidon on the day of judgment than for you. And you, Capernaum, will you be lifted up to the skies? No, you will go down to the depths. If the miracles that were performed in you had been performed in Sodom, it would have remained to this day. But I tell you that it will be more bearable for Sodom on the day of judgment than for you.[49]

One of the ideas here seems to be that, among those people who reject God, those who are presented with greater evidence for certain theistic beliefs accrue more moral guilt than those who are presented with less evidence. Yes, the opportunity that comes from clear theistic evidence and from having true beliefs about God can turn out to be a blessing in that it can move one toward a fulfilling personal relationship with God. But such opportunities also can turn out to have the opposite effect.

7.4 *Divine hiddenness and theodicy*

Schellenberg might at this point press the same type of objection he makes against Pascal: why would God not provide clear evidence for theism to those people for whom such evidence *will* serve to move them toward a fulfilling relationship with God? Implicit in this question is the suggestion that a perfectly loving God would always provide a person with clear theistic evidence if he knew that the person would respond positively to it. We have already noted that the Christian religion affirms that God's chief purpose for us is that we take part in a fulfilling and personal relationship with him. So why would God not provide a person with clear theistic evidence if he knew that that person would respond positively to it and thereby move toward the kind of (explicit) personal relationship with God for which the person was created?

In sketching a theodicy on this point, there seem to be three types of responses that the Christian theist might plausibly offer. First, the Christian theist might suggest that God does not in fact know for certain just when people will and will not respond positively to clear theistic evidence. Granted, not all Christian theists would want to take such a line. However, there are at present a growing number of Christian writers who argue that human decisions cannot be free (on the libertarian definition of freedom) if God knows in advance what these decisions will be. Proponents of the so-called 'open view' of God suggest that the Christian religion's traditional understanding of God's omniscience has long been unduly influenced by Greek philosophical ideas. Specifically, they point to the Greek idea that change denotes imperfection. And they submit that, in order to resist the notion that change might occur within God as he comes to acquire new knowledge by observing what humans freely do, the Christian tradition has tended to embrace a much stronger picture of divine immutability than is warranted by the Christian scriptures.[50]

If God does not know with certainty whether a person will respond positively to further theistic evidence at a given point in time, then he will not know with certainty whether the introduction of further evidence at that time will move the person toward or away from a positive, personal relationship with himself. It is true that God could still know whether a person is *inclined* to respond in a positive way to further evidence. But we must also consider that for one who already has good tendencies, a decision to break with these tendencies may change significantly the shape of one's moral orientation. Conversely, a decision to follow the tendencies one already has does not have the potential to reshape one's character to as great an extent. So, the fact that God may know people's tendencies to respond positively or negatively to a certain piece of theistic evidence does not mean that he knows whether the introduction of this evidence would, all things considered, tend to be a good thing. We conclude, then, that the appeal to the incompatibility of (libertarian) free decisions with God's advance knowledge of those decisions provides one way for the Christian theist to defend God's goodness in the face of God's hiddenness.

A second type of response the Christian theist might offer draws upon the Christian understanding of the universal nature of human sin. Schellenberg's line of argument stipulates that God would provide evidence for his existence sufficient for theistic belief to those who are 'capable' of a relationship with him.[51] By 'capable' Schellenberg means something like: 'able to enter positively into'. In response to Schellenberg, the Christian theist might grant that perhaps many nonbelievers are not so resistant at a time *t* to the truth about God that they are incapable of entering into *some* kind of beneficial relationship with God were they to have more evidence for theism. At the same time, the Christian theist might insist that the introduction of further evidence at time *t* may nonetheless in many cases make more difficult the kind of deep, long-term personal relationship with God commended by the Christian religion. In other words, the Christian theist need not assert that nonbelievers, if they were to possess clear evidence for God's existence, would fail to form *any* relationship with God by which they might receive certain benefits. Instead, the Christian theist might make the more modest suggestion that many nonbelievers would, upon considering clear evidence, fail to form the kind of deep and trusting relationship with

God that is his ultimate purpose for each person. This suggestion is
quite natural when we consider the Christian theist's position that
all humans on earth – believers and nonbelievers alike – have sinful
tendencies and thus resist the kind of loving and completely self-
giving relationship with God for which they were created and which
the redeemed in heaven enjoy.

If God's ultimate goal in providing theistic evidence is to draw
people into this kind of deep and self-giving relationship with him,
then the Christian theist might suggest that, in many cases, clear
theistic evidence best draws a person into this kind of deep, personal
relationship only after the person's character becomes developed in
certain ways. Thus, for the purpose of helping to make people ready
for the kind of deep, personal relationship he wishes to have with
them, God may remove the obstacle of unbelief only after their
wilful resistance to him has been mitigated by a pattern of good
moral choices through which they become more capable of such a
deep, personal relationship. Put another way, moral growth may be
best achieved among many people when they first make certain
moral decisions at earlier stages in their moral development, and
then at later stages are presented with clear theistic evidence.

It is not uncommon in human examples for one person to delay
making to another person an explicit invitation to become involved
in a certain kind of loving relationship. Even though a positive –
albeit more superficial – relationship through which the beloved can
benefit might be possible early on, a person might still wait until the
beloved is judged to be in various senses more 'ready' to take part in
the deeper relationship the person wishes to have with the beloved.
In the case of human readiness to commit every aspect of life
unhesitatingly into the hands of God, obstacles to such readiness
may take any number of forms. We have already discussed how
pride can undermine the kind of relationship with God that he
endeavours to have with people. Other obstacles may include a fear
of commitment, a lack of understanding of the ways in which one
needs a saviour and the tendency to backslide from an existing
relationship where one does not appreciate just how valuable that
relationship is. Again, if the Christian theist is correct in affirming
the universal nature of sin, then all people will face such obstacles to
the kind of deep relationship with God for which the Christian
religion affirms they were created.

Schellenberg might at this point want to expand on a previously
noted rejoinder of his and insist that non-epistemic obstacles to a
deep and fully self-giving relationship with God are best overcome
within an existing, explicit relationship with God. He appeals at one
point to the Christian theist's understanding of God's 'infinite
resourcefulness in addressing human need' and notes 'the testimon-

ials of those who claim that precisely *through* relationship with God all manner of ills of the sort that might be introduced here – such as initial resistance to God or fear of God – have been defeated and indeed turned into good'.[52]

But it seems far from clear that an explicit, but less-than-ideal, relationship with God would always lead one in the direction of the kind of deep, self-giving relationship with God for which Christians maintain we were created. Suppose that a nonbeliever received clear evidence that God does exist and has issued the commands contained throughout the New Testament. Responding to her new beliefs about what God commands of her, suppose the person responds positively to God's commands on stealing, forgiving, making peace and caring for widows and orphans – yet resists God's commands regarding lying, sexual behaviour and finances. Thus, in some respects she becomes more like the kind of person who can enter into the deep and trusting relationship with God for which the Christian religion affirms she was created. On the other hand, she also resists in some ways this type of relationship and thereby solidifies her resistance to some aspects of the relationship God endeavours to have with her. So, has the original introduction of clear evidence led her, all things considered, *toward* or *away from* the kind of relationship with God commended by the Christian religion? This question seems difficult to answer. At the very least, it is not obviously correct that resistance to a deep and completely self-giving relationship with God is generally best overcome after epistemic obstacles are first removed. And so it remains possible for the Christian theist plausibly to argue that God, as he works to help us shape our character so that we can participate in the kind of relationship with him in which we will find ultimate fulfilment, will not see it as necessarily a good thing that we enter into an explicit but less-than-ideal relationship with him during the early stages of our development.

A third type of response open to the Christian theist is to emphasize that people's relationships with God are enhanced by the fact that, in a world where God's existence and character are not obvious to all, people must help one another to learn about God. The Christian religion has always emphasized that God works through people to spread the gospel message. Jesus's reference to how he envisioned the spread of the gospel is recorded in the gospel of John, where we find Jesus praying 'for those [i.e., people throughout the world] who will believe in me through their [i.e., his disciples'] message'.[53] Accordingly, we find Timothy encouraged by the person who shared the gospel message with him to share in turn the gospel message with others: 'What you heard from me, keep as the pattern of sound teaching, with faith and love in Christ Jesus . . .

And the things you have heard me say in the presence of many witnesses entrust to reliable men who will also be qualified to teach others'.[54] In relying on the testimony of others to learn about the character and promises of God – as well as in turn testifying to others about these things – one learns what it is to be in a relationship where one person depends on another for direction in religious matters. That is, one learns what it is to be in the kind of dependent relationship into which, according to the Christian religion, God invites us. And only if God remains to some extent hidden from us do we have the opportunity to rely on others – and have others rely on us – in obtaining spiritual direction in the form of true beliefs about God's existence, character, promises and directives.

Continuing this third line of response, the Christian theist can insist that the testimony of others does not merely provide *a* way for people to gain knowledge about God. Rather, the testimony of others provides an essential way if we are to enjoy fully the relationships for which we were created. The 'communion of saints' is an important notion in the Christian religion, which affirms that humans were created in such a way that their relationships with God are, in a sense, actualized through their relationships with others. While maintaining that humans were created to be in relationship with God, the Christian theist can also affirm that humans were created such that their proper development and well-being require things like physical contact with other people and a sense of belonging to a community. As we relate to one another within a community where human touch and supporting acceptance are present, we find a kind of fulfilment we would otherwise not find. In God-centred, loving relationships with one another, the Christian theist may emphasize, we experience the love of God as we relate to the 'image' of God within one another. On the understanding that the Holy Spirit infuses those in right relationship with God with God's presence and with God-like characteristics such as self-giving love, the saints in heaven relate positively to God as they relate positively to one another. Thus it is open to the Christian theist to argue that people were created in such a way that they find ultimate fulfilment in their relationships with God by being in right relationship with God *and* with one another.

The relationships within the community of saints in heaven are meant to reflect the loving, self-giving, interdependent relationships within the members of the Trinity. If the saints in heaven are not in some ways dependent upon, and responsible for, their fellow saints, then their relationships with one another will not be characterized by interdependence. Clearly, they could not depend on one another for things only God can provide – such as atonement for sins and sanctifying grace. However, among those spiritually significant things the saints *can* provide for one another are instruction and insights into the nature of God and his interaction in human history. And clearly, if the saints are to be dependent upon, and responsible for, one another with respect to learning about God, then God will need to limit private revelations and other ways of helping people to learn about him that do not involve the activity of others.

While each of the three lines of response we have discussed provides a plausible way for the theist to defend God's goodness in the face of Schellenberg's general argument from divine hiddenness, the third line of response may have the most explanatory potential. For it involves God's *general* reasons for creating a world that contains a certain amount of religious ambiguity. In defending this third line of response, the Christian theist can acknowledge that God may have reasons for granting special revelations to certain people at certain times. For example, the Christian theist may see St Paul's encounter with Jesus Christ on the road to Damascus as part of God's plan to use Paul to preach to the Gentiles. But while such special, private revelations to certain people may be necessary for specific purposes God has, the Christian theist can still maintain that it is God's general intention for people to learn about him with the help of one another. In taking this third line of response, then, the Christian theist need not be bothered by the fact that some people receive clearer theistic evidence in this life than others. The Christian theist need not point to any moral characteristic within nonbelievers that accounts for the fact that God may have made less theistic evidence available for them than for others. Rather, the Christian theist can account for divine hiddenness by pointing to God's general intention that people should learn about him from others.

Conclusion

We began this chapter by considering the following argument put forward by J.L. Schellenberg:

(1) A perfectly loving God would desire a reciprocal relationship always to obtain between himself and every human capable of it.

(2) But a logically necessary condition of such a relationship is belief in God's existence.

(3) Hence, a loving God would bring it about that those not resistant to the truth are in possession of sufficient evidence showing that God exists. (From (1) and (2))

(4) Yet the available evidence is not of this sort, as evidenced by inculpable nonbelief.
(5) Hence, a perfectly loving God does not exist. (From (3) and (4))

We explored the possibility that premise (4) might be challenged on the grounds that *all* nonbelief is in fact culpable nonbelief. However, we found that, even if inculpable nonbelief does not exist, Schellenberg's argument can be amended slightly in the following way so as to render this challenge inadequate:

(1) A perfectly loving God would desire a reciprocal relationship always to obtain between himself and every human capable of it.
(2) But a logically necessary condition of such a relationship is belief in God's existence.
(3)′ Hence, a loving God would bring it about that those not resistant to the truth (to the extent that no amount of evidence would convince them) are in possession of sufficient evidence showing that God exists. (From (1) and (2))
(4)′ Yet the available evidence is not of this sort.
(5) Hence, a perfectly loving God does not exist. (From (3) and (4))

We then proceeded to explore how the Christian theist might respond to this amended form of Schellenberg's argument. We discussed Pascal's contention that theistic belief – if it does not stem from a humble search for God – leads to pride, which actually hinders the development of a positive, reciprocal relationship with God. This contention might be used as a basis for claiming that (3)′ does not follow from (1) and (2). At the same time, we noted Schellenberg's rejoinder that Pascal's contention leaves unaddressed the question of why God does not provide stronger evidence for theism to those nonbelievers who *do* humbly search for God.

We next considered an alternative line of argument designed to show that (3)′ does not follow from (1) and (2). We outlined Swinburne's explanation why moral probation – through which one can reshape one's character and grow into the kind of person fit for heaven – becomes possible as God remains to some extent hidden. We then noted Schellenberg's general objection to the idea that God would use the intellectual probation associated with divine hiddenness to provide an opportunity for moral probation: namely, that there exist *other* ways in which God might provide opportunities for moral probation *within* an existing human–divine relationship.

After discussing just how bad a thing it really is for God to allow inculpable nonbelief to occur in this life, we sketched three types of responses the Christian theist might offer to the objection that a perfectly good God would remove epistemic obstacles to theistic belief in this life for those who would respond positively to this belief. First, the Christian theist might maintain that God's advance knowledge of human free decisions is incompatible with these decisions actually being free (in the libertarian sense). On this line of response, God simply does not know who will respond positively to the beliefs that would follow from his introduction of clear evidence for theism. Second, the Christian theist might argue that, while some nonbelievers might be capable of a relationship with God that has some positive aspects to it, they are nonetheless resistant – as all people are – to at least some aspects of the kind of loving and completely self-giving relationship with God that is God's ultimate purpose for all people. As God attempts to draw people into this kind of deep relationship with him, it may often be best that epistemic obstacles to this relationship are removed only after other, non-epistemic obstacles are removed through the person's own good moral choices. Finally, it seems open to the Christian theist to argue that divine hiddenness makes possible a world where people must depend on, and be responsible for, one other as they learn about God. In depending on one another for this aspect of their spiritual growth, the saints in heaven experience an interdependency within their God-centred community through which they find fulfilment and through which their relationships with God, himself, are in part actualized.

We conclude, then, that the Christian theist has resources for developing an adequate response to Schellenberg's line of argument. Divine hiddenness in this life does not by itself undermine God's goodness. Of course, God's goodness *would* be undermined if divine hiddenness made it impossible for some people to attain heaven in the *next* life. And so we reiterate here that the Christian theist, if she is to meet the objection outlined at the end of Part 1, must still address the important question of whether inculpable nonbelief compromises the possibility of the heavenly relationship with God for which all people were created. So let us turn finally to consider how the Christian theist might seek to give an account of the fate of nonbelievers.

Notes

[1] Schellenberg 1993: 2–3.
[2] Calvin 1559: I, iii, 3.
[3] Calvin 1559: I, ii, 2.
[4] Tertullian c. 197: XVII, §5. Tertullian went on in this passage to make the more

specific and bold claim that 'the witness of the soul [is] in its very nature Christian' (XVII, §6).

[5] See Talbot (1989), especially 166–8. Talbot's reference to sin is to a person's *own* sin.

[6] Talbot 1989: 166.

[7] Schellenberg 1993: 66.

[8] Morris 1992: 97.

[9] Hume 1779: Pt III.

[10] Hume 1779: Pt III.

[11] Hanson 1971: 314.

[12] Butler 1729: XV, §8. Butler's quotation is from Ps. 97.2.

[13] Butler 1729: XV, §5.

[14] Butler 1729: XV, §4.

[15] Butler 1729: XV, §15.

[16] Schellenberg 1993: 90. See 88–91 for Schellenberg's full response to the appeal to divine inscrutability.

[17] See Luther 1513–15: III: 575, 25–6 and 1515–16: 5, 105–6.

[18] Peter Lombard 1145–51: Bk II, xlii, 7.

[19] Wesley 1771a: §7, 629.

[20] Cf. Wesley 1782: §1.

[21] Butler 1729: XV, §9.

[22] Augustine 397: Bk III, Ch. viii, 16.

[23] Pascal 1670: §234.

[24] Pascal 1670: §446.

[25] Pascal 1670: §449.

[26] Pascal 1670: §449.

[27] Inasmuch as there exist 'arrogant philosophers', Pascal would have to concede that divine hiddenness does not always prevent the prideful from forming (at least some) Christian beliefs.

[28] Pascal 1670: §149.

[29] Schellenberg 1993: 148.

[30] Schellenberg 1993: 148.

[31] Lewis 1961: 63.

[32] Schellenberg 1993: 140.

[33] Ps. 22.2.

[34] Isa. 45.15.

[35] Augustine 397: Bk I, Ch. v, 5.

[36] Anselm 1077–78: Ch. I.

[37] Pascal 1670: §427.

[38] Morris 1992: 102.

[39] Swinburne 1998: 178.

[40] Though we earlier noted Joseph Butler's appeal to the inscrutability of God's reasons for remaining hidden, he did offer a line of argument similar to (though less developed than) Swinburne's here: 'The evidence of religion not appearing obvious, may constitute one particular part of some men's trial in the religious sense: as it gives scope for a virtuous exercise, or vicious neglect of their understanding, in examining or not examining into that evidence' (1736: II, vi, 8).

[41] Swinburne 1998: 86.

[42] Swinburne 1998: 84.

[43] Swinburne 1998: 88.

[44] Cf. Swinburne 1998: 251.

[45] Schellenberg 1993: 203.

[46] Schellenberg 1993: 28–9.

[47] Cf. Adams (1986) on the benefits associated with the 'inner peace or sense of security' that comes when one 'both loves God and trusts in God's love' (184).

[48] Schellenberg 1993: 18.
[49] Mt. 11.21-4.
[50] For an introduction to this line of thought, see Pinnock, Rice, Sanders, Hasker and Basinger (1994).
[51] See Schellenberg 2002: 49.
[52] Schellenberg 2002: 50.
[53] Jn 17.20.
[54] 2 Tim. 1.13, 2.2.

8

THE FATE OF NONBELIEVERS

In our Introduction we stipulated that the Christian theist will want
to assign to Jesus Christ a unique role in the process of human
reconciliation to God. More specifically, we are assuming that the
Christian theist understands the atoning work of Jesus Christ to
constitute the one and only means by which sinful humans can be
reconciled to God. In sum, the perfect life of Christ 'covers' or
'applies to' the sinful earthly life of the redeemed person in the sense
that the redeemed person is accepted by God into heaven on the
basis of the merits of Christ's – rather than the person's own – life.
Such an assumption, though, does not settle the question of what
fate awaits those who in this life do not hold explicitly Christian
beliefs about God. For this assumption only provides an answer to
the question: what is the means through which God has chosen to
reconcile sinful people to himself? Granting that reconciliation with
God occurs only as one's life is accepted by God on the merits of
Christ's atoning work, our interest in this chapter is with the further
question: *whose* lives are accepted by God on the merits of Christ's
atoning work?

8.1 *The possibility of implicit faith*

Theologians within the Christian tradition have often affirmed that
there are definite propositions, or 'articles of faith', that must be
believed by anyone striving to exercise Christian faith. Indeed, the
Christian Church has often tested the authenticity of one's faith by
observing whether one affirms key propositions about God. Thomas
Aquinas's writings on the articles of faith are illustrative here.
Aquinas identified fourteen articles of faith, all having to do either
with the Incarnation of Jesus Christ or with the triune Godhead.
These articles focus on such subjects as the virginal birth of Jesus;
his death, resurrection and ascension; the creation of the world; the
sanctification of man; and life everlasting.[1] In describing the person
who fails to believe all fourteen articles, Aquinas declared: 'Neither
living nor lifeless faith remains in the heretic who disbelieves one
article of faith'.[2]

Aquinas's insistence that virtuous faith demands belief of all articles of faith stems from his understanding of the authoritative role played by the Church. Aquinas understood divine truth to be manifested in the teachings of the Church; and if a person 'is not prepared to follow the teaching of the Church in all things', then it is evident that that person 'has not the habit of faith' indicative of one who submits to divine truth.[3] According to Aquinas, the *reason* one believes the articles of faith is of telling importance. He maintained that 'if, of the things taught by the Church, [a person] holds what he chooses to hold, and rejects what he chooses to reject, he no longer adheres to the teaching of the Church as to an infallible rule, but to his own will'.[4] For Aquinas, as Terence Penelhum summarizes, 'faith is the willing acceptance of the articles on authority'.[5] And a person not willing to believe all the articles of faith on the Church's authority is a person without the proper commitment of faith.

Notwithstanding Aquinas's own reasons for insisting that faith is possible only as one holds a number of explicitly Christian beliefs, other Christian writers have stressed what seems to be a more fundamental reason for insisting that reconciliation with God is possible only as one holds explicitly Christian beliefs. We might roughly characterize this reason as involving the view that a person's sin cannot properly be 'dealt with' through the atoning work of Christ unless the person responds in some way specifically to that atoning work. Put another way, the idea here is that one cannot attain salvation through the merits of Christ if one does not explicitly plead to God Christ's passion as atonement for one's own sins.

In his epistle to the Romans, St Paul quotes the Old Testament passage, 'Everyone who calls on the name of the Lord will be saved'.[6] He then asks, 'How, then, can they call on the one they have not believed in? And how can they believe in the one of whom they have not heard?'[7] Picking up on this passage, Augustine comments on the New Testament story of Cornelius, whom St Luke describes as a 'devout and God-fearing' man who 'gave generously to those in need and prayed to God regularly'[8] and who embraced Peter's subsequent presentation to him of the Christian gospel message:

> it is often said, 'He deserved to believe, because he was a good man even before he believed'. Which may be said of Cornelius since his alms were accepted and his prayers heard before he had believed on Christ ... But if he could have been saved without the faith of Christ the Apostle Peter would not have been sent as an architect to build him up.[9]

Again adopting St Paul's language in Romans 10, Luther asserted that 'where Christ is not preached, there is no Holy Spirit to create, call, and gather the Christian Church, and outside it no one can come to the Lord Christ ... [O]utside the Christian Church (that is, where the Gospel is not) there is no forgiveness, and hence no holiness'.[10] Calvin was no less explicit in commenting on the fate that awaited those without specific beliefs as to the person or atoning work of Jesus. He affirmed that 'by excluding the reprobate either from the knowledge of his name or the sanctification of his Spirit, [God] by these marks in a manner discloses the judgment which awaits them'.[11] Whatever else these Christian writers might want to include in their respective accounts of faith, they agree on the necessity of holding explicitly Christian beliefs – e.g. that Jesus, as God incarnate, made atonement for human sin – if reconciliation with God is to be possible.

At the same time, even the most ardent defenders of the necessity of explicitly Christian beliefs have acknowledged that some individuals from before the time of Christ are counted among the redeemed in heaven. After all, the eleventh chapter of Hebrews commends to its Christian readers as examples of faith the lives of Old Testament characters who anticipated their own heavenly reward. As to the possibility of salvation for those living *after* the time of Christ who do not hold explicitly Christian beliefs, the Christian tradition as a whole has moved from general pessimism to greater optimism over the last millennium. We can recognize this shift by surveying official documents within the Roman Catholic Church. The Fourth Lateran Council (1215) under Innocent III – in keeping with the general consensus among the Church Fathers and medieval theologians – maintained that 'One indeed is the universal Church of the faithful, outside which no one at all is saved'.[12] And the Council of Florence (1442) declared that 'those not living within the Catholic Church, not only pagans, but also Jews and heretics and schismatics cannot become participants in eternal life'.[13] However, moving forward several centuries, one can find what may initially seem to be contradictory statements within Roman Catholic documents, such as the 1863 encyclical of Pope Pius IX, which stated that

> they who labor in invincible ignorance of our most holy religion and who, zealously keeping the natural law and its precepts engraved in the hearts of all by God, and being ready to obey God, live an honest and upright life, can, by the operating power of divine light and grace, attain eternal life.[14]

More recently, the Second Vatican Council (1962–65) affirmed that 'God in ways known to himself can lead those inculpably ignorant of the gospel to that faith without which it is impossible to please him'.[15]

In explaining this apparent shift regarding the possibility of salvation for those without explicitly Christian beliefs in this life, it would be a mistake to conclude that earlier Christian writers as a whole did not share the working assumption that God would not withhold salvation from the morally inculpable. Aquinas is representative in avowing that 'it pertains to divine providence to furnish everyone with what is necessary for salvation, provided that on [one's] part there is no hindrance'.[16] Instead, the shift in question is most plausibly explained in terms of the failure of earlier Christian writers to take very seriously the possibility of inculpable nonbelief among those living after the time of Christ.[17] We find, for example, Aquinas in his early writings dismissing the possibility that any person might fail through no fault of his own to hold those beliefs necessary for salvation.[18]

> even if someone is brought up in the forest or among wild beasts ... if someone so brought up followed the direction of natural reason in seeking good and avoiding evil, we must most certainly hold that God would either reveal to him through inner inspiration what had to be believed, or would send some preacher of the faith to him as he sent Peter to Cornelius (Acts 10.20).[19]

In sum, we can note that earlier Christian writers were more pessimistic than those of modern times about the possibility of salvation for those who lived after the coming of Christ and who did not hold orthodox Christian beliefs. Yet, it seems plausible to attribute this pessimism primarily to an understanding that any person after the time of Christ who fails to belong to the body of Christian believers wilfully and sinfully chooses to resist those truths that Christians affirm.

In support of this explanation of earlier pessimism in Christian thought regarding the fate of those outside the Christian Church, we can note how the Second Vatican Council viewed its own statements on the matter as continuous with the earlier Christian tradition: 'Basing itself upon sacred Scripture and tradition, [this sacred Synod] teaches that the Church ... is necessary for salvation ... Whoever, therefore, knowing that the Catholic Church was made necessary by God through Jesus Christ, would refuse to enter her or to remain in her could not be saved'.[20] The understanding here seems to be that we should read earlier pessimism as to the possibility of salvation for those 'outside the Church' in terms of pessimism regarding those *culpably* outside the Church'.[21] Again, these two terms for many earlier Christian writers were synonymous because it was generally assumed that all people after the time of Christ were given the resources to form Christian beliefs if they were so willing. In other words, the two terms were synonymous because the possibility of inculpable nonbelief was not seriously considered. However, where the possibility of inculpable nonbelief *has* been taken seriously, the Christian tradition – in keeping with the assumption that moral culpability presupposes free and wilful decisions – *has* tended to allow for the possibility that those without explicitly Christian beliefs in this life might yet attain salvation through the merits of Christ.

In affirming both the unique role of Christ's atoning work in salvation and the possibility that those without Christian beliefs might yet attain salvation, the Christian theist may at this point appeal to the notion of 'implicit' Christian faith. In recent times, Karl Rahner has been widely associated with the notion of the 'anonymous Christian' and has provided a theology of salvation whereby people from other religious traditions can nonetheless exercise implicit Christian faith. The account of implicit faith I shall advance in this section leads to the same general conclusion that Rahner reaches: namely, that salvation remains possible for those who do not in this life hold explicitly Christian beliefs. At the same time, Rahner's account of implicit faith differs from the account I shall advance in at least one obvious way. Rahner focuses on people's participation in their own social religion, emphasizing that the differing religions of various communities can for their participants be 'a positive means of gaining the right relationship to God and thus for attaining of salvation'.[22] By contrast, the account of implicit faith I shall advance focuses on an individual's personal response to divine messages – whatever the form (social or not) in which these messages come.

This difference has at least two important implications for our discussion. First, Rahner seems to allow that salvation can be attained through another religion only when one is not aware of the Christian religion, which he calls the 'absolute religion':[23]

> Until the moment when the Gospel really enters into the historical situation of an individual, a non-Christian religion ... contains also supernatural elements arising out of the grace which is given to men as a gratuitous gift on account of Christ. For this reason a non-Christian religion can be recognized as a *lawful* religion.[24]

On the further question of whether a person who thoughtfully considers the Christian religion can still attain salvation through a non-Christian religion, Rahner states that 'Wherever in practice Christianity reaches man in the real urgency and rigour of his actual existence, Christianity – once understood – presents itself as the only still valid religion for this man, a necessary means for his salvation'.[25] On the account of implicit faith I shall advance, what will be important is simply whether a person's nonbelief is culpable or non-culpable. Failure to be exposed to the Christian gospel message is one clear way in which a person may not be culpable for a failure to hold Christian beliefs, but it is not the only way. Indeed, I shall claim that there may be nonbelievers who *have* been exposed to the gospel message and who nevertheless exercise implicit Christian faith. If Rahner's account of implicit faith does not allow for this scenario – and it is not clear to me that it does[26] – then his account will be at odds with the account I shall advance.

Second, it is not clear whether Rahner thinks that one can attain heaven without *first* – even if after life on earth – explicitly pleading Christ's passion as atonement for one's own sins. In commenting on what is required of someone in another religious community, Rahner states that we should not 'expect from someone who lives outside the Christian religion that he should have exercised his genuine, saving relationship to God absolutely outside the religions which society offered him'.[27] If one accepts Rahner's claim that a person can have a 'genuine, saving relationship to God' without explicitly holding Christian beliefs, then it might be suggested that a person can attain heaven without ever first explicitly pleading Christ's passion. Such a suggestion, however, is at odds with our assumption in the Introduction that full and final reconciliation with God can occur only when one explictly pleads Christ's passion as atonement for one's own sins.

While Rahner is perhaps the best-known contemporary defender of the idea of implicit faith among those outside the community of earthly Christian believers, we should note that this idea is hardly new within the Christian tradition. Consider the second-century writings of Justin Martyr, who addressed as follows the fate of Gentiles who lived before Christ.

> We have been taught that Christ was First-begotten of God (the Father) and we have indicated ... that He is the Word [*Logos*] of whom all mankind partakes. Those who lived by reason (*logos*) are Christians, even though they have been considered atheists: such as, among the Greeks, Socrates, Heraclitus and others like them.[28]

Justin's appeal to *logos* in spelling out how implicit faith is possible attests to his training as a philosopher in the Platonic tradition. Other Christian writers have offered different accounts of how implicit faith is possible.

Augustine seemed to take the line that all people of virtuous faith – even those who lived well before the coming of Christ – *have* had some kind of awareness of Christ and his work. Augustine suggests that the story of Job was divinely provided for the Christian canon so that 'from this one case we might know that among other nations also there might be men pertaining to the spiritual Jerusalem who have lived according to God and have pleased Him'.[29] Augustine is quick to add, though, that 'it is not to be supposed that this was granted to any one, unless the one Mediator between God and men, the Man Christ Jesus, was divinely revealed to him; who was pre-announced to the saints of old as yet to come in the flesh'.[30]

Calvin took a similar line in suggesting that the people of faith who lived before Christ knew more about the person of Christ than we might be inclined to suppose is plausible. He notes that Naaman of Aram[31] is 'commended for his piety' and that 'this must have been the result of faith'.[32] In commenting further on the faith of Naaman and other biblical characters before Christ thought to be among the redeemed, Calvin states:

> I admit that, in some respect, their faith was not explicit either as to the person of Christ, or the power and office assigned him by the Father. Still it is certain that they were imbued with principles which might give some, though a slender, foretaste of Christ ... [A]lthough their knowledge of Christ may have been obscure, we cannot suppose that they had no such knowledge at all.[33]

Apart from Calvin's subsequent allusion to Old Testament prophets who spoke about the coming Messiah, he does not provide many details as to what the 'obscure' knowledge of ancient people of faith might have amounted to. It seems rather difficult to imagine, though, that the people of faith before the time of Christ – especially Job, Noah, Abraham and other characters thought to have lived early in human history – each had some sort of knowledge about the person of Jesus Christ.

Like Calvin, Aquinas affirmed that some people who lived before the time of Christ exercised a kind of implicit Christian faith. Commenting on the Gentiles who lived before Christ's coming, Aquinas stated that 'If some Gentiles were saved, without receiving any revelation [about Christ], they were not saved without faith in the Mediator. Because even though they did not have explicit faith, they did have a faith that was implicit ...'[34]

In Aquinas's account of how implicit faith is possible, he focuses on how an individual might hold *implicit beliefs*. He did affirm 'belief of some kind in the mystery of Christ's Incarnation was necessary at all times and for all persons'.[35] Yet, he added that 'this belief differed according to differences of times and persons',[36] explaining that 'whatever those who lived later have believed, was contained, albeit implicitly, in the faith of those Fathers who preceded them'.[37] Specifically, belief in 'the existence of God includes all that we believe to exist in God eternally'; and belief in 'the Redemption of mankind includes belief in the Incarnation of Christ, His Passion, and so forth'.[38] As to the explicit beliefs that

God exists and that he providentially governs the world, Aquinas was uncompromising, stating that 'It must be said that in every age and for everyone, it has always been necessary to believe explicitly in these two things.'[39] For it is these beliefs, in Aquinas's view, that amount to implicit belief in Christ and his atoning work. And for Aquinas it is implicitly Christian beliefs that make implicit Christian faith possible.

There does seem to be empirical reason to question Aquinas's views on the implicitly Christian nature of theistic beliefs relating to God's existence and the redemption of humankind. After all, someone from another religious tradition – e.g. Judaism or Islam – may affirm God's existence and the redemption of humans and yet explicitly deny the Christian doctrines of the Trinity and the Incarnation. So, it is unclear in what sense we should understand the beliefs of Old Testament characters such as Noah and Abraham as implicitly containing specific articles of faith related to the person and work of Jesus.

Apart from any specific difficulties with Aquinas's account of implicit belief, the general notion that implicit faith can be analysed in terms of implicit belief does not help to address our larger question of how nonbelievers might yet voluntarily exercise some sort of virtuous faith. For, as we concluded in Chapter 2, belief is involuntary. Thus, among those people who do not hold explicitly Christian beliefs, we cannot account for any voluntary exercise of implicit faith by pointing to a purported decision 'to believe' certain general theistic propositions that implicitly contain the more specific Christian articles of faith. Instead, if the Christian theist is to maintain that God rightly holds nonbelievers responsible for whether or not they exercise faith, we will have to look for some other type of decision – available to all people – that amounts to an implicit making of the decision that lies at the heart of Christian faith.

In Chapter 3 I provided an account of Christian faith as the acceptance of the authoritative claims that accompany God's invitational statements to a person. Might the decision to accept God's authority be implicitly made in other decisions a person – even a nonbeliever – voluntarily makes? Though Christian writers have perhaps not characterized Christian faith in the terms I have used, the notion of something like an 'implicit decision' I am describing is by no means new within the Christian tradition. Consider Richard Swinburne's summary of the patristic and scholastic doctrine of *limbus partum*: 'According to this doctrine, the Old Testament patriarchs were consigned to an intermediate state, *limbus patrum*, until Christ "descended into Hell" to preach to them the redemption which he had won for them on Calvary'.[40]

What is most important for our purposes is the understanding that the Old Testament patriarchs did not *become* men of faith only subsequent to Christ's preaching. Rather, they performed virtuous acts of faith during their earthly lives – acts of faith for which they are commended in the eleventh chapter of Hebrews. Their response to Christ's preaching is not, it seems clear, to be understood as a moral decision with which they in any way wrestled. Rather, their response was inevitable, given the kinds of people into which they had developed by their repeated decisions to perform certain acts – acts, again, that the Christian tradition has understood to be acts of virtuous faith. As Swinburne comments:

> Once they accepted [Christ's preaching] (as they were already geared to do in virtue of their good will), they inherited its benefits – Heaven. Their inability, through ignorance, to plead Christ's sacrifice alone barred them from Heaven; when it was remedied, they could avail themselves of that sacrifice and Heaven was theirs.[41]

The specifics of the doctrine of *limbus patrum*, and whether it was at the time of Christ's earthly death that the Old Testament patriarchs heard the gospel message about Christ, are not vital to our overall discussion. What is important for our purposes is that the Old Testament patriarchs *at some point* after their earthly lives were given the opportunity to make an explicit response to Christ's atoning work – i.e. plead Christ's passion – and thereby be finally reconciled with God. And, again, it is important for our purposes to note that this response was an inevitable one given the kinds of people they had become through their earthly patterns of decisions.

In the next section we shall explore whether there are types of decisions – available to people today without specifically Christian beliefs – through which one might become like the Old Testament patriarchs: the kind of person who would inevitably respond positively to Christ's atoning work once the truth about Christ became clear. Put another way, and in keeping with the account of faith offered in Chapter 3, we shall explore whether there might be decisions available to nonbelievers that would constitute a kind of 'implicit' decision to accept God's authority.

8.2 *The criteria for implicit faith*

While affirming the unique role Christ's atoning work plays in the salvation of sinful humans, the Christian tradition has always held that the recognition of the person and work of Jesus Christ in itself by no means guarantees the exercise of virtuous faith. Indeed, St Matthew records Jesus making reference to people who profess to perform acts of faith in his name but yet who do not exercise the kind of faith that lies at the heart of the kind of relationship into which God invites people.

> Not everyone who says to me, 'Lord, Lord', will enter the kingdom of heaven, but only he who does the will of my Father who is in heaven. Many will say to me on that day, 'Lord, Lord, did we not prophesy in your name, and in your name drive out demons and perform many miracles?' Then I will tell them plainly, 'I never knew you. Away from me, you evildoers!'[42]

The people described here do use the name of Jesus when praying to God and when performing acts that they, themselves, no doubt consider to be acts of faith. Yet, Jesus does not consider their actions to be acts of virtuous faith. So, we must be careful about what we conclude from biblical passages stating that salvation awaits 'everyone who calls on the name of the Lord',[43] or who 'believe on him',[44] or who 'believe in him',[45] or who 'believe that Jesus is the Christ'.[46] However we interpret such proclamations,[47] we cannot conclude from them – in the light of the group of people described in Matthew 7 – that addressing God by the right particular name constitutes the criterion by which God assesses whether or not a person is exercising virtuous faith.

To see why it is that the people described by Jesus in Matthew 7 do not exercise virtuous, Christian faith despite using the name of Jesus in their acts of service, let us turn to some comments made by Richard Swinburne on the nature of faith. Swinburne observes that, if faith is equated with mere belief[48] and/or trust,[49] then 'the perfect scoundrel may yet be a man of faith'.[50] To see why this is so, consider the historical case of Abraham, who, when God stated to him that his offspring would be as numerous as the stars, 'believed the Lord, and he credited it to him as righteousness'.[51] For the purpose purely of a thought experiment, suppose that Abraham had previously decided at some point that he was going to spend his life cheating people out of money. Upon hearing God's testimony to him, he might then have thought to himself, 'I do *believe* that God will in fact give me many descendants, and this will greatly help in my goal of cheating people. For if my descendants are in places of power, I'll be less likely to be punished or held accountable for my unlawful acts.' In such a case, Abraham, eager to cheat people in whatever land he finds himself, might have been happy to demonstrate *trust* – i.e. act on the assumption that God's statement is true – following God's call to move to a not yet identified foreign land where his household will prosper.

Swinburne points out that of vital importance in acts of faith are the *purposes* one seeks to achieve. In our thought experiment, the ultimate purposes we imagine Abraham as seeking to achieve are clearly not virtuous ones. And this is why he does not exercise commendable faith when he entrusts his future to God and follows God's direction. As for the people described in Matthew 7, perhaps their ultimate purpose in prophesying in Jesus's name is to manipulate people. Perhaps their ultimate purpose in working to facilitate miraculous healing in others is to draw undue attention to themselves. There may be any variety of reasons that account for the lack of virtuous faith on the part of these individuals who profess the name of Jesus and do works of service in his name. Yet, the reasons will all have to do with the purposes they ultimately seek to achieve.

Toward seeing more clearly that the purposes one pursues are of more fundamental importance to a relationship with God than is the correct identification of God's name and God's specific works, we might consider a passage from C.S. Lewis's *The Last Battle*, the final book in his *Chronicles of Narnia*. In Lewis's stories, Aslan is the one true God. Contrastingly, Tash is described as a 'false God of the pagan Calormenes', whose character is evil and of whom Aslan says, 'We are opposites.' Aslan states at one point:

> I and he are of such different kinds that no service which is vile can be done to me, and none which is not vile can be done to him. Therefore if any man swear by Tash and keep his oath for the oath's sake, it is by me that he has truly sworn, though he know it not, and it is I who reward him. And if any man do cruelty in my name, then, though he says the name Aslan, it is Tash whom he serves and by Tash his deed is accepted.[52]

The people described by Jesus in Matthew 7 do perform works in his name. But they clearly do not pursue the kinds of ultimate purposes that he himself pursues and intends for them to pursue; and so he essentially tells them that they have nothing in common with him.

If, contrary to this line of argument, we suppose that God *were* to judge the lives of people on the basis of their beliefs instead of on the basis of the purposes they pursue, we would be left with some odd consequences indeed. First, as the Christian tradition has always recognized, one who holds true beliefs about the person and work of Jesus Christ, but who pursues purposes antithetical to the establishment of the loving, self-giving relationships God invites people to have with him and with others, will not be fit for heaven. In order for such a person to take her part in the heavenly community, her very character – which is the result of her systematic pursuit of certain purposes – will need to be radically overhauled. In a sense, God would need unilaterally to override and reverse the moral orientation she has developed through a lifetime of moral choices – a scenario that seems hard to reconcile with the affirmation that

God honours people's free choices as to the kinds of people they want to become and how they want to be related to God. Now, a person who does *not* hold true beliefs about God, but who *has* developed a virtuous character through the pursuit of purposes jointly pursued by the heavenly community, will not, of course, exercise explicit Christian faith. However, when she comes to see the truth about God – perhaps after her earthly life, as was the case with the Old Testament patriarchs – she will naturally fit in very well with the heavenly community. No radical overhaul of her character will be needed.

Second, as already discussed at length, belief is involuntary in that one cannot hold a belief simply by deciding to hold it. On the other hand, the decision to pursue one purpose over another can indeed be a voluntary decision. Where the decision between pursuing purposes involves a choice between following the leading of one's moral beliefs or following the inclinations of contrary desires, the decision is a morally significant one. On the assumption that people are morally responsible only for their free, moral decisions, what people are responsible for is not, strictly speaking, what they believe. Rather, they are responsible for the purposes they seek to achieve in the light of what they believe.[53] We conclude, then, that when God judges whether individuals possess the kind of virtuous faith that leads to salvation, his judgments will be based on the purposes they decide to pursue.

In exploring the kinds of purposes the pursuits of which are indicative of virtuous Christian faith, we can begin by noting the significance within the Christian religion of pleading Christ's passion. Clearly, Christ's atoning work *itself* is central to the Christian religion because it is seen as the divinely given means by which sinful humans can be reconciled to God and enjoy the kind of loving and eternal personal relationship with God for which they were created. Apart from this fact, a person's *decision* to plead Christ's atoning work is also seen as having great significance as an indicator of the moral direction of that person's life. The reason such a decision is viewed as especially indicative of one's moral direction is best explained in terms of the purposes to which the decision seems to indicate that one is committed.

To turn to God and plead Christ's passion is to perform, according to the Christian religion, an act of 'repentance'. Repentance essentially contains two elements, both of which play a vital role in the establishment of the kind of personal relationship into which God invites people. First, we acknowledge our past wrongdoings – particularly our failure to meet our obligations toward God – and our inability by ourselves to make amends for them. Admitting this fact about ourselves, we ask that God accept us on the merits of Christ's life – and not on the merits of our own lives. Second, we pledge to live our lives in the future as God wants us to live them. With these two elements, then, we profess Jesus Christ as both 'Saviour' and 'Lord'.[54]

Of course, as our thought experiment involving Abraham showed, one's decision to turn to God as Saviour and Lord must be in the context of pursuing further purposes that are not antithetical to the kind of relationship into which God invites people.[55] Presuming that this is the case, one's decision to plead Christ's passion amounts to an explicit acceptance of the terms on which God invites people to relate to him. Having sketched the kind of response to God that lies at the heart of virtuous Christian faith, we can now ask: might someone make a decision that *implicitly* amounts to this kind of response to God?

Let us suppose that a person forms a moral belief regarding her obligations to God, if he exists. Specifically, let us suppose that she comes to believe that, if she does owe her existence to a creator, then she has an obligation to relate to him as Lord. Despite not being sure as to exactly what God requires of her, if he even exists, perhaps she makes a solemn vow to be a person who meets all her obligations toward her creator (again, if she does have a creator) and who acts in accordance with whatever God commends. Put in the terms adopted in Chapter 6, she makes the decision to respond positively to the truth about God wherever the truth lies. In such a case it seems appropriate to describe her decision as implicitly containing the decision to accept God's authority.[56] For, if she remains faithful to this decision, then she will go about responding positively to whatever directives she believes God to have given her (and will do so because it is God who has given the directives). Thus, once she comes to hold true beliefs about God's enjoinment to plead Christ's passion – perhaps, like the Old Testament patriarchs, sometime after her earthly life – she will have no moral struggles with doing so. Given her original decision and a life lived faithful to it, she will – again like the Old Testament patriarchs – inevitably respond in a positive way to the gospel message once she hears it and forms the belief that it is true. In the meantime, apropos our discussions in Chapter 6, if she is faithfully responding positively to the truth about God as she sees it, then any failure to form the belief that God enjoins us to plead Christ's passion will not be the result of a self-deceptive process. Rather, it will be the result of inculpable ignorance. In sum, then, her original decision in a real sense implicitly contains the decision to exercise Christian faith.

The person who exercises implicit Christian faith need not *know* that her decisions are making her fit for heaven and that they in fact amount to the exercise of implicit Christian faith. Christian theists affirm that the relationships those in heaven have with God and with one another are characterized by mutually loving and self-giving service for the sake of the other person. Inasmuch as a person in her earthly life works to help and serve others, she pursues those goals also pursued by the heavenly community. Within the broad class of actions that might constitute loving service to others, one might pursue such purposes as ensuring that the oppressed receive justice, that the repentant receive mercy and that the alienated receive support. In the end, there may be any number of purposes one might pursue that would contribute to one becoming the kind of person (or unlike the kind of person) who possesses the moral orientation of those in the heavenly community. Similarly, when we consider the specific invitation to relate to God as Saviour and Lord, there may be any number of moral decisions one might make that would make one more (or less) inclined to accept this relationship where one must live in dependence on God's grace and submission to his will. Yet, one does not need to be aware of these implications of one's moral decisions in order for one's moral decisions in fact to have these implications.

Sometimes people do make a momentous moral decision that signifies a sort of 'conversion', in that the decision dramatically changes the set of morally significant goals toward which they subsequently work. In the example we have considered, we supposed that a person makes a considered decision to accept, or respond positively to, the truth about God, and that all her subsequent actions reflect this decision. It is clear to see in this case how her decision constitutes (at least implicitly) a decision to be the kind of person who would plead the passion of Christ if this action is what God commends and expects. However, the morally significant decisions people make are ordinarily not nearly so clear-cut as to the implications they have for implicit faith. We may face any number of morally significant decisions each day. Sometimes our moral decisions are good ones; at other times they are not. Each moral decision may make us either more or less like the Old Testament patriarchs whose acceptance of the Christian gospel message was the inevitable result of the kind of people they had become.

As to God's criteria in determining whether a person's implicit faith is sufficient for salvation, the Christian theist will probably not want to attempt to give too many specifics. We have already noted that becoming fit for heaven will involve the pursuit of purposes consistent with agapeistic love and with a willingness to embrace God as Saviour and Lord. Offering anything more specific is difficult. There are any number of different kinds of decisions that are available to some people and not to others. For example, theists who are not Christian theists may still face decisions as to whether to turn to God in repentance as they pursue their various purposes in life. Atheists may not understand such a course of action even to be an option. Atheists may, though, like theists, face decisions as to whether the ultimate purposes they seek to achieve are consistent with agapeistic love and with a willingness to fulfil any obligations they might have. Given, then, the vast web of moral decisions that may and may not be available to a person, and given the potential complications involved in determining whether any single action merits praise or blame, it seems an exceedingly complex matter to evaluate a person's moral character as formed by his voluntary moral choices. And even if we did see clearly the status of one's moral character, we would still not fully understand exactly which character traits are most essential to participation in the heavenly community.

The Christian theist would, of course, have a much more tidy answer to the question 'Whose lives are covered by Christ's atoning work?' if she could identify this group of people with those who in their earthly lives explicitly recognize the person of Jesus and subsequently plead his passion. But, as we saw in the previous section, such an answer is clearly inadequate as the criterion for identifying those people whose lives are accepted by God on the merits of Christ's life. Can the Christian theist, though, offer some kind of general criterion God might use in determining the overall moral 'trajectory' of a person's life as he judges where their fate lies in the afterlife?

Given the Christian religion's understanding that no human is without sin, it would seem to follow that no human has, for all her life, pursued only those purposes consistent with heavenly life, where sin is understood to play no part. Returning to the terminology of Chapter 3, we can say that no one has accepted God's authority as Lord with perfect consistency. We noted in Chapter 3 that where a person does not fully accept the authoritative claims of lordship that lie behind God's statements of invitation to a relationship, God will have to decide whether he is willing to accept a relationship with the person on these terms. In explaining God's decision-making process here – a process that must, as we assumed in the Introduction, be consistent with perfect goodness – the Christian theist may appeal to the question of whether an ongoing relationship with God would help to achieve the purposes a person has decided to pursue. The Christian religion describes an everlasting relationship with God as a very good thing. But to a person whose purposes remain such that an everlasting relationship with God will not achieve them, such an everlasting relationship will prove more a source of frustration than joy. If God honours people's free, self-determinative decisions as to which purposes they seek to achieve, then it seems that God could refuse to accept a relationship with someone on the grounds that such a relationship will not, given their decisions, be a source of fulfilment for them.

8.3 *Response summary*

We are now in a position to summarize the line of response open to the Christian theist with respect to the objection raised at the end of Part 1. I defended an account of faith in Part 1 according to which the exercise of Christian faith amounts to the acceptance of the authoritative claims that accompany God's invitational statements. I went on to identify two beliefs one must hold if one is to exercise Christian faith. First, one must have a belief$_m$, which is the belief that a particular message comes from God. Second, one must have a belief$_p$, which is the belief that there exists no more likely means of achieving a purpose one is pursuing than the acceptance of God's authority. We concluded Part 1 by pressing the following objection against the Christian theist who affirms that faith in the Christian God is necessary for a person to be reconciled to God and enjoy eternal life in heaven: 'If one cannot exercise Christian faith without first having certain beliefs, and if belief is involuntary, then how can the Christian theist rule out the possibility of some people failing to exercise Christian faith due to an involuntary lack of belief and hence through no fault of their own?'

In outlining the Christian theist's possible response to this challenge, we have in no way denied our working assumption that explicit Christian faith is necessary for full and final reconciliation with God, or that explicit Christian faith requires a belief$_m$ and a belief$_p$. We have not, that is, denied the Christian understanding that it is through faith in Jesus Christ – specifically, in the areas of his general lordship and his specific atoning work – that salvation comes. However, we *have* denied that there is sufficiently good reason to think that Christ's atoning work can only be applied to the lives of those who understand *in this life* the person and work of Christ. People without specifically Christian beliefs in this life may still, through the right kinds of moral choices, become the kinds of people who – like the Old Testament patriarchs – would readily accept the Christian gospel message if they came to see the truth of it. If God's moral evaluation of one's life is based on the voluntary decisions one makes, then it seems open for the Christian theist to affirm that God will allow such people – again, as with the Old Testament patriarchs – some time after they die to hear and recognize the truth of the Christian gospel message, which they will then readily embrace, given the kinds of people they have become through their earthly decisions. While explicit Christian faith may not be possible for all people here on earth, implicit Christian faith nonetheless is.[57]

For those who do not in this life hold beliefs$_m$, implicit faith remains an option. By pursuing in this life those purposes God pursues and intends for all people to pursue, one can become the kind of person who would readily follow the direction of God in the next life. Indeed, on the understanding that the pursuit of these purposes amounts to following the leading of one's moral beliefs – which themselves are instances of divine communication – one would already be responding to God's direction in this life even if one was unaware of this fact. Through this exercise of implicit faith one becomes the kind of person who would exercise explicit Christian faith as outlined in Chapter 3 – if only one came to see that certain messages (most importantly, the message that recon-ciliation with God is possible by pleading Christ's passion) do in fact come from God.

So much for the lack of belief$_m$ impeding implicit Christian faith. What about belief$_p$? Clearly, if one does not have any beliefs of the belief$_m$ sort, then one will also not have a belief$_p$. For if one does not believe that a particular message comes from God, then when one considers available options as to how best to achieve one's purposes, the option of accepting the authoritative claims that accompany God's message will not even present itself. Still, we might imagine a case where one *does* believe that certain messages come from God – and yet does not form a belief$_p$. Rather than denoting a lack of implicit faith, though, such lack of belief may in some cases actually be *indicative* of implicit faith. Suppose that a person misunderstands the kinds of purposes to which the Christian God is committed and which God directs people to seek to achieve. Perhaps her misun-derstanding stems from inaccurate teaching about the nature of God or from making assumptions about God's commitments based on the less-than-virtuous patterns of behaviour she observes from professing Christians. Even though she may seek to achieve the very kinds of purposes to which God and the heavenly community are actually committed, she may (wrongly) think that the Christian God is not committed to these kinds of purposes. So, it would not be surprising if such a person failed to believe that the noble purposes dear to her were not best achieved by following the direction of the Christian God. Of course, once she came to hold true beliefs about the goals God is committed to helping people to achieve, then she would naturally respond positively to the direction of an all-knowing and all-powerful God as she pursues those purposes to which she now knows he is also committed.

I conclude, then, that the Christian theist can adequately meet the objection against her as outlined in Part 1. Although *belief* is involuntary, this does not mean that people are not free to exercise *faith*. For all people – at least if they are to be called by God to account for their earthly lives – possess some set of moral beliefs. And faced with decisions whether to follow the leading of certain kinds of these moral beliefs, even those who have never heard the Christian gospel message have the opportunity to exercise at least implicit Christian faith.

8.4 *Possible theological objections*

While I have suggested a line of argument the Christian theist might use to rebut the objection outlined against her in Part 1, there might be various theological reasons why some Christian theists would be reluctant to adopt my suggestion. One source of hesitation might be that the possibility of implicit faith as I have described it undermines the importance of both Christian conversion and evangelism. After all, if nonbelievers can exercise faith – albeit implicit faith – then what ultimately distinguishes the Christian from the non-Christian in this life? And if those who exercise this implicit faith have the opportunity to plead Christ's passion at some time after their earthly lives, then where is the impetus for evangelism?

As to the first question, the Christian theist, if she adopts the line of response I have outlined in Part 2, can still maintain that those with explicit Christian faith in this life are related to God in a very different way from those nonbelievers with merely implicit faith. After all, the Christian view is that it is not until one explicitly pleads Christ's passion that one can be fully reconciled to God. Accordingly, the Christian theist is free to maintain that it is not until such a time that certain profound, spiritual changes occur within an individual. For example, the Christian theist can maintain that one's spiritual gifts[58] are not released until such a time. Also, the Christian theist can point to divinely ordained means of grace, such as the sacraments of baptism and eucharist, in explaining how only Christian believers have access to certain kinds of divine anointing. More generally, the Christian theist can point out that, inasmuch as we must cooperate with God's grace in order to receive its benefits,[59] and inasmuch as cooperation may involve explicitly asking for help from God,[60] nonbelievers who exercise merely implicit faith in no way can attain in this life the same spiritual depth as is possible for Christian believers. Thus, my account of implicit faith need not threaten the Christian theist who seeks to affirm the special standing of Christians in this life.

As to the importance of evangelism, I acknowledge that Christian

mission work has often been motivated largely by the belief that the
unevangelized in this life have no hope of attaining salvation. Yet, I
think there is good reason to question this postulation. Apart from
the arguments of this chapter that one's pursuit of certain purposes
is more important to being in a positive relationship with God than
is the holding of true beliefs about God, it may prove telling to
review Jesus's recorded words in issuing the 'Great Commission' in
St Matthew's gospel. In Jesus's final recorded words in this gospel,
he commissions his followers to 'go and make disciples of all
nations, baptizing them in the name of the Father and of the Son
and of the Holy Spirit, and teaching them to obey everything I have
commanded you'.[61] But the reason Jesus gives for doing so is not
that those who remain unconverted and unbaptized in this life have
no hope of heaven. Rather, the reason seems to be given in the
prefixed statement: 'All authority in heaven and on earth have been
given to me. Therefore go and make disciples of all nations ...'[62]
The context of the Great Commission, then, seems to involve the
task set before Jesus's followers to announce his reign, which
encompasses both heaven and earth. Put another way, Jesus's
followers have the task of bearing witness to the reality of the
kingdom of God, where Jesus Christ is Lord. Though much of the
world might not recognize – at least, not until his second coming –
that Jesus is the sovereign head over all we see and that the fate of
those who oppose Jesus has been sealed by his triumph over death,
Christians in this life are called to bear witness to this fact.

While I have suggested that the exercise of implicit faith might
occur in the everyday decisions one makes as one responds to divine
communication in the form of one's moral beliefs, this in no way
undermines the possibility that many people might have singular
conversion experiences where the moral orientation of their lives is
dramatically changed. By spelling out the eternal consequences of
our moral decisions, evangelism may help others to make those
kinds of momentous decisions that dramatically alter their own
moral orientation and relationship with God.

We might mention here a further question about the role of
evangelism – though it involves an issue on which the Christian
theist is not forced to take a particular stand if she adopts the line of
response I have outlined in Part 2. The question is whether a person
can, through evangelism, play a causal role in determining *whether*
someone else attains salvation. Put more broadly, would God allow
one person's eternal fate ultimately to hinge in part on whether a
second person chose to perform some act – such as preaching the
gospel to the first person? The majority of the Christian tradition
has been inclined to answer 'yes' to this question, though some
Christian writers[63] have argued that the answer must be 'no'. The

Christian theist who adopts the line of response I have outlined in Part 2 is free to affirm either that we can or that we cannot through interaction with others spur others on to make a particular moral decision at a particular time that changes their moral orientation in a way that would otherwise never occur. In taking my suggested line of response, the Christian theist, of course, will not affirm that nonbelievers in this life are *ipso facto* excluded from the possibility of salvation. But the Christian theist can still affirm (though she need not) that we can influence what eternally significant moral decisions other people make to the extent that their eternal fate would ultimately have been different if not for our influence.

We might also note here that, in adopting my suggested line of response, the Christian theist need not be committed to a particular view as to whether someone who rejects God's grace in this life might have an opportunity to accept God's grace in some future state. It is true that, in taking the line of response I have suggested, the Christian theist will affirm that those who exercise implicit faith in this life will – like the Old Testament patriarchs – have the opportunity at some time in the afterlife to see the truth about God, to recognize that the moral commitments they made in their earthly lives were implicit commitments to exercise faith in the Christian God, and then to confirm explicitly these implicit commitments by pleading Christ's passion. As to the further question of whether people are given the opportunity after their earthly lives to make morally significant decisions by which they might *change* their overall moral orientation, the Christian theist need not commit herself to one particular view in adopting my suggested line of response.

Turning now to consider a different kind of possible theological objection, exception might be taken to my account of faith on the grounds that it makes faith out to be a kind of 'work'. For, if saving faith is a matter of pursuing the right kinds of purposes, then salvation, it might be argued, ceases to be a gift freely given by God. Rather, salvation becomes something one earns by performing certain good actions.

In assessing this charge of 'works righteousness', it may be instructive to consider how the doctrine of 'justification by faith' has been interpreted within the Christian tradition. Alister McGrath, in his historical survey of the doctrine of justification, makes clear that throughout the medieval period Christian writers understood justification 'as the process by which a man is made righteous, subsuming the concepts of "sanctification" and "regeneration"'.[64] McGrath goes on to add that 'the medieval period was astonishingly faithful to the teaching of Augustine on the question of the nature of justification, where the Reformers departed from it'.[65] As to the specific point of departure here, Jerry Walls explains that the Protestant Reformers – or at least many of their followers – 'departed from the catholic consensus in seeing justification as a forensic or legal declaration that the believer is *declared* righteous, rather than as a process whereby he is actually *made* righteous'.[66]

If salvation is seen as fundamentally a process of regeneration, as opposed to a kind of legal standing, then transformation – and not simply God's forgiveness – is needed in order for one to attain heaven.[67] When salvation is understood in these terms, then the need for a positive response to God – which, as we have seen, will require the pursuit of virtuous purposes – becomes clear. For, given that one must cooperate with God's transforming grace in order to be fully transformed, one must make a positive response to God in order to become the kind of person fit for heaven. As outlined in Chapter 3, such a positive response may come in the form of explicit Christian faith, where one accepts the authoritative claims that lie behind the Christian God's invitational statements. Alternatively, as I have suggested in this chapter (8.2), nonbelievers may still make a kind of preliminary and 'implicit' response to God in which the nonbeliever responds positively to those divinely placed moral beliefs of hers through which God seeks to communicate to her.

Do these kinds of responses to God amount to performing good *works*, which God then rewards by granting heaven to those who perform them? A Christian theist who is concerned to stress the free nature of the gift of God's grace might still object that *any* human response to God – however this response is construed – must not be viewed as necessary to the attainment of heaven. Otherwise, a person's positive response to God becomes a good work, which God would then be seen to reward by granting the person heaven. Such an objection, though, rests on what I take to be a mistaken understanding of the Christian view of heaven. In some other religions, heaven may be viewed as containing good things that are separate from, and are rewards for, one's positive response to God's directives. Such rewards might include exotic foods or sexual pleasures. However, the Christian explanation of heavenly rewards must take into account the understanding that humans – created in the image of God, who is in his nature triune and therefore relational – find ultimate fulfilment in being in right relationship with God (and with others). Accordingly, the rewards of heaven must be understood in terms of people enjoying the kind of personal relationship with God for which they were created.

I have sought to characterize faith in terms of certain kinds of responses to God. In exercising explicit Christian faith one responds to invitational statements which one recognizes as coming from God. In exercising implicit faith one may merely respond to one's moral beliefs – not realizing that these beliefs are forms of divine communication aimed at conforming one to the image of Christ. The general point here about the exercise of faith is that, when one positively responds to God, one moves toward the kind of personal relationship with God which the redeemed in heaven enjoy and in which the Christian theist will affirm that humans find ultimate fulfilment. Thus, the proper Christian understanding of heavenly rewards is not that they are additional good things – like exotic foods or sexual pleasures – given out to those who respond positively to God and thereby move into a positive, personal relationship with him. Rather, the Christian understanding of heavenly rewards must be that the moving into a positive, personal relationship with God *is* the reward of making a positive response to God. Heaven is merely the place where this positive and ongoing relationship takes place. Zachary Hayes offers an analysis along similar lines in his discussion of merit:

> The issue of 'merit' for good works, then, does not mean that we receive something extrinsic to the work itself. We receive nothing other than the very self-gift of God. And in the reception of that gift, we are profoundly changed. What we 'get,' then, is the intrinsic effect of God's presence on the human person.[68]

In the end, the proper Christian understanding of salvation and heavenly rewards must be that they are fruits of the kind of personal relationship with God for which humans were created. And we have seen in earlier chapters that, in exercising the kind of faith that establishes a positive relationship with God, one will need to pursue certain virtuous purposes. Thus, to object that the link between faith and the pursuit of virtuous purposes amounts to a kind of 'works righteousness' is to fail to understand that salvation and heavenly rewards can only be achieved – and cannot *but* be achieved – through the pursuit of certain purposes.

Turning now to consider a different and final possible theological objection to my suggested line of response in Part 2, the Christian theist might question whether my account of implicit faith is really an account of *faith* at all. Much of our discussion has been on the type of response to God that establishes the kind of relationship with God commended by the Christian religion. And I have argued that this response is not the decision 'to believe' certain things about God; rather, this response involves the decision to pursue certain purposes in the light of what one already believes. Indeed, on my account of implicit faith it would be possible for one who inculpably fails to hold Christian beliefs nonetheless to exercise implicit Christian faith by pursuing purposes in line with one's moral beliefs. But if a *nonbeliever* can exercise (implicit) faith, then have we done justice to the term 'faith'? Put another way, it might be objected that the nonbeliever I have described here does not exercise *faith* – implicit or otherwise. Rather, the inculpable nonbeliever simply demonstrates a pattern of performing morally good actions and at most a *potential* to exercise faith.

In response to this line of argument I should first emphasize that, on my account of faith, it is not any pattern of performing morally good actions that *itself* provides final reconciliation with God. Throughout our discussion I have in no way denied the working assumption that final reconciliation with God is possible only as one explicitly pleads Christ's passion to God as atonement for one's own sins. I have merely suggested that a nonbeliever who responds positively to the truth about God as she sees it in this life may – like the Old Testament patriarchs – have the opportunity at some point after this life to plead Christ's passion.

But should we say that such a nonbeliever can exercise (implicit) *faith* in this life? The answer, I think, is 'yes'. As the nonbeliever follows the leading of her moral beliefs – which, again, the Christian theist can plausibly construe as a form of divine communication – she pursues certain purposes. These purposes might include ensuring that the oppressed receive justice; that the downtrodden receive encouragement; and that the lonely feel loved and welcomed. Now, the pursuit merely of these kinds of purposes perhaps does not by itself show that a nonbeliever is implicitly exercising the kind of faith outlined in Chapter 3. For a nonbeliever who pursues these kinds of loving purposes might nevertheless be a person who would be hesitant to give up final control of her life by relating to God as Lord. However, the nonbeliever's adherence to her moral beliefs might lead her to pursue *other* kinds of purposes as well. These other purposes might include ensuring that all her obligations toward others are met; that she offer proper cooperation to others dedicated to morally good goals; and that she defer to others who are in better positions to know how moral progress should be sought. The continued pursuit of purposes such as these would be akin to making a determined decision to meet all one's obligations toward God, if God exists, and to act in accordance with whatever God commends. And we saw in section 8.2 how such a decision implicitly contains the decision to relate to God as Lord. Thus, because even non-theists can make the types of decisions that amount to the implicit decision to relate to God as Lord, it seems only appropriate to describe these kinds of decisions as the exercise of implicit faith.

I should like to emphasize one final point about possible objections to the line of argument I offer in Part 2, and that is that they should be considered in relation to the objection outlined in Part 1. The objection raised in Part 1, which was directed against

Christian theism, was that the involuntary nature of belief decisively undercuts the Christian affirmation that our eternal fate hinges on whether we voluntarily put our faith in God. This affirmation I take to be absolutely fundamental to the Christian religion. In order to defend this affirmation from the objection outlined in Part 1, and in order to do so in a way that preserves God's goodness, my contention is that something like the line of argument I put forward in Part 2 is needed. In the absence of any other adequate rebuttal to the objection posed in Part 1, the Christian theist should, I contend, adopt my line of argument. For, whatever theological issues one might want to press in response to this line of argument, it has the merit of preserving the Christian affirmation that faith is voluntary. And this affirmation is simply too central a claim in the Christian religion to dispense with.

Conclusion

If the Christian theist adopts the line of response I have suggested, she will have to concede that the Christian tradition has, with respect to the question of saving faith, often placed too great an emphasis on what a person believes.[69] I have argued that, with respect to becoming the kind of person fit for heaven, the matter of what a person believes is not as important as the matter of what moral decisions a person makes, given what he believes. If this is right, then the Christian evangelist, rather than urging nonbelievers 'to believe' the gospel message, ought perhaps instead to urge nonbelievers to consider the question of whether they want the gospel message to be true. That is, the Christian evangelist ought perhaps to urge nonbelievers to ask themselves the question: '*if* I believed the Christian gospel message to be true in its description of the kind of relationship into which God invites me, would I be willing to accept the terms of that relationship?' This question is one about a person's willingness to accept the truth about God wherever the truth lies. Of course, one who engages in such self-examination can nonetheless be self-deceived about one's own openness to the truth – especially in religious matters where the truth may require one to change very personal habits or to admit one's faults and ask for forgiveness. Still, such self-examination is perhaps the best one can do to guard against resistance to the truth – and thus to guard against self-deception. Given that self-deception lies at the heart of any morally culpable failure to hold Christian beliefs (as argued in Chapter 6), the Christian evangelist who encourages nonbelievers to guard against self-deception has worked to prevent morally culpable nonbelief.

Still, because the term 'faith' is so commonly linked with

'belief',[70] it may be difficult for the reader to shake off the feeling
that one's beliefs play a more critical role in the kind of response
God seeks to elicit from us than I have allowed. H.H. Price suggests
a reason for the derision be believes has been directed at the so-
called Agnostic's Prayer: 'O God, if there be a God, save my soul, if
I have a soul':

> ... a Theist does not merely recommend us to view the world 'as if' there
> were a God who created it and loves each person whom He has created
> ... He asserts that God does actually exist, and even that he exists in a
> sense in which nothing else does. *Qui est*, 'He who is', is one of the
> descriptions which Theists have given of him.[71]

Perhaps we can think back to the general appeal of the line of
argument stemming from Kierkegaard's writings on the need for
certainty of belief, as discussed in section 4.2. The argument there
was that the nature of Christian faith is such as to be incompatible
with anything less than firm belief. Kierkegaard might have
imagined something like the following response one might offer to
God: 'God, I've read the Bible, which says that I'm a sinner and that
Jesus Christ died to make it possible for me to make atonement for
my failings and to be reconciled to you. I'm not sure if all that's true,
but I think it might be true. I think there is perhaps a 50–75 per cent
chance that I'm a sinner, and I think there's roughly that same
chance that Jesus was in fact divine and died for my sins.'
Kierkegaard would no doubt want to insist that such a scenario
does *not* represent true repentance or a firm commitment to seek
forgiveness.

But the line of argument I have outlined in Part 2 suggests that a
different type of scenario may be a closer analogy to at least some
initial (and authentic) acts of commitment and virtuous faith.
Imagine that you are taking a walk in a park one winter evening.
There is a frozen pond nearby on which children sometimes skate.
You know the frozen pond is there, although you can't see the pond
at the moment because there are bushes between you and the pond.
As you are walking along, you seem faintly to hear the sound of a
child's voice coming from the direction of the pond, and the voice
seems to be saying, 'Help!' You cannot tell if it really is the faint cry
for help of a child who perhaps has fallen through the ice. You think
it might have been the wind whistling through the bushes, or
perhaps some bird from far away that chirped on a certain pitch that
sounded like the tone of a child's cry. Perhaps, you think, the cry
was just your own imagination. You clearly don't know for certain
that you *did* hear a child's cry for help; you may not even think that
you *probably* did. But you nonetheless rush through the bushes to
the frozen pond to make sure that there is not some child who has

fallen through the ice. Your commitment to go to the pond stems from your commitment to be a person who does not stand idly by when a child is in desperate need of help.

Now, let us think about your state of mind immediately before you go through the bushes to the frozen pond. You may think to yourself: 'I'm not sure the voice I thought I heard was real. Maybe it was the wind. Maybe the voice was just a figment of my imagination. To take a Freudian theme, maybe my desire to be a hero has led me to believe wrongly that there is a child who has fallen through the ice and needs me to rescue him.' Even *if* you think all these things, even if you think that your belief that you heard a voice might be the result of wishful thinking, you still are going to go through the bushes to make sure that there is not a child drowning. Why? Again, because you are the kind of person who could not live with yourself if you let a child drown instead of reaching out to save the child. If you go through the bushes and it turns out that the voice you thought you might have heard was not real after all – well, you can live with that.

Similarly, it seems open for the Christian theist to encourage others to make the following commitment: '*If* there is a God, and *if* Jesus Christ is the way to reconciliation and eternal life with him, then I am going to be a person who pleads the passion of Christ and follows God's directives. If the voice I think might be God speaking to me (through prayer, through the Bible, through my conscience, and so forth) turns out not to be real – well, I can live with that.' Although the *beliefs* requisite for explicit Christian faith are not voluntary, it is open to the Christian theist to point out that this type of *faith* decision certainly is.

Notes

[1] Aquinas 1265–73: II–II, i, 8. Cf. II–II, ii, 8.
[2] Aquinas 1265–73: II–II, v, 3.
[3] Aquinas 1265–73: II–II, v, 3.
[4] Aquinas 1265–73: II–II, v, 3.
[5] Penelhum 1989: 129.
[6] Rom. 10.13. The quoted passage is from Joel 2.32.
[7] Rom. 10.14.
[8] Acts 10.2. The term 'God-fearing' in this context denotes one who was not a full Jewish proselyte but who acknowledged one God and who followed central ethical teachings of the Jewish tradition.
[9] Augustine 428: Ch. 12 [VII].
[10] Luther 1538: 416, 418.
[11] Calvin 1559: III, xxi, 7.
[12] *Enchiridion Symbolorum* 1957: 430.
[13] *Enchiridion Symbolorum* 1957: 714.
[14] *Enchiridion Symbolorum* 1957: 1677.
[15] *The Documents of Vatican II* 1966: 593.

[16] Aquinas 1256–59: XIV, xi, ad. 1.

[17] As to how explorations of unevangelized parts of the world began to increase sensitivity toward the possibility of inculpable nonbelief, see Sullivan (1992) Ch. 5. Similarly, Sanders (1992) states that 'The magnitude of the problem [that some people might remain unevangelized throughout their earthly lives] became evident only after the great explorations and discoveries of new lands in the fifteenth and sixteenth centuries'.

[18] Aquinas's teacher, Albert the Great, indicates that this view was indeed widespread, affirming that 'Theologians in general teach that it is impossible that a man, who performs adequately all in his power to do to prepare himself, should not receive a revelation from God, or instruction from men who have been themselves inspired, or some sign of a Mediator'.

[19] Aquinas 1256–59: XIV, xi, ad. 1. Sanders (1992) concludes that 'Aquinas believed that there was only a handful of people who remained unevangelized in his day, and consequently he did not give a great deal of attention to formulating a view concerning their destiny' (156–7). At the same time, in his later writings Aquinas (1265–73) did perhaps make allowances for the possibility of inculpable nonbelief, distinguishing between (a) the person who fails to believe an article of faith due to ignorance of the teachings of the Church and (b) the person who disbelieves an article of faith owing to a refusal to follow the teachings of the Church. While the latter person falls into heresy, the former is merely in error (II–II, v, 3); and the failure of people in error to hold Christian beliefs is something that 'is no fault of theirs' (II–II, ii, 6, ad. 2).

[20] *The Documents of Vatican II* 1966: 32–3.

[21] Note that the reference in Vatican II is to the group of people outside the Church who *refuse* to enter or remain in it.

[22] Rahner 1961: 66–7.

[23] Cf. Rahner 1961: 56; 59.

[24] Rahner 1961: 60–1.

[25] Rahner 1961: 59.

[26] On the question of when the Christian gospel 'really enters' into the 'historical situation' of a person participating in a non-Christian religion, Rahner (1961) states that the criteria 'for a more exact determination of this moment in time' remains in some respects 'an open question' (59). Elsewhere, Rahner indicates that a person's own non-Christian religion continues to be the appropriate way to express his relationship with God and arrive at this salvation until such a time as it becomes a mortal sin not to accept Christianity. See Sullivan 1992: 171f.

[27] Rahner 1961: 71.

[28] Justin Martyr c. 150a: Ch. 46. As Sullivan (1992) points out, living according to reason (*logos*) meant, for Justin, keeping the natural law (15). Justin was by no means alone among the Church Fathers in offering this line of thought. See, e.g., Clement of Rome c. 97: Ch. 7; Irenaeus c. 180: Bk IV, 22, 2; and Clement of Alexandria c. 202: Bk V, Chs 5 and 13.

[29] Augustine 426: Bk 18, Ch. 47.

[30] Augustine 426: Bk 18, Ch. 47.

[31] Cf. 2 Kgs 5.

[32] Calvin 1559: II, ii, 32.

[33] Calvin 1559: II, ii, 32.

[34] Aquinas 1265–73: II–II, ii, 7, ad. 3.

[35] Aquinas 1265–73: II–II, ii, 7.

[36] Aquinas 1265–73: II–II, ii, 7.

[37] Aquinas 1265–73: II–II, i, 7.

[38] Aquinas 1265–73: II–II, i, 7.

[39] Aquinas 1265–73: II–II, ii, 8, ad. 1.

[40] Swinburne 1989: 192. Though this doctrine is not popular among many Christian

writers today, MacCulloch (1930) concludes from his analysis of the doctrine in
Patristic times that 'From at least the second century there was no more well-known
and popular belief' than that associated with Christ's 'descent to Hades, the
overcoming of Death and Hades, the Preaching to the Dead, and the Release of
Souls' (45). See, e.g. Justin Martyr c. 150b: Ch. 72; Irenaeus c. 180: I, 27, 3; IV, 27, 2;
V, 31, 1; Clement of Alexandria c. 202: Bk VI, Ch. 6; Tertullian c. 220: Chs 7 and 55;
Hippolytus c. 230: §26, 45; Origen c. 248: Bk II, Ch. 56; Athanasius c. 369: §lix.

[41] Swinburne 1989: 192.

[42] Mt. 7.21-3.

[43] Acts 2.21, quoting Joel 2.32.

[44] Phil. 1.29.

[45] Jn 3.16.

[46] 1 Jn 5.1.

[47] Rather than reading them as the first premise of a syllogism designed to specify
exactly who it is that will eventually be saved, perhaps they are better read simply as
exhortations to turn to God because God is one who responds with mercy and love to
those who turn to him.

[48] We defined 'belief' at length in Chapter 1.

[49] Where 'trust' is defined as follows: 'To trust a man is to act on the assumption
that he will do for you what he knows that you want or need, when the evidence gives
some reason for supposing that he may not and where there will be bad consequences
if the assumption is false' (Swinburne 1981: 111).

[50] Swinburne 1981: 113.

[51] Gen. 15.6.

[52] Lewis 1956: 166.

[53] These purposes, of course, may include the taking of steps in an attempt to
acquire true beliefs.

[54] God's role as Lord seems logically primary to his role as Saviour. A person comes
to plead Christ's passion as atonement for her own sins because she believes that God
has prescribed this course of action. Her act, then, is an act she performs as part of
her commitment to relate to God as Lord by following his direction. Also, that we
may need a saviour is a contingent fact – contingent on our moral failures toward
God and our subsequent need for forgiveness and reconciliation if we are to relate to
him as he intended from creation. However, any creatures God creates who are able
to take on obligations cannot but take on the obligation to relate to God as Lord.

[55] We discussed in section 3.4 the general limits to the kinds of ultimate purposes
that are consistent with a person's decision to exercise Christian faith as a means to
those purposes.

[56] I use the term 'accept' here in the sense specified in section 3.3.

[57] Of course, all Christian theists will want to affirm that having true Christian
beliefs can help one to lead a virtuous life of faith. Through having such beliefs one
can better see what moral goodness amounts to and what goals one should seek to
achieve. One can also find encouragement to make the kinds of decisions one needs to
make in order to lead a virtuous life of faith and to attain salvation. That much is
uncontroversially true for Christian theists. The point at issue in our discussion here,
however, is whether the *nature* of the kind of response God seeks to elicit from us is
such that the exercise of any kind of faith – even implicit faith – is impossible without
true, Christian beliefs.

[58] Cf. 1 Cor. 12, which lists some of these gifts before going on to speak of the
connection between the proper use of one's spiritual gifts and one's participation in
the community of believers, or Christ's 'body' .

[59] I have in mind here benefits such as spiritual insight and wisdom (cf. 1 Cor. 2.
6–16) and the 'fruit of the Spirit' (Gal. 5.22-3).

[60] Cf. Mt. 7.7, 'Ask and it will be given to you; seek and you will find; knock and the
door will be opened to you.' Jas 4.2, 'You do not have, because you do not ask God.'

[61] Mt. 28.19-20.

[62] Mt. 28.19.

[63] See, e.g. Walls (1992), especially Ch. 5.

[64] McGrath 1986: I.184.

[65] McGrath 1986: I.185.

[66] Walls 2002: 40.

[67] For a good discussion of why we should affirm that salvation *is* a matter of regeneration, or transformation, see Walls (2002) 37–62.

[68] Hayes 1992: 116.

[69] Though see Smith (1977), especially Part II and Smith (1979) Ch. 6 as to how the meaning of 'belief' has changed since its origination in Middle English. Under the original meaning of belief – to hold dear, to love – the exhortation to religious belief becomes more understandable and less problematic.

[70] The close association of faith with belief in Christian discussions is no doubt largely attributable to the fact that πίστις in the New Testament is often translated into the English word 'belief'. In section 3.1, however, we observed that πίστις when its various contexts within the New Testament are considered, may carry the connotation of belief, obedience, commitment, an authentic Christian walk, and more. Recognizing, then, that the Greek word πίστις has a different etymology from the English word 'belief', we must be careful what we infer from the New Testament exhortation to 'belief'. Additionally, there is the added complication that, as observed in the previous note, the term 'belief' in the English language has changed significantly over time.

[71] Price 1969: 465. Price's own view is that the Agnostic's Prayer 'is a perfectly sensible prayer for an Agnostic to offer, and unless he begins by praying in some such way, one cannot see how he is ever to begin praying at all, nor how he is ever to be converted from Agnosticism to Theism' (484).

BIBLIOGRAPHY

Adams, Robert, 1972 'Must God Create the Best?', repr. in *The Virtue of Faith and Other Essays in Philosophical Theology* (Oxford: Oxford University Press, 1987).

——1976 'Kierkegaard's Arguments against Objective Reasoning in Religion', repr. in *The Virtue of Faith and Other Essays in Philosophical Theology* (Oxford: Oxford University Press, 1987).

——1984 'The Virtue of Faith', repr. in *The Virtue of Faith and Other Essays in Philosophical Theology* (Oxford: Oxford University Press, 1987).

——1985 'Involuntary Sins', *Philosophical Review* 94: 3–31.

——1986 'The Problem of Total Devotion', in Robert Audi and William Wainwright (eds), *Rationality, Religious Belief, and Moral Commitment* (Ithaca, NY: Cornell University Press).

——1987 'The Leap of Faith', in *The Virtue of Faith and Other Essays in Philosophical Theology* (Oxford: Oxford University Press).

——1999 *Finite and Infinite Goods* (Oxford: Oxford University Press).

Alston, William, 1988 'The Deontological Conception of Epistemic Justification', repr. in *Epistemic Justification* (Ithaca, NY: Cornell University Press).

——1994 'Swinburne on Faith and Belief', in Alan Padgett (ed.), *Reason and the Christian Religion* (Oxford: Clarendon Press).

——1996 'Belief, Acceptance, and Religious Faith', in Jeff Jordan and Daniel Howard-Snyder (eds), *Faith, Freedom, and Rationality* (Lanham, MD: Rowman & Littlefield).

Anselm, 1077–78 *Proslogion*, trans. M.J. Charlesworth (Oxford: Clarendon Press, 1965).

Aquinas, Thomas, 1256–59 *De Veritate*, repr. in *Truth*, 3 vols, trans. Robert W. Mulligan (Indianapolis, IN: Hackett, 1994).

——1261–64 *Summa Contra Gentiles*, trans. English Dominican Fathers (London: Burns, Oates & Washbourne, 1923–29).

——1265–73 *Summa Theologica*, trans. Fathers of the English Dominican Province (Westminster, MD: Christian Classics, 1981).

Aristotle, n.d. *Nicomachean Ethics*, trans. David Ross (Oxford: Clarendon Press, 1925).

Athanasius, c. 369 'Letters of Athanasius', in Philip Schaff (ed.), *The Nicene and Post-Nicene Fathers*, series 2, Vol. 4, trans. Philip Schaff and Henry Wace (Albany, OR: Sage Software, 1996).

Audi, Robert, 1972 'The Concept of Believing', *The Personalist* 53: 43–62.

——1998 *Epistemology* (London: Routledge).

Augsburg Confession, 1530 repr. in *The Book of Concord*, trans. and ed. Theodore G. Tappert (Philadelphia, PA: Fortress Press, 1959).

Augustine of Hippo, 388 *On the Morals of the Catholic Church*, repr. in *The Nicene and Post-Nicene Fathers* series 1, Vol. 4, ed. Philip Schaff, trans. Richard Strothert. (Albany, OR: Sage Software, 1996).

——389–91 'De vera religione', repr. in *Corpus Christianorum, series Latina XXXII* (Turnholt: Brepols, 1962).

——397 *Confessions*, repr. in *The Nicene and Post-Nicene Fathers* series, Vol. 1, ed. Philip Schaff, trans. J.G. Pilkington (Albany, OR: Sage Software, 1996).

——426 *The City of God*, repr. in *The Nicene and Post-Nicene Fathers* series, Vol. 2, ed. Philip Schaff. trans. Marcus Dods (Albany, OR: Sage Software, 1996).

——428 'On the Predestination of the Saints', repr. in *The Nicene and Post-Nicene Fathers* series 1, Vol. 5, ed. Philip Schaff, trans. P. Holmes, R.E. Wallis and B.B. Warfield (Albany, OR: Sage Software, 1996).

Bacon, Francis, 1620 *Novum Organon*, trans. G.W. Kitchin (Oxford: Oxford University Press, 1855).

Baier, Annette, 1971 'The Search for Basic Actions', *American Philosophical Quarterly* 8: 161–170.

——1993 'Trust and Anti-Trust', in Joram Graf Haber (ed.), *Doing and Being* (New York: Macmillan).

Bain, Alexander, 1859 *The Emotions and the Will* (London: John W. Parker).

Baker, Lynne Rudder, 1987 *Saving Belief* (Princeton, NJ: Princeton University Press).

Barnes, G.W., 1983 'The Conclusion of Practical Reasoning', *Analysis* 43: 193–9.

Barth, Karl, 1953 'The Doctrine of Reconcilation', in *Church Dogmatics*, Vol. 4, Pt I, ed. G.W. Bromiley and T.F. Torrance, trans. G.W. Bromiley (Edinburgh: T&T Clark, 1956).

Basil of Caesarea, 361 'On Faith', repr. in *Fathers of the Church* series, Vol. 9, trans. Monica Wagner (Washington, DC: The Catholic University of America Press, 1962).

Bem, Daryl, 1972 'Self-Perception Theory', *Advances in Experimental Social Psychology* 6: 1–62.

Blackburn, Simon, 1984 *Spreading the Word* (Oxford: Clarendon Press).

Bonaventure, 1254–57 *Disputed Questions on the Mystery of the Trinity*, trans. Zachary Hayes (St Bonaventure, NY: The Franciscan Institute, repr. 1979).

Bonhoeffer, Dietrich, 1937 *The Cost of Discipleship* (London: SCM Press, 1959).

Braithwaite, R.B., 1933 'The Nature of Believing', *Proceedings of the Aristotelian Society* 33: 129–46.

Brink, David O., 1989 *Moral Realism and the Foundations of Ethics* (Cambridge: Cambridge University Press).

Brümmer, Vincent, 1993 *The Model of Love* (Cambridge: Cambridge University Press).

Bultmann, Rudolph, 1948–53 *Theology of the New Testament*, trans. Kendrick Grobel (London: SCM Press, 1952–55).

Butler, Joseph, 1729 Fifteen Sermons Preached at the Rolls Chapel, repr. in J.H. Bernard (ed.), *The Works of Bishop Butler*, Vol. I (London: Macmillan, 1900).

——1736 *The Analogy of Religion*, repr. in J.H. Bernard (ed.), *The Works of Bishop Butler*, Vol. II (London: Macmillan, 1900).

Calvin, John, 1559 *Institutes of the Christian Religion* trans. Henry Beveridge (Albany, OR: Sage Software, 1996).

Chisholm, Roderick, 1968 'Lewis' Ethics of Belief', in P.A. Schilpp (ed.), *The Philosophy of C.I. Lewis* (La Salle, IL: Open Court).

Clark, Kelly James, 1990 *Return to Reason* (Grand Rapids, MI: Eerdmans).

Clarke, Murray, 1986 'Doxastic Voluntarism and Forced Belief', *Philosophical Studies* 50: 39–51.

Classen, H.G., 1979 'Will, Belief and Knowledge', *Dialogue* 18: 64–72.

Clement of Alexandria, c. 202 *Stromata*, in *The Ante-Nicene Fathers*, Vol. 2, ed. A. Roberts and J. Donaldson, trans. William Wilson (Albany, OR: Sage Software, 1996).

Clement of Rome, c. 97 First Epistle to the Corinthians, in *The Ante-Nicene Fathers*, Vol. 1, ed. and trans. A. Roberts and J. Donaldson (Albany, OR: Sage Software, 1996).

Clifford, W.K., 1877 '*The Ethics of Belief*', repr. in Gerald D. McCarthy (ed.), *The Ethics of Belief Debate* (Atlanta, GA: Scholars Press, 1986).

Code, Lorraine, 1987 *Epistemic Responsibility* (Hanover, NH: University Press of New England).

Cohen, Jonathan, 1989 'Belief and Acceptance', *Mind* 98: 367–89.

Collins, A.W., 1969 'Unconscious Belief', *Journal of Philosophy* 66: 667–80.

Craig, William Lane, 1989 'No Other Name: A Middle Knowledge Perspective on the Exclusivity of Salvation through Christ', *Faith and Philosophy* 6: 172–88.

Danto, Arthur, 1965 'Basic Actions', *American Philosophical Quarterly* 2: 141–8.

Davidson, Donald, 1970 'How is Weakness of the Will Possible?', repr. in *Essays on Actions and Events* (Oxford: Clarendon Press, 1980).

Demos, Raphael, 1960 'Lying to Oneself', *The Journal of Philosophy* 57: 588–95.

Descartes, René, 1642 *Meditation II*, in *The Philosophical Works of Descartes*, Vol. I, trans. E.S. Haldane and G.R.T. Ross (London: Dover, 1955).

The Documents of Vatican II, 1966 Gen. ed. Walter M. Abbott, trans. and ed. Joseph Gallagher (London: Geoffrey Chapman).

Dulles, Avery, 1994 *The Assurance of Things Hoped For* (Oxford: Oxford University Press).

Dummett, Michael, 1973 *Frege: Philosophy of Language* (London: Duckworth).

Duns Scotus, John, 1300–07 *Ordinatio*, in *Duns Scotus on the Will and Morality*, sel. and trans. Allan B. Wolter (Washington, DC: The Catholic University of America Press, 1986).

Edwards, Jonathan, 1746 *A Treatise Concerning Religious Affections*, repr. in John E. Smith (ed.), *The Works of Jonathan Edwards*, Vol. 2 (New Haven, CT: Yale University Press, 1959).

——1758 'Original Sin', repr. in Clyde A. Holbrook (ed.), *The Works of Jonathan Edwards*, Vol. 3 (New Haven: Yale University Press, 1970).

Enchiridion Symbolorum, 30th edn, 1957, ed. Henry Denzinger, trans. Roy J. Defarrari (St Louis, MO: Herder).

Evans, C. Stephen, 1990 'The Relevance of Historical Evidence for Christian Faith: A Critique of a Kierkegaardian View', *Faith and Philosophy* 7: 470–85.

——1992 *Passionate Reason: Making Sense of Kierkegaard's* Philosophical Fragments (Bloomington, IN: Indiana University Press).

——1996 *The Historical Christ and the Jesus of Faith: The Incarnational Narrative as History* (Oxford: Oxford University Press).

——1998 *Faith Beyond Reason* (Edinburgh: Edinburgh University Press).

——2000 'Kierkegaard on Religious Authority: The Problem of the Criterion', *Faith and Philosophy* 17: 48–67.

Evans, Donald D., 1980 *Faith, Authenticity, and Morality* (Toronto: University of Toronto Press).

Feuerbach, Ludwig, 1841 *The Essence of Christianity,* trans. George Eliot (New York: Harper & Row, 1957).

Fingarette, Herbert, 1969 *Self-Deception* (London: Routledge & Kegan Paul).

——1985 'Alcoholism and Self-Deception', in Mike W. Martin (ed.), *Self-Deception and Self-Understanding* (Lawrence, KS: University Press of Kansas).

Foot, Philippa, 1978 *Virtues and Vices* (Oxford: Basil Blackwell).

Formula of Concord, 1577 repr. in *The Book of Concord*, trans. and ed. Theodore G. Tappert (Philadelphia, PA: Fortress Press, 1959).

Foster, John, 1991 *The Immaterial Self* (London: Routledge).

Freud, Sigmund, 1900 'The Interpretation of Dreams', in *The Standard Edition of the Complete Works of Sigmund Freud*, Vols. 4 and 5, gen. ed. James Strachey, trans. James Strachey and Anna Freud (London: Hogarth Press, 1953–74).

——1901 'The Psychopathology of Everyday Life', in *The Standard Edition of the Complete Works of Sigmund Freud*, Vol. 6, gen. ed. James Strachey, trans. James Strachey and Anna Freud, (London: Hogarth Press, 1953–74).

——1915 'The Unconscious', in *The Standard Edition of the Complete Works of Sigmund Freud*, Vol. 14, gen. ed. James Strachey, trans. James Strachey and Anna Freud (London: Hogarth Press, 1953–74)

——1915–17 'Introductory Lectures on Psycho-Analysis', in *The Standard Edition of the Complete Works of Sigmund Freud*, Vols. 15 and 16, gen. ed. James Strachey, trans. James Strachey and Anna Freud (London: Hogarth Press, 1953–74).

——1927 'The Future of an Illusion', in *The Standard Edition of the Complete Works of Sigmund Freud*, Vol. 21, gen. ed. James Strachey, trans. James Strachey and Anna Freud (London: Hogarth Press, 1953–74).

Gergen, Kenneth J., 1985 'The Ethnopsychology of Self-Deception', in Mike W. Martin (ed.), *Self-Deception and Self-Understanding* (Lawrence, KS: University Press of Kansas).

Gilbert, Daniel T. and Cooper, Joel, 1985 'Social Psychological Strategies of Self-Deception', in Mike W. Martin (ed.), *Self-Deception and Self-Understanding* (Lawrence, KS: University Press of Kansas).

Govier, Trudy, 1976 'Belief, Values, and the Will', *Dialogue* 15: 642–63.

Greenwald, Anthony G., 1980 'The Totalitarian Ego', *American Psychologist* 35: 603–18.

Haight, M.R., 1980. *A Study of Self-Deception* (Brighton: Harvester Press).

——1985 'Tales from a Black Box', in Mike W. Martin (ed.), *Self-Deception and Self-Understanding* (Lawrence, KS: University Press of Kansas).

Hanson, Norwood Russell, 1961 'The Agnostic Dilemma', repr. in Terence Penelhum (ed.), *Faith* (New York: Macmillan, 1989).

——1971 'What I Don't Believe', in *What I Do Not Believe, and Other Essays* (Dordrecht: Reidel).

Hare, R.M., 1952 *The Language of Morals* (Oxford: Clarendon Press).

——1955 'Universalizability', *Proceedings of the Aristotelian Society* 55: 295–312.

——1963 *Freedom and Reason* (Oxford: Clarendon Press).

Hayes, Zachary, 1992 'The Purgatorial View', in William Crockett (ed.), *Four Views on Hell* (Grand Rapids, MI: Zondervan).

Heil, John, 1982 'Seeing Is Believing', *American Philosophical Quarterly* 19: 229–40.

——1983a 'Believing What One Ought', *Journal of Philosophy* 80: 752–64.

——1983b 'Doxastic Agency', *Philosophical Studies* 43: 355–64.

——1984 'Doxastic Incontinence', *Mind* 93: 56–70.

Helm, Paul, 1994 *Belief Policies* (Cambridge: Cambridge University Press).

——2000 *Faith With Reason* (Oxford: Oxford University Press).

Herbert, R.T., 1961 'Two of Kierkegaard's Uses of "Paradox" ', *Philosophical Review* 70: 41–55.

Hick, John, 1983 'Seeing-As and Religious Experience', in Terence Penelhum (ed.), *Faith* (New York: Macmillan, 1989).

Hippolytus, c. 230 *Dogmatic and Historical Treatise on Christ and Anti-Christ*, in *The Ante-Nicene Fathers* series, Vol. 5, *The Extant Works and Fragments of Hippolytus, Part II*, ed. A. Roberts and J. Donaldson, trans. S.D.F. Salmond (Albany, OR: Sage Software, 1996).

Hoitenga, Dewey, 1991 *Faith and Reason from Plato to Plantinga: An Introduction to Reformed Epistemology* (Albany, NY: SUNY Press).

Holyer, Robert, 1983 'Belief and Will Revisited', *Dialogue* 22: 273–90.

Hookway, Christopher, 1981 'Conscious Belief and Deliberation', *Proceedings of Aristotelian Society*, suppl. vol. 55: 75–89.

Howard-Snyder, Daniel and Moser, Paul (eds), 2002 *Divine Hiddenness: New Essays* (Cambridge: Cambridge University Press).

Hume, David, 1739–40 *A Treatise of Human Nature*, ed. L A. Selby-Bigge and Revd P.H. Nidditch (Oxford: Clarendon Press, 2nd edn, 1978).

——1748 *Enquiry Concerning Human Understanding*, ed. L.A. Selby-Bigge and Revd P.H. Nidditch (Oxford: Clarendon Press, 3rd edn, 1975).

——1777 *The Natural History of Religion*, in H.E. Root (ed.), *David Hume: The Natural History of Religion* (London: Adam & Charles Black, 1956).

——1779 *Dialogues Concerning Natural Religion*, ed. Richard H. Popkin (Indianapolis, IN: Hackett, 1980).

Irenaeus, c. 180 'Against Heresies', in *The Ante-Nicene Fathers* series, Vol. 1, ed. and trans. A. Roberts and J. Donaldson (Albany, OR: Sage Software, 1996).

James, William, 1896 'The Will To Believe', in *The Will to Believe and Other Essays in Popular Philosophy* (New York: Dover Publications, 1956).

Jones, Edward E., 1979 'The Rocky Road from Acts to Dispositions', *American Psychologist* 34: 107–17.

Jones, Edward E. and Berglas, Steven, 1978 'Control of Attributions about the Self through Self-Handicapping Strategies: The Appeal of Alcohol and the Role of Underachievement', *Personality and Social Psychology Bulletin* 4: 200–6.

Jones, Edward E. and Harris, Victor A., 1967 'The Attribution of Attitudes', *Journal of Experimental Social Psychology* 3: 1–24.

Justin Martyr, c. 150a *First Apology*, in *Fathers of the Early Church* series, Vol. 6, ed. Ludwig Schopp, trans. Thomas B. Falls (New York: Christian Heritage, 1948).

——c. 150b *Dialogue with Trypho*, in *The Ante-Nicene Fathers* series, Vol. 1, ed. and trans. A. Roberts and J. Donaldson (Albany, OR: Sage Software, 1996).

Kahneman, Daniel and Tversky, Amos, 1972 'Subjective Probability: A Judgment of Representativeness', *Cognitive Psychology* 3: 430–54.

——1973 'Availability: A Heuristic for Judging Frequency and Probability', *Cognitive Psychology* 5: 207–32.

Kant, Immanuel, 1781 *Critique of Pure Reason*, trans. Norman Kemp Smith (London: Macmillan, 1929, repr. 1965).

——1785 *Grounding for the Metaphysics of Morals*, repr. in *Ethical Philosophy: The Complete Texts of Grounding for the Metaphysics of Morals and Metaphysical Principles of Virtue*, trans. James W. Ellington (Indianapolis, IN: Hackett, 1981).

——1793 *Religion within the Limits of Reason Alone*, trans. Theodore M. Greene and Hoyt H. Hudson (New York: Harper & Row, 1960).

——1797 *The Metaphysics of Morals*, Pt. 2, in *The Doctrine of Virtue*, trans. Mary J. Gregor (Philadelphia, PA: University of Pennsylvania Press, 1964).

Kierkegaard, Søren, 1844 *Philosophical Fragments*, ed. and trans. Howard V. and Edna H. Hong (Princeton, NJ: Princeton University Press, 1985).

——1846 *Concluding Unscientific Postscript,* ed. Walter Lowrie, trans. David F. Swenson (Princeton, NJ: Princeton University Press, 1941).

——1846–47 'On Authority and Revelation: The Book on Adler', in *The Book on Adler*, trans. Howard V. and Edna H. Hong (Princeton, NJ: Princeton University Press, 1998).

Kipp, David, 1985 'Self-Deception, Inauthenticity, and Weakness of Will', in Mike W. Martin (ed.), *Self-Deception and Self-Understanding* (Lawrence, KS: University Press of Kansas).

Kirk, Kenneth E., 1931 *The Vision of God* (London: Longmans, Green).

Kornblith, Hilary, 1983 'Justified Belief and Epistemically Responsible Action', *Philosophical Review* 92: 33–48.

Kvanvig, Jonathan, 1993 *The Problem of Hell* (Oxford: Oxford University Press).

Lehrer, Keith, 1990 *Theory of Knowledge* (London: Routledge).

Lewis, C.S., 1956 *The Last Battle* (London: Bodley Head).

——1961 *The Screwtape Letters* (New York: Macmillan).

Locke, John, 1690 *An Essay Concerning Human Understanding*, ed. Peter H. Nidditch (Oxford: Oxford University Press, 1975).

Luther, Martin, 1513–15 'Lectures on the Psalms', in *D. Martin Luthers Werke*, Vols 3 and 4 (Weimar: Hermann Böhlau, 1885–86).

——1515–16 'Lectures on Romans', in *Luther: Lectures on Romans*, Library of Christian Classics series, Vol. 15, trans. and ed. Wilhelm Pauck (London: SCM Press, 1961).

——1520a 'A Brief Explanation of the Ten Commandments, the Creed, and the Lord's Prayer', in *Works of Martin Luther*, Vol. 2., ed. A. Spaeth, trans. H.E. Jacobs (Philadelphia, PA: Muhlenberg Press, 1943).

——1520b 'The Freedom of a Christian', in *Luther's Works*, Vol. 31, ed. H.J. Grimm, trans. W.A. Lambert (Philadelphia, PA: Muhlenberg Press, 1957).

——1522 'Preface to the Epistle of St Paul to the Romans', in *Reformation Writings of Martin Luther*, Vol. 2, trans. B.L. Woolf (London: Lutterworth Press, 1952).

——1538 'Large Catechism', in *The Book of Concord*, trans. Theodore G. Tappert (Philadelphia, PA: Fortress Press, 1959).

MacCulloch, J.A., 1930 *The Harrowing of Hall: A Comparative Study of an Early Christian Doctrine* (Edinburgh: T&T Clark).

MacDonald, Scott, 1993 'Christian Faith', in Eleonore Stump (ed.), *Reasoned Faith* (Ithaca, NY: Cornell University Press).

MacIntyre, Alasdair, 1957 'What Morality is Not', *Philosophy* 32: 325–35.

Mackie, J.L., 1982 *The Miracle of Theism* (Oxford: Clarendon Press).

Malcolm, Norman, 1977 'The Groundlessness of Belief', repr. in Terence Penelhum (ed.), *Faith* (New York: Macmillan, 1989).

Martin, Mike W. (ed.), 1985 *Self-Deception and Self-Understanding* (Lawrence, KS: Kansas University Press).

Mavrodes, George, 1986 'Intellectual Morality in Clifford and James', in Gerald D. McCarthy (ed.), *The Ethics of Belief Debate* (Atlanta, GA: Scholars Press).

McLeod, Mark, 1993 *Rationality and Theistic Belief* (Ithaca, NY: Cornell University Press of Kansas).

McGrath, Alister, 1986 *Iustitia Dei: A History of the Christian Doctrine of Justification* (Cambridge: Cambridge University Press).

McTaggart, J.M.E., 1906 'The Establishment of Dogma', repr. in Terence Penelhum (ed.), *Faith* (New York: Macmillan, 1989).

Mele, Alfred R., 1987 *Irrationality* (Oxford: Oxford University Press).

Moltmann, Jürgen, 1965 *Theology of Hope*, trans. James W. Leitch (London: SCM Press; 5th edn, 1967).

Montmarquet, James A., 1986 'The Voluntariness of Believing', *Analysis* 46: 49–53.

Morris, Thomas V., 1992 *Making Sense of it All* (Grand Rapids, MI: Eerdmans).

Moser, Paul, 2002 'Cognitive Idolatry and Divine Hiding', in Daniel Howard-Snyder and Paul Moser (eds), *Divine Hiddenness: New Essays* (Cambridge: Cambridge University Press).

Muyskens, James, 1979 *The Sufficiency of Hope* (Philadelphia, PA: Temple University Press).

Myers, David G., 1998 *Psychology* (New York: Worth).

Newman, John Henry, 1853 'On the Certainty of Faith', repr. in J. Derek Holmes (ed.), *The Theological Papers of John Henry Newman on Faith and Certainty* (Oxford: Clarendon Press).

——1872 'Faith and Reason, Contrasted as Habits of Mind', in *Fifteen Sermons Preached before the University of Oxford between A.D. 1826 and 1843*, 3rd edn, repr. in *Fifteen Sermons* (Notre Dame, IN: University of Notre Dame Press, 1997).

Nietzsche, Friedrich, 1886 *Beyond Good and Evil: Prelude to a Philosophy of the Future*, trans. Walter Kaufmann (New York: Vintage Books, 1989).

——1892 *Thus Spoke Zarathustra*, trans. Walter Kaufmann (Harmondsworth: Penguin, 1978).

Nisbett, Richard and Ross, Lee, 1980 *Human Inference: Strategies and Shortcomings of Social Judgment* (Englewood Cliffs, NJ: Prentice-Hall).

O'Hear, Anthony, 1972 'Belief and the Will', *Philosophy* 47: 95–111.

Origen, c. 248 *Against Celsus*, in *The Ante-Nicene Fathers*, Vol. 4, ed. A. Roberts and J. Donaldson, trans. Frederick Crombie (Albany, OR: Sage Software, 1996).

Pascal, Blaise, 1670 *Pensées*, trans. A.J. Krailsheimer (Harmondsworth: Penguin, 1966).

Passmore, John, 1970 *The Perfectibility of Man* (London: Duckworth).

Pears, David, 1984 *Motivated Irrationality* (Oxford: Clarendon Press).

Peirce, C.S., 1877 'The Fixation of Belief', in Nathan Houser and Christian Kloesel (eds), *The Essential Peirce*, Vol. 1 (Bloomington, IN: Indiana University Press, 1992).

Penelhum, Terence, 1989 'The Analysis of Faith in St Thomas Aquinas', in Terence Penelhum (ed.), *Faith* (New York: Macmillan).

Peter Lombard, 1145–51 *Sentences*, in J.P. Migne (ed.), *Patrologiae Cursus Completus*, Vol. 192 (Paris: Garnier frères, 1854).

Pinnock, Clark, Rice, Richard, Sanders, John, Hasker, William and Basinger, David, 1994 *The Openness of God* (Downers Grove, IL: InterVarsity Press).

Plantinga, Alvin, 1983 'Reason and Belief in God', in Alvin Plantinga and Nicholas Wolterstorff (eds), *Faith and Rationality* (Notre Dame, IN: University of Notre Dame Press).

——2000 *Warranted Christian Belief* (Oxford: Oxford University Press).

Plantinga, Alvin and Wolterstorff, Nicholas (eds), 1983 *Faith and Rationality* (Notre Dame, IN: University of Notre Dame Press).

Platts, Mark de Bretton, 1979 *Ways of Meaning* (London: Routledge & Kegan Paul).

——1991 *Moral Realities: An Essay in Philosophical Psychology* (London: Routledge).

Pojman, Louis, 1979 'Rationality and Religious Belief', *Religious Studies* 15: 159–72.

——1984 'A Critique of Holyer's Volitionalism', *Dialogue* 23: 695–700.

——1986 *Religious Belief and the Will* (London: Routledge & Kegan Paul).

Price, H.H., 1954 'Belief and Will', *Proceedings of the Aristotelian Society*, suppl. vol. 28: 1–26.

——1965 'Belief "In" and Belief "That"', *Religious Studies* 1: 5–27.

——1969 *Belief* (London: Allen & Unwin).

Quattrone, George A. and Tversky, Amos, 1984 'Causal Versus Diagnostic Contingencies: On Self-Deception and on the Voter's Illusion', *Journal of Personality and Social Psychology* 46: 237–48.

Quinn, Philip, 1985 'In Search of the Foundations of Theism', *Faith and Philosophy* 2: 468–86.

Rahner, Karl, 1954–84 *Theological Investigations*, 23 vols, trans. Karl-H. Kruger, et al. (London: Darton, Longman & Todd, 1961–92).

——1961 'Christianity and the Non-Christian Religions', in John Hick and Brian Hebblethwaite (eds), *Christianity and Other Religions* (Glasgow: Collins).

Reichenbach, Bruce, 1999 'Inclusivism and the Atonement', *Faith and Philosophy* 16: 43–54.

Ricoeur, Paul, 1970 *Freud and Philosophy*, trans. Denis Savage (New Haven, CT: Yale University Press).

Roberts, Robert C., 1992 'Emotions as Access to Religious Truths', *Faith and Philosophy* 9: 83–94.

Rovane, Carol, 1998 *The Bounds of Agency* (Princeton, NJ: Princeton University Press).

Sanders, John, 1992 *No Other Name* (Grand Rapids, MI: Eerdmans).

Sartre, Jean-Paul, 1943 *Being and Nothingness* [*L'Etre et le néant*], trans. Hazel E. Barnes (London: Methuen, 1957).

Schellenberg, J.L., 1993 *Divine Hiddenness and Human Reason* (Ithaca, NY: Cornell University Press).

——2002 'What the Hiddenness of God Reveals: A Collaborative Discussion', in Daniel Howard-Snyder and Paul Moser (eds), *Divine Hiddenness: New Essays* (Cambridge: Cambridge University Press).

Schlesinger, George N., 1984 'Evidence and Religious Belief', *Faith and Philosophy* 1: 421–36.

Sessions, William, 1994 *The Concept of Faith* (Ithaca NY: Cornell University Press).

Smith, Michael, 1994 *The Moral Problem* (Oxford: Blackwell).

Smith, Wilfred Cantwell, 1977 *Belief and History* (Charlottesville, VA: University Press of Virginia).

——1979 *Faith and Belief* (Princeton, NJ: Princeton University Press).

Snyder, C.R., 1985 'Collaborative Companions: The Relationship of Self-Deception and Excuse Making', in Mike W. Martin (ed.), *Self-Deception and Self-Understanding* (Lawrence, KS: University Press of Kansas).

Snyder, C.R., Higgins, Raymond L. and Stucky, Rita J., 1983 *Excuses: Masquerades in Search of Grace* (New York: John Wiley).

Stocker, Michael, 1979 'Desiring the Bad: An Essay in Moral Psychology', *Journal of Philosophy* 76: 738–53.

——1982 'Responsibility Especially for Beliefs', *Mind* 91: 398–417.

Sullivan, Francis, 1992 *Salvation Outside the Church? Tracing the History of the Catholic Response* (London: Geoffrey Chapman).

Swinburne, Richard, 1981 *Faith and Reason* (Oxford: Clarendon Press).

——1989 *Responsibility and Atonement* (Oxford: Clarendon Press).

——1997 *The Evolution of the Soul*, rev. edn (Oxford: Clarendon Press).

——1998 *Providence and the Problem of Evil* (Oxford: Clarendon Press).

Szabados, Béla, 1973 'Wishful Thinking and Self-Deception', *Analysis* 33: 201–5.

Talbot, Mark R., 1989 'Is it Natural to Believe in God?', *Faith and Philosophy* 6: 155–71.

Tennant, F.R., 1943 'Faith', in Terence Penelhum (ed.), *Faith* (New York: Macmillan, 1989).

Tertullian, c. 197 *Apology*, trans. T.R. Glover (Cambridge, MA: Harvard University Press, 1960).

——c. 200 'The Prescription against Heretics', in *The Ante-Nicene Fathers* series, Vol. 3, ed. A. Roberts and J. Donaldson, trans. Peter Holmes (Albany, OR: Sage Software, 1996).

——c. 220 *A Treatise on the Soul*, in *The Ante-Nicene Fathers* series, Vol. 3, ed. A. Roberts and J. Donaldson, trans. Peter Holmes (Albany, OR: Sage Software, 1996).

Tesser, Abraham and Smith, Jonathan, 1980 'Some Effects of Task Relevance and Friendship on Helping: You Don't Always Help the One You Like', *Journal of Experimental Social Psychology* 16: 582–90.

Tillich, Paul, 1948 *The Shaking of the Foundations* (New York: Charles Scribner's Sons).

Wainwright, William, 1995 *Reason and the Heart* (Ithaca, NY: Cornell University Press).

Wallace, G. and Walker, A.D.M. (eds), 1970 *The Definition of Morality* (London: Methuen).

Walls, Jerry L., 1992 *Hell: The Logic of Damnation* (Notre Dame, IN: University of Notre Dame Press).

——2002 *Heaven: The Logic of Eternal Joy* (Oxford: Oxford University Press).

Walster, Elaine, 1966 'Assignment of Responsibility for an Accident', *Journal of Personality and Social Psychology* 3: 73–9.

Wesley, John, 1742 'Journal from August 12, 1738 to Nov. 1, 1739', repr. in W. Reginald Ward (ed.), *The Works of John Wesley*, Vol. 19 (Nashville, TN: Abingdon Press).

——1771a 'Original Sin', in *Sermons on Several Occasions* (London: Wesleyan Methodist Book-Room, 1800).

——1771b 'The Nature of Enthusiasm', in *Sermons on Several Occasions* (London: Wesleyan Methodist Book-Room, 1800).

——1782 'On the Fall of Man', in Thomas Jackson (ed.), *The Works of John Wesley, A.M.*, sermon LVII (London: Wesleyan Conference Office, 1872).

Westminster Confession of Faith, 1646 ed. S.W. Carruthers (Glasgow: Free Presbyterian Publications, 1978).

Westminster Shorter Catechism, 1648 repr. in *The Confessions of Faith, The Larger and Shorter Catechisms* (Glasgow: John Roberson, 1756).

Westphal, Merold, 1993 *Suspicion and Faith* (Grand Rapids, MI: Eerdmans).

Wilkes, K.V., 1981 'Conscious Belief and Deliberation', *Proceedings of Aristotelian Society*, suppl. vol. 55: 91–107.

Williams, Bernard, 1970 'Deciding to Believe', repr. in *Problems of the Self* (Cambridge: Cambridge University Press, 1973).

Wilson, Timothy, 1985 'Self-Deception without Repression: Limits on Access to Mental States', in Mike W. Martin (ed.), *Self-Deception and Self-Understanding* (Lawrence, KS: University Press of Kansas).

Wilson, Timothy, Snyder, C.R., and Perkins, Suzanne, 1983 'The Self-Serving Function of Hypochondriacal Complaints: Physical Symptoms as Self-Handicapping Strategies', *Journal of Personality and Social Psychology* 44: 787–97.

Winters, Barbara, 1979 'Believing at Will', *Journal of Philosophy* 76: 243–56.

Wolterstorff, Nicholas, 1981 'Is Reason Enough?', repr. in R.D. Geivett and B. Sweetman, (eds), *Contemporary Perspectives on Religious Epistemology* (Oxford: Oxford University Press, 1992).

——1995 *Divine Discourse* (Cambridge: Cambridge University Press).

Zagzebski, Linda, 1996 *Virtues of the Mind* (Cambridge: Cambridge University Press).

INDEX